The Harcombe Diet®

The Recipe Book

D1341355

First published by Columbus Publishing Ltd 2011
November 2012 edition

www.columbuspublishing.co.uk

ISBN 978-1-907797-07-1

Copyright © Zoë Harcombe 2011

The Harcombe Diet® is a registered trademark of Zoë Harcombe.

Zoë Harcombe has asserted her right to be identified as the author of this work in accordance with the Copyright, Designs and Patents Act 1988.

A CIP record of this book is available from the British Library.

Cover design by Lewis Kokoc

The advice offered in this book, although based on the author's experience and over twenty years of research, is not intended to be a substitute for the advice of your personal physician. Always consult a medical practitioner before embarking on any diet. Neither the author nor the publisher can be held responsible for any loss or claim arising from the use or misuse of this book.

COLUMBUS PUBLISHING

Thank You...

Thank you to our friends Lyn Johnson and Sam McFadzean for your wonderful recipe contributions.

Thank you to Zoë's parents, John and Verna Dent, for passing down so many real food creations.

Thank you to members of The Harcombe Diet Club – Helen, Kimberley, Lird, Mat, Melissa, Naomi and Splodge – for your delicious recipes and for testing so many of the others.

Thank you Andy for being the chef in our household and for feeding us great food three times a day!

Further Information...

www.zoeharcombe.com

www.theharcombediet.com

www.theharcombedietclub.com

www.theobesityepidemic.org

CONTENTS

(P2) Introduction & How to use this book

(P7) Summary of The Harcombe Diet

Phase 1 & 2

(P20) Breakfasts

(P30) Carb Main Meals (Vegetarian)

(P50) Fat Main Meals

(P126) Side Dishes & Sauces

(P166) Soups, Starters & Lite Bites

Phase 2

(P190) Breakfasts

(P202) Carb Main Meals (Vegetarian)

(P222) Fat Main Meals

(P289) Side Dishes & Sauces

(P303) Soups, Starters & Lite Bites

(P330) Desserts

Phase 3

(P342) Main Meals

(P356) Healthy cheats

(P379) Useful Tables

(P382) The Index

INTRODUCTION

This recipe book is the perfect accompaniment to the growing collection of "The Harcombe Diet" books. We are passionate about helping people to eat food – real food. This is the definitive collection of the favourite recipes dating back to "Why do you overeat? When all you want is to be slim" and many new recipes contributed by the wonderful members of The Harcombe Diet Club.

The recipes from "Stop Counting Calories & Start Losing Weight" have been included in this book – so that you can keep your healthy recipes together in one handy reference book. However, they have been included in addition to, not instead of, over 200 other recipes, just to make sure that you get great value from this bumper book.

This recipe book assumes that you are familiar with The Harcombe Diet and know the three phases of the diet and the three medical conditions, which we need to keep under control. However, just after "how to use this book", there is a summary of what you can eat in Phase 1 and Phase 2 and a quick reminder of the three conditions. We refer to the phases and the conditions quite a bit throughout the book, so we hope that you find these summaries handy for reference.

Please read the notes in the next few pages, as they really will help you to get the most out of this book.

Andy and I hope that the book reawakens an interest in cooking for lapsed cooks and introduces total novices to the joys of making and eating real food. Bon Appétit!

Zoë Harcombe

HOW TO USE THIS BOOK

There are approximately 250 recipes in this book and we hope that the following notes may be of help:

The tick boxes at the bottom of each recipe:

There is a tick box table at the bottom of each recipe to give you a quick glance guide to the following:

- In which phase of the diet you can eat the dish (Phase 1 & 2; Phase 2; Phase 3).

- If the recipe is a carb or fat meal (or OK for either).

- If the recipe is suitable for Vegetarians (V). (This means no meat, fish, gelatine, cochineal, Worcestershire sauce etc).

- If the recipe is suitable for people with Candida (C) (This means no vinegar or pickled foods, no bread or breadcrumbs and no mushrooms). We have ticked recipes with wine as suitable for Candida as so little is used in cooking and the alcohol cooks off anyway.

- If the recipe is suitable for people with Hypoglycaemia (H) (This means no high sugar fruits or high glycaemic index carbs).

- If the recipe is Wheat-free (✓).

- If the recipe is Dairy-free (✓) (This means no cheese, milk, cream, butter or yoghurt but we have included eggs).

As an example, the following table is for a chicken dish (obviously not vegetarian), which can be eaten in Phase 1 or 2, is suitable for people with Candida or Hypoglycaemia and is wheat-free and dairy-free.

Phase	Meal	V	C	H	Wheat free	Dairy free
1 & 2	Fat		✓	✓	✓	✓

General notes on the recipes:

- The book is structured by Phase, as this should be your starting point e.g. "I'm in Phase 1, what can I have for dinner?"

- Phase 1 allows mixing of fats and carbs for two main reasons: a) the first five days can be really tough, so we don't want to make it any tougher than we need to and b) the weight loss in Phase 1 is so good, that the mixing doesn't make much difference. In this recipe book, however, we have focused on Phase 1 recipes that *don't* mix, so that they are automatically suitable for Phase 2. We have only included one Phase 1 recipe that does mix and this is at the end of the Phase 1 main meal section.

- Within each section ("Phase 1 Fat Main Meals", for example) the vegetarian recipes come first, then the fish recipes and then the meat recipes. All carb meals and some fat meals are vegetarian.

- We have approximately 30 recipes that are currently written for Phase 2, but can be easily modified for Phase 1. These recipes have (1 &) 2 in the first column of the tick box table and we state clearly what needs to be left out, or modified, to make the recipe suitable for Phase 1. We have put these at the end of the Phase 1 recipes (again, vegetarian first, then fish, then meat).

- Where we put '3' in the first column, this means that the recipe doesn't meet the 'rules' for Phase 2 so it should be avoided by adults trying to lose weight. Phase 3 dishes can be eaten by children at any time and they can be enjoyed by adults either when they are getting close to their natural weight, and are starting to 'cheat', or for special. Our Phase 3 recipes are still very healthy, but they either mix fats and carbs (which breaks rule 2 in Phase 2) or

4

they may have a bit of sugar, dried fruit or fruit juice in them – all refined carbohydrates.

- We have tried to make the index at the back as helpful as possible. Dishes are listed more than once, so that, for example, you can find a chicken salad under chicken and salads.

- All of the recipes are in metric. We use universal references, like "1 onion" or "2 tablespoons olive oil", as much as possible to minimise any gram and ml/litre measures. There are conversion tables at the back of the book for weights and volumes.

- When we list weights or volumes for ingredients, these are always pre-cooked weights and volumes. Hence "100g brown rice" on the ingredients list will be 100g of brown rice grains straight from the packet – the weight will approximately double when cooked for this particular ingredient. 200g of spinach, on the contrary, will reduce in weight a little and substantially in volume, when it is cooked.

- We list Fahrenheit, Celsius and gas marks on every recipe to make sure that the setting for your own oven is always to hand, without the need to convert. There is also a useful oven conversion table at the back of the book for other recipes you may have.

- Most recipes are designed to serve four people. Please adjust the quantities to suit your family size and/or to make some leftovers for another meal.

- To make the recipes easy to follow, we have listed all the ingredients in the order that you will use them.

- Many of our recipes refer to a large frying pan. This can be a wok – whatever you normally use to fry things with minimal olive oil.

General notes on the ingredients:

- If there is anything you don't like in a recipe, leave it out or swap it for something similar (one spice for another, one vegetable for another etc). Recipes are meant to be adapted to suit your tastes.

- The addition of salt and freshly ground black pepper is mentioned in most dishes. Black pepper is highly recommended, but added salt is not necessary and can easily be left out – nature puts sodium (salt) and potassium in balance in foods, so it is a good idea to respect that balance.

- Please check any tins or packets for unnecessary ingredients. There is never a need for added sugar or salt. Tins of tomatoes usually have citric acid as an added ingredient – this is fine as a preservative. Tinned fish, kidney beans, chickpeas and so on are valuable items to keep in stock – not everything has to be fresh.

- Similarly, frozen vegetables are fine as an alternative to fresh vegetables and useful to keep in stock.

- We always recommend live/bio yoghurt and this is important for Phase 1. For Phase 2 recipes, it's OK to use normal yoghurt, if you can't get live yoghurt.

- We use stock in many recipes. We have recipes for home-made meat and vegetables stocks, which are ideal for cooking. However, in the interests of ease and speed we do appreciate that you may want to use bought stock cubes. Please check that they don't have added sugar (if you are really struggling to find one without sugar then pick one that has sugar lowest down the list of ingredients, as this indicates that there is less sugar in it than other ingredients).

PHASE 1 SUMMARY

Phase 1 was designed to be the perfect diet to overcome the three conditions – Candida, Food Intolerance and Hypoglycaemia – which cause insatiable food cravings. The diet was not intended to produce spectacular weight loss – but it does. The current record is 17 pounds in five days.

Phase 1 lasts for just five days. In such a short time you can kick-start a new way of eating and have a significant impact on the three conditions and therefore food cravings.

You can eat whenever you want during Phase 1, but it really is best to get into the habit of eating three main meals a day and only having snacks in between meals if you are genuinely hungry. However, the most important thing with Phase 1 is to complete it, so eat to make sure that you are not hungry and can stick to the eating plan for the full five days.

You can eat as much as you want of everything on the 'allowed' list, except brown rice for which allowances are given. You really can have a large plate of bacon and eggs for breakfast (just make sure the bacon has no added ingredients) and you can have as much meat, fish, salad and vegetables as you need for main meals.

If you need to snack between your three main meals then you can have cold meats, hard-boiled eggs, celery sticks, raw carrots, Natural Live Yoghurt or a tin of tuna – whatever it takes to keep hunger at bay.

Phase 1 is the start to a life style change in the way that you eat, but it is also the perfect quick fix diet. If you have been cheating a bit too much and a bit too often and feel the cravings return, Phase 1 is your five day rescue plan whenever you need it.

These are the foods that you can eat in Phase 1. Please see notes (1-6) after the tables:

Vegetables		Herbs & Spices
Alfalfa	Marrow	Basil
Artichoke	Mustard greens	Bay leaves
Asparagus	Okra	Caraway
Aubergine	Onions	Cardamom
Bamboo shoots	Parsnip	Chervil
Bean sprouts	Peas	Chives
Beetroot	Peppers (any)	Cinnamon
Broccoli	Pumpkin	Cloves
Brussels sprouts	Radish	Coriander
Bok choy	Rocket	Cumin
Cabbage (any)	Salsify	Dill
Carrots	Shallots	Ginger
Cauliflower	Sorrel	Marjoram
Celeriac	Spinach	Mint
Celery	Spring onions	Nutmeg
Chicory	Squashes	Oregano
Chillies (any)	Swiss chard	Paprika
Courgettes	Swede	Parsley
Cucumber	Turnip	Pepper
Dandelion	Watercress	Rosemary
Endive	Water chestnuts	Saffron
Fennel		Sage
Garlic		Salt
Green beans		Tarragon
Kale		Thyme
Leeks		Turmeric
Lettuce (any)		
Mange tout		

White Fish (1)	White Meat & Birds (2)	Other
Cod	Chicken	Eggs (3)
Coley	Duck	Natural Live
Haddock	Goose	(Bio) Yoghurt
Halibut	Guinea Fowl	Tofu (4)
Monkfish	Pheasant	Quorn (4)
Plaice	Quail	Brown rice (5)
Sea bass	Rabbit	
Sole	Turkey	
Turbot		**Fruit**
Whiting		Tomato
Seafood	**Red Meat**	Olives
Clams	Bacon	
Crab	Beef	**Misc**
Lobster	Gammon	Butter
Mussels	Ham	Olive oil
Oysters	Lamb	Lemon juice
Prawns	Pork	
Winkles	Veal	**Drinks** (6)
Oily Fish	Venison	Water – still or sparkling
Anchovies		Decaf coffee
Herring		Decaf tea
Mackerel		Any herbal teas
Pilchards		Any 'fruit' teas
Salmon		
Sardines		
Tuna		
Trout		

Notes:

1) Provided of course that you don't have a food allergy to any fish or seafood. Fresh, frozen or tinned fish is all fine – just no breadcrumbs or added ingredients.

2) Ideally get all your meat from a local butcher that you come to know and trust. Animals need to be living naturally – grazing on grass in sunlight – for meat to be nutritious. If you do buy any packaged or tinned meats, please check the ingredients list carefully and avoid any with sugars (the 'oses') or other unnecessary ingredients. A preservative is the only acceptable added ingredient.

3) Provided that you are *not* intolerant to, or allergic to, eggs. Eggs should also be from animals able to graze freely on grass in the sunlight.

4) Provided that you are OK with vegetarian protein alternatives. Tofu is a soy product, and soy is a common Food Intolerance – especially in the US. Quorn is made from a type of fungus and so it is best to avoid this if you suffer from Candida.

5) The only food that is limited in quantity is the brown rice. You can have up to 50g (dry weight – before cooking) of brown rice per day. If you are vegetarian or vegan you can have up to 150g (dry weight before cooking) of brown rice per day to make sure that you get enough to eat.

Since first writing "Stop Counting Calories & Start Losing Weight" a couple of suitable alternatives to the brown rice have been added:

a) Puffed brown rice cereal is already listed as one swap option. Brown rice pasta (literally pasta spirals made from brown rice) is another. Both can be swapped, gram for gram dry weight, with the carnivore or vegetarian brown rice allowance. If you suffer Hypoglycaemia, you should avoid the brown rice cereal, as it will likely be too high a glycaemic food for you. For this reason, don't swap the brown rice allowance for rice cakes – they are even more 'puffed' than the cereal and could upset blood glucose levels unnecessarily.

b) Quinoa can also be swapped gram for gram with the brown rice allowance – this is a rarely eaten grain and, therefore, one of the least likely grain intolerances.

c) Porridge oats have also been found to be safe with clients with whom I have worked. This is a really useful breakfast option, especially for people who don't eat eggs.

Don't eat anything that is not on the above list during Phase 1 – no fruit, no other grains, no milk, cheese or other dairy products, no sugar/ sweeteners, no processed food or drink.

6) For drinks, you may drink as much bottled or filtered water and herbal teas as you like during Phase 1, but no alcohol, caffeine or canned drinks (even low calorie drinks) or fruit juices. You can also have any decaffeinated coffee or tea, but without milk, sugar or sweeteners. Any herbal teas are fine – even the fruit versions (like blackcurrant) – they are fruit infusions, rather than fruit itself.

PHASE 2 SUMMARY

These are the foods that you can add in Phase 2 **with Carb meals**:

Whole-grains	Kidney beans	High sugar fruit
Barley	Lentils (all colours)	Bananas
Basmati rice	Lima beans	Dates (fresh)
Brown (whole-grain) rice	Pinto beans	Figs (fresh)
Brown pasta	Soy beans	Grapes
Brown rice pasta		Guavas
Buckwheat	**Vegetables**	Kumquat
Bulghar wheat	Potatoes	Kiwi fruit
Corn	Sweet potatoes	Lychees
Millet	Yams	Mango
Oats		Melons
Quinoa	**Low sugar fruit**	Papaya
Rye	Apples	Passion fruit
100% Wholemeal bread	Apricots	Pineapple
100% Whole wheat cereal	Cherries	Pomegranates
	Clementines	Sharon fruit
	Grapefruit	Tropical fruits
Beans & Pulses	Nectarines	
Aduki beans	Oranges	
Black eyed beans	Peaches	
Broad beans	Pears	
Butter beans	Satsumas	
Chickpeas	Tangerines	
Flageolet		

These are the foods that you can add in Phase 2 **with meals, as shown**:

With either meal	With either meal	With fat meals
Fruit – Berries	**Low-fat Dairy**	**Dairy Products**
Blackberries	(Very) low-fat milk	Cheese
Blackcurrants	(Very) low-fat yoghurt	Cream
Blueberries		Milk
Cranberries		Yoghurt
Gooseberries		
Lemons		
Limes		
Loganberries		
Raspberries		
Strawberries		

The three rules of Phase 2 are:

1) Don't eat processed foods;

2) Don't eat fats and carbohydrates at the same meal;

3) Don't eat foods that cause your cravings.

Again – really try *not* to snack – you need to give your body the chance to burn its own fat and eating all day long is not going to help with this.

Here is a really useful list to show which foods can be eaten as a fat meal and which can be eaten as a carbohydrate meal and which can be eaten with either:

(Don't forget – fats had 'faces' or come from things with faces – meat, fish, eggs, cream, milk etc. Carbs tend to come from trees and the ground – fruit, grains, potatoes etc. That is the quick way to remember the difference between fats and carbs).

FAT MEALS	CARB MEALS
Any unprocessed meat (2) – bacon, beef, chicken, duck, goose, guinea fowl, ham, lamb, pheasant, pork, quail, rabbit, turkey, veal, venison.	All **Fruit**
	Whole-grains – brown rice, brown pasta, brown rice pasta, 100% whole wheat bread, quinoa, millet etc.
Any unprocessed fish (1) – cod, haddock, halibut, mackerel, plaice, pilchards, salmon, seafood (1), trout, tuna, whiting etc. Includes tinned fish in only oil, salt and/or water.	**Whole wheat cereal** – porridge oats, brown rice cereal, Shredded Wheat, other sugar-free cereal.
	Beans & Pulses – lentils, broad beans, kidney beans, chickpeas.
Eggs – chicken, duck etc. (3)	
Dairy Products – cheese, milk, butter, cream, yoghurt (ideally Natural Live Yoghurt)	Baked **Potatoes** in their skins.

EAT WITH EITHER A FAT OR CARB MEAL
Salads – alfalfa, bean sprouts, beetroot, celery, chicory, cress, cucumber, endive, all types of lettuce, radish, rocket, spring onions etc.
Vegetables – artichoke, asparagus, aubergine/eggplant, bamboo shoots, broccoli, Brussels sprouts, cabbage, carrot, cauliflower, celeriac, chillies, courgettes/zucchini, garlic, green/French beans, kale, leek, mange tout, marrow, okra, onions, parsnip, peas, peppers (any colour), pumpkin, salsify, shallots, spinach, squashes, swede, turnip, water chestnuts etc.
Tofu/Quorn – vegetarian protein alternatives. (4)
Certain **Fruits** – olives, tomatoes & berries.
Very low-fat dairy products – milk, cottage cheese & yoghurt.
Herbs, Spices & Seasoning – basil, chives, coriander, cumin, dill, fennel, mint, oregano, paprika, parsley, pepper, rosemary, sage, salt, thyme. Olive oil for cooking.

Notes 1 to 4 in the Phase 1 summary also apply to the above table.

How to use this list:

1) You can eat anything on the 'fat' list with anything on the 'eat with either' list. You can eat anything on the 'carb' list with anything on the 'eat with either' list.

2) You cannot eat anything on the fat and carb lists at the same meal i.e. nothing on the fat list at the same time as something on the carb list.

3) Generally, when fat is removed from a product something else needs to be put back in to replace it. The exception to this is with animal fat products where fat can be removed and nothing needs to be put back in its place. So, where there are low-fat alternatives to standard products like milk and yoghurt, these low-fat alternatives can be eaten with carb meals. This lets us have (very) low-fat milk with whole wheat cereals and low-fat cottage cheese with baked potatoes. The key is to keep fat away from carbs so carbs can be eaten with (very) low-fat alternatives to dairy products.

PHASE 3 SUMMARY

The rules of Phase 3 are:

1) Don't 'cheat' too much;

2) Don't 'cheat' too often;

3) Be alert and stay in control.

Some of the recipes in this book are 'cheats', but they show you how to cheat healthily and how to continue to eat real food in a way that can help you maintain your weight loss.

Just a final food table, before we move on to the conditions...

The following are very nutritious foods but they contain both fats and carbohydrates, in reasonable quantities, so they should not be eaten while you are trying to lose weight. They are fine for using sparingly in cooking and they are good as snacks for children. They are also really healthy for Phase 3, when you start mixing fats and carbs again, as they are nature's natural mixed foods...

Raw Nuts	Seeds	Misc
Almonds	Flax	Avocados
Brazil nuts	Pumpkin	
Cashews	Sesame	
Hazelnuts	Sunflower (more fat than carbohydrate, but has both)	
Chestnuts		
Pecans		
Pine nuts		
Pistachios		
Walnuts		

THE MEDICAL CONDITIONS

Candida – is a yeast, which lives in all of us, and is normally kept under control by our immune system and other bacteria in our body. It usually lives in the digestive system. Candida serves no useful purpose. If it stays quiet, and in balance, it causes no harm. The problem starts if Candida multiplies out of control and then it can create havoc with our health and wellbeing.

Candida causes cravings for bread, sugary foods, yeasty foods, vinegar and pickled foods and these are the foods that must be avoided by people with Candida overgrowth. The key 'every day' ingredients for people with Candida to avoid are mushrooms and vinegar.

Food Intolerance – means, quite simply, not being able to tolerate a particular food. This is different to Food Allergy – Food Allergy is the really serious, life threatening, condition where people have nut, or strawberry allergies, for example. Food Intolerance develops when you have too much of a food and too often and your body just gets to the point where it can't cope with that food any longer. Food Intolerance can also make a person feel horribly unwell.

Food Intolerance causes cravings for the food(s) to which you are intolerant. There is quite a complex medical explanation for this but the simplest way to understand why this happens is that you develop addiction to foods that you eat too much of and too often. You then crave the foods, not to make you feel good, but because you get headaches and other withdrawal symptoms if you don't have the food. The most common Food Intolerances are to wheat, sugar and dairy products. Every one of the following recipes indicates whether or not it has wheat or dairy products in it.

Hypoglycaemia – is literally a Greek translation from "*hypo*" meaning 'under', "*glykis*" meaning 'sweet' and "*emia*" meaning 'in the blood together'. The three bits all put together mean low blood sugar. Hypoglycaemia describes the state the body is in if your blood sugar levels are too low. When your blood sugar levels are too low, this is potentially life threatening and your body will try to get you to eat.

People with Hypoglycaemia find that their blood glucose levels are all over the place and difficult to keep stable. They find that they crave carbohydrates – sometimes 'good' carbs, like fruit, and often 'bad' carbs, like sweets and biscuits. They crave carbohydrates because they are trying to get their blood glucose level back to normal. The trouble is, people with Hypoglycaemia have such sensitive blood glucose mechanisms that, eating any carbohydrates can send their blood glucose level off balance again and they are back craving more carbohydrates.

The following cravings are likely to indicate the following conditions:

- Bread & Cereal – Candida and wheat Food Intolerance;

- Sugar & sugary foods – usually all three conditions;

- Fruit – Candida and Hypoglycaemia;

- Pickled foods – Candida;

- Cheese – Dairy Food Intolerance & (possibly) Candida.

Phase 1

(P20) Breakfasts

(P30) Carb Main Meals (Vegetarian)

(P50) Fat Main Meals

(P126) Side dishes & Sauces

(P166) Soups, Starters & Lite Bites

PHASE 1 – BREAKFASTS

The single best tip that we have, to make Phase 1 as easy as possible, is to drop preconceived ideas of what 'should' be eaten at breakfast. Think of having three meals a day and all Phase 1 options open up to you. Many Asian populations are role models for this – they eat noodle, rice and vegetable dishes, with any meat and fish available, three times a day. They don't think of breakfast as being different to other meals and nor should you. You can have any Phase 1 main meal for breakfast – the key thing will be what you can get your head around eating first thing in the morning.

The second best tip is to think of breakfast as just fuel. Zoë has had porridge every day for 15 years and Andy bacon & eggs. You just need some fuel to start the day – you don't need culinary delights, or even variety.

The cereal breakfast options for Phase 1 are puffed brown rice cereal (now available in most supermarkets, as well as health food shops) and porridge oats. The brown rice cereal should be eaten dry – it is crunchy and many people feed back that they really enjoy it. The simplest way to do porridge oats is to measure out your 50g dry weight (remember, this is a swap for your brown rice allowance in Phase 1) and literally pour boiling water over the oats, stir and eat while hot and chewy. You may like to microwave or boil the oats in hot water, stirring regularly, if you like a less coarse consistency.

Natural Live Yoghurt is another quick and simple breakfast option. You will find normal yoghurt (not low fat) more filling and more likely to see you through until lunch time.

Other breakfast options will largely be based around eggs, bacon and fish – variations of kippers and salmon being perfectly acceptable starts to the day.

Poached Egg Salad

Poached eggs are one of the simplest, yet most difficult, dishes to master. The secret to success is in getting the water to the right temperature before adding the eggs.

Ingredients:

25g mixed salad leaves, chopped	Knob of butter
½ red pepper, finely sliced	2 eggs
1 tablespoon olive oil	Salt & ground black pepper
200ml water	

Method:

1) Place the salad leaves on a medium plate and add the finely sliced red pepper. Drizzle olive oil over the salad and put it to one side.

2) Add the water to a frying pan and heat to boiling point. Add the knob of butter and then reduce the heat until the water occasionally bubbles.

3) Crack the eggs into the boiling water and tease the whites towards the yolks to keep them in an egg shape. Cook for 3-4 minutes, making sure that you keep the eggs moving in the bubbling water.

4) Remove the eggs from the pan with a slotted spoon and place them on the ready prepared salad. Season to taste and serve immediately.

Serves 1

Phase	Meal	V	C	H	Wheat free	Dairy free
1 & 2	Fat	✓	✓	✓	✓	

Spanish (Squash) Omelette

The traditional Spanish omelette is not Harcombe Diet friendly, as it is based on eggs and potatoes and therefore it mixes. This variation uses butternut squash instead of potatoes and encourages you to use up any leftover vegetables from the night before.

Ingredients:

4 tablespoons olive oil	50g frozen peas
250g butternut squash, peeled, deseeded & thickly sliced	6 eggs, beaten
	3 tablespoons parsley, chopped
1 onion, chopped	Salt & ground black pepper
200g leftover vegetables - broccoli, carrots, peppers work well	

Method:

1) Heat the oil in a large frying pan. Add the butternut squash slices and onion and cook gently, partially covered, for 30 minutes, stirring occasionally until the squash is softened.

2) Add the leftover vegetables and peas and stir until they are warmed through.

3) Strain the vegetables through a colander into a large bowl (set the strained oil aside).

4) Add the beaten eggs to the vegetables. Add the parsley and plenty of seasoning.

5) Heat a little of the strained oil in an omelette pan (any frying pan approximately 25-30cm diameter). Pour the mixture into the pan and cook on a moderate heat, using a spatula to shape the omelette into a fluffy round 'cushion'.

6) When almost set, invert on a plate and slide back into the pan and cook a few more minutes. Invert twice more, cooking the omelette briefly each time and pressing the edges to keep the cushion shape. Slide onto a plate and serve immediately.

TIP 1 – This is also great served cold and can therefore be taken to work as a lunch option.

Serves 2 – scale up on the basis of allowing 3 eggs per person

Phase	Meal	V	C	H	Wheat free	Dairy free
1 & 2	Fat	✓	✓	✓	✓	✓

The Harcombe Protein Shake

Who needs expensive, processed protein shakes, with so many unrecognisable ingredients, when nature provides natural vitamins, minerals, protein and fat in eggs and yoghurt?

Ingredients:

4 eggs, separated 1-2 teaspoons ground cinnamon	500ml thick Natural Live Yoghurt

Method:

1) Separate the egg yolks and whites. Put the yolks in one mixing bowl and the whites in another.

2) Using an electric whisk beat the egg yolks until they are mixed. Continue whisking for 1-2 minutes, until the yolks turn pale yellow.

3) Stir in the cinnamon to your liking.

4) Whisk the egg whites until stiff peaks form.

5) Fold the egg whites into the egg yolk mixture.

6) Gently fold the thick NLY into the mixture.

7) Serve in a glass, as if a milkshake, and sprinkle a dash of cinnamon on top.

TIP 1 – Swap the NLY for half milk and half real whipped cream and add 100ml of bourbon or brandy for a 'close to Phase 2' "Eggnog".

Serves 2

Phase	Meal	V	C	H	Wheat free	Dairy free
1 & 2	Fat	✓	✓	✓	✓	

Haddock with Fennel

This would be a wonderful breakfast to do at the weekend. Don't be put off by the idea of fish for breakfast – it's just a Phase 1 version of kippers.

Ingredients:

50g butter	½ small fennel bulb, approximately 75g, finely chopped
4 haddock fillets, each approximately 200g	
1 lemon, quartered	Freshly ground pepper

Method:

1) Preheat the oven to 400° F, 200° C, gas mark 6.

2) Melt half the butter in a frying pan and cook the haddock fillets for 2-3 minutes on each side. Transfer the fillets to a shallow oven-proof dish.

3) Squeeze the juice from 1 lemon quarter over each fillet and place the squeezed quarter on top of each fish. Bake in the oven for approximately 15 minutes. Turn off the oven and leave the fish inside to keep warm.

4) To make the sauce, add the remaining butter to the frying pan with the chopped fennel. Cook for about 4 minutes and season to taster.

5) Transfer the haddock fillets to warm plates and pour the fennel and butter sauce over them. Serve immediately.

Serves 4

Phase	Meal	V	C	H	Wheat free	Dairy free
1 & 2	Fat		✓	✓	✓	

The Perfect 'Fat' Breakfast

The perfect start to any day is the dish commonly known as "The Full English". The real "Full English" can include bacon, eggs, sausages, black pudding, tomatoes, baked beans and fried bread, making it a fat storing concoction with unnecessarily added wheat and sugar. For our Phase 1 version we can have any of the following:

- Bacon: Ideally get your meat from the local butcher – best for your community and for your health. The butcher's meat is hard to beat for quality and reduced chance of added ingredients. Choose bacon that is *not* smoked, sweetened or processed in any unnecessary way. Cured bacon is fine – that's the natural drying/preserving process for meat. Real bacon should look pale in colour and it will *not* naturally have a long shelf life. If in any doubt, use any slice of pork from the leg or rib instead of bacon. It's just pig & egg at the end of the day. Bacon can be grilled, or fried in butter or olive oil.

- Eggs: (provided of course that you are tolerant to eggs) – scrambled, fried (in butter or olive oil), poached, boiled eggs & crudités soldiers etc.

- Steak: or any other pure meat, if you fancy it.

- A few mushrooms and tomatoes fried in olive oil (no mushrooms if Candida is a problem for you and only a couple of tomatoes, as they are carbohydrates).

Avoid:

- Sausages, as they are almost always packed with other ingredients. If you can get pure meat sausages from the butcher, with meat and animal products, but no wheat or other carb fillers, these will be fine to have with your fat breakfast.

- All carbohydrates, other than tomatoes or mushrooms. No bread, no baked beans etc.

- All sauces e.g. tomato sauce, ketchup, brown sauce etc. – as these are all laden with sugar and often other refined carbohydrates too.

The "Middle Eastern" breakfast is also a great fat meal. The Phase 1 version can include a selection of cold meats and hard-boiled eggs. Cheese slices can be added in Phase 2.

Here are three of the basic Phase 1 versions of our favourite fat breakfasts:

Simple Bacon & Eggs

Ingredients (per person):

2 rashers of back bacon (unsmoked, unsweetened) Knob of butter	2 eggs Freshly ground black pepper

Method:

1) Heat a frying pan to a warm heat and add the bacon rashers. Cook them for 2-3 minutes on each side, in their own fat, and then transfer them to a plate and keep them warm under a grill.

2) Melt a knob of butter in the frying pan and, when it begins to bubble, crack the eggs into the butter. Cook for about 3 minutes until the whites become opaque, or longer if you prefer a firmer yolk.

3) Serve immediately on the warmed plate and then grind some freshly ground pepper over the eggs.

Phase	Meal	V	C	H	Wheat free	Dairy free
1 & 2	Fat		✓	✓	✓	

Phase 1 Omelette (No Milk)

We have a couple of classic egg breakfast recipes, made without milk, to be suitable for Phase 1.

Ingredients (per person):

2-3 eggs	Freshly ground black pepper
½ teaspoon mixed herbs	Knob of butter

Method:

1) Crack 2-3 eggs per person into a mixing bowl and beat with a fork, or an electric whisk, until fluffy.

2) Add the mixed herbs and black pepper.

3) Melt a knob of butter in a frying pan and add the whisked eggs.

4) Cook slowly until the mixture becomes firm. (You can tilt the pan to move the mixture around to make sure it covers the pan, but don't stir it or you will end up with scrambled eggs).

TIP 1 – For a flavoured omelette, add some of your favourite ingredients to the whisked eggs before pouring them into the frying pan. The classic options are ham in Phase 1 and cheese and mushrooms in Phase 2 (no mushrooms for Candida).

TIP 2 – This can be served with a mixed salad for a main meal.

TIP 3 – To make a Phase 2 omelette, add about 30ml of milk (or cream) to the eggs at step 1.

Phase	Meal	V	C	H	Wheat free	Dairy free
1 & 2	Fat	Can be	✓	✓	✓	

Phase 1 Scrambled Eggs (No Milk)

The traditional way to serve scrambled eggs invariably involves toast. This introduces wheat at breakfast – not a good start to the day for likely Food Intolerance and Candida. Try this recipe on a bed of crispy lettuce – for the same crunchy effect. Or, serve on top of plain, unadulterated bacon, for a far tastier base.

Ingredients (per person):

2-3 eggs	Dash of Tabasco (optional)
Freshly ground black pepper	Knob of butter

Method:

1) Crack 2-3 eggs per person into a mixing bowl and beat with a fork, or an electric whisk, until fluffy.

2) Season to taste.

3) Melt a knob of butter in a frying pan and add the whisked eggs.

4) Continually stir the eggs in the pan (with a wooden spoon) until they become the consistency that you like. The longer you cook them the firmer they will get.

TIP 1 – To make scrambled eggs, for Phase 2, add the same volume as the eggs, in milk (or cream), when you first crack the eggs into a bowl.

Phase	Meal	V	C	H	Wheat free	Dairy free
1 & 2	Fat	✓	✓	✓	✓	

PHASE 1 – CARB MAIN MEALS

Spinach & Sun Dried Tomato Risotto

This uses just a couple of vegetables – spinach and sun-dried tomatoes – but both of these ingredients have a rich taste, almost unparalleled in the vegetable world. This recipe also uses brown rice, instead of risotto rice, so that it is perfect for all stages of the diet. You can even do this in Phase 1 with your rice allowance.

Ingredients:

600ml vegetable stock	100g sun-dried tomatoes
225g brown rice (dry weight)	A pinch of dried basil
	A pinch of dried oregano
2 tablespoons olive oil	Salt & ground black pepper
2 onions, finely chopped	
225g spinach	

Method:

1) Make the stock either from scratch using a recipe in this book or by crumbling a stock cube into 600ml boiling water.

2) Put this in a saucepan and cook the brown rice in the stock for 30 minutes.

3) Meanwhile, a) put the olive oil in a large frying pan, and fry the onions until soft and b) boil the spinach in a separate saucepan, in as little water as you can get away with, until it wilts. This should take only a couple of minutes.

4) As soon as the spinach is wilted, drain it, let it cool and chop it into fine pieces.

5) Drain off any excess water in the rice pan and then add the rice into the pan with the onions.

6) Add the spinach, sun-dried tomatoes, basil, oregano, salt & pepper and give it a good stir.

7) Ideally serve straight away, but the dish can be kept for up to an hour if you cover it, to seal the moisture in, and keep it warm in a very low oven.

8) Garnish with parsley.

TIP 1 – Risottos are great served with a peppery rocket side salad.

TIP 2 – Add a pinch of saffron to the rice, when you begin to add the stock, for a great flavour and colour.

Serves 4

Phase	Meal	V	C	H	Wheat free	Dairy free
1 & 2	Carb	✓	✓	✓	✓	✓

Mediterranean Quinoa

Quinoa can be swapped, gram for gram dry weight, with the Phase 1 brown rice allowance. It would be virtually unheard of for someone to be intolerant to this unusual and versatile grain. This can be an especially useful dish for vegetarians in Phase 1.

Ingredients:

750ml vegetable stock	1 red pepper, deseeded & chopped
3–4 sprigs of fresh thyme	
200g quinoa	200g cherry tomatoes
2 tablespoons olive oil	200g tinned tomatoes, chopped
1 red onion, chopped	
2 garlic cloves, crushed	2 tablespoons tomato purée
1 aubergine, diced	Salt & ground black pepper
1 courgette, chopped	

Method:

1) Preheat the oven to 375° F, 190° C, gas mark 5.

2) Place the stock, thyme sprigs and quinoa in a saucepan and bring to the boil. Cover and simmer gently for approximately 20 minutes until the quinoa is cooked.

3) Meanwhile heat the olive oil in a frying pan and stir-fry the onion, garlic, aubergine, courgette and pepper until slightly blackened.

4) Add the (whole) cherry tomatoes and cook for approximately 2 minutes, or until the skins start to burst. Remove from the heat.

5) When the quinoa is cooked, drain away any left over stock, remove the thyme sprigs and put the

quinoa in an oven-proof dish. Add the stir-fried vegetables, tinned tomatoes and seasoning and gently mix the ingredients together.

6) Cover with tin foil, to retain the moisture, and bake for approximately 30 minutes, until the vegetables are soft to a fork touch.

TIP 1 – For a great Phase 3 variation, add 200g of goats or feta cheese, cut into cubes, at stage 5 of the method. This will make the meal more substantial and filling.

TIP 2 – For a Phase 1 mixing option – add diced meat to the frying pan at stage 3 of the method and seal the meat as you slightly blacken the vegetables.

Serves 4 (vegetarians may like to increase the quinoa portion to 100g per person)

Phase	Meal	V	C	H	Wheat free	Dairy free
1 & 2	Carb	✓	✓	✓	✓	✓

Southern Indian Vegetable Curry

This is a really special vegetarian curry with a wonderful mixture of vegetables and spices. Phase 1 works well with butternut squash as the staple ingredient. Phase 2 can work well using potatoes, instead of the squash, for a variation. (Watch the potatoes if you are very carb sensitive, as they have a high glycaemic index). This does mix fats and carbs a bit, with the coconut milk. However, each serving ends up with just one tablespoon of coconut milk so this is not going to make any difference to your weight loss.

Ingredients:

2 tablespoons of oil	¼ teaspoon of chilli powder
1 teaspoon of mustard seeds	6 tomatoes, chopped
2 green chillies, deseeded & chopped	1 butternut squash, peeled, deseeded & diced
1 bunch of curry leaves (ideally fresh, if not dried or see TIP 4)	1 aubergine, diced
2 onions, finely chopped	100ml unsweetened coconut milk
½ teaspoon of ground coriander	75g French beans
A pinch of cumin seeds	75g peas
½ teaspoon of garam masala	75g okra
¼ teaspoon of turmeric	Salt & ground black pepper

Method:

1) Heat the oil in a pan and fry the mustard seeds for 2-3 minutes or until they start to pop.

2) Add the chillies, curry leaves, onions, coriander, cumin seeds, garam masala, turmeric, and chilli powder. Stir and cook until the onion is soft.

3) Add the chopped tomatoes.

4) Add the butternut squash (or potatoes – see TIP 3) and aubergine to the sauce.

5) Pour in the coconut milk and cook until the butternut squash (or potato) is soft. This will take about 20-30 minutes.

6) Add the beans, peas and okra.

7) Season and cook for a few more minutes until everything is tender.

TIP 1 – This can be served with brown rice, as it is a carb meal.

TIP 2 – As with the butternut squash curry, this is suitable for Phase 1, as coconut milk is non dairy and has anti-Candida properties.

TIP 3 – This can be done with 2 sweet potatoes, peeled & diced and 2 new potatoes, peeled & diced instead of the butternut squash.

TIP 4 – Curry leaves are a unique and distinctive ingredient in Southeast Asian cooking. You should be able to get some on line or in Asian shops. If you can't get some, either leave them out or try basil leaves. Basil will give a different flavour – nothing can substitute properly for curry leaves.

Serves 4

Phase	Meal	V	C	H	Wheat free	Dairy free
1 & 2	Carb	✓	✓	✓	✓	✓

Butternut Squash Curry

This has proved to be the single most popular Harcombe recipe ever. We have had more comments about this than most other recipes put together. If you haven't tried it yet – you must. Even the most ardent carnivores rave about this – Andy's best creation.

Butternut squash is like the meat of the vegetable kingdom. This is the most luxurious Phase 1 dish possible as it uses creamed coconut for flavouring. Creamed coconut is non-dairy and coconut oil has natural anti-Candida properties.

Ingredients:

2 tablespoons olive oil	500ml vegetable stock
3 onions, finely chopped	100g block of creamed coconut
4 cloves garlic, crushed	
2 teaspoons each of turmeric, cumin, paprika, coriander, chilli powder, curry powder (medium or hot depending on your preference)	1kg of mixed vegetables, peeled & diced (cauliflower, courgettes, broccoli, carrots etc)
	1 butternut squash, peeled, deseeded & diced
2 x 400g tins of chopped tomatoes	

Method:

1) Heat the olive oil in a large saucepan and then gently fry the onions and garlic until soft.

2) Add the spices and gently fry for 1-2 minutes.

3) Add the tomatoes and vegetable stock and bring to the boil. Simmer for 5 minutes and then remove it from the heat and allow the mixture to cool slightly.

4) Using a hand blender, blend the mixture until smooth.

5) Return the mixture to the heat and stir in the creamed coconut block until it is completely dissolved.

6) You now have a delicious curry sauce to which you can add all the vegetables. Put the lid on the saucepan and simmer gently until the vegetables are cooked to your liking (approximately 30 minutes).

TIP 1 – This can be served with brown rice, as a carb meal. It could also be served with chicken as a fat meal – the butternut squash is a coloured vegetable and therefore higher in carbohydrate, but this should be fine for most people. Alternatively you can replace the butternut squash and so many mixed vegetables with 500-750g of diced meat (chicken, beef or lamb) and 250-500g of mixed vegetables.

TIP 2 – If you are very carb sensitive, make the sauce without the butternut squash and with 500g of lower carb vegetables (cauliflower, courgettes and broccoli for example) and use 500g of diced chicken for a chicken curry. You can stir-fry the chicken pieces along with the onions and garlic.

Serves 4-6

Phase	Meal	V	C	H	Wheat free	Dairy free
1 & 2	Either	✓	✓	✓	✓	✓

Mild Korma Curry

This can be done with any vegetables in season, or any left over vegetables. It is done here as a vegetable curry, but you can also do a meat curry version if you would prefer. If you make a meat version then eat it on its own, not with brown rice, to keep the carbs and fats separate. If you do make a meat version you can use full fat or Greek yoghurt to make the recipe richer and creamier.

Ingredients:

2 tablespoons olive oil	1 tablespoon ground cumin
1 red onion, coarsely chopped,	¼ teaspoon ground coriander
2 carrots, peeled & thickly sliced	1 teaspoon garam masala
1 cauliflower, broken into florets	1 teaspoon salt
1 green chilli, deseeded & chopped	150ml vegetable stock
	100g frozen or fresh peas
2 cloves garlic, crushed	6 tablespoons Natural Live Yoghurt
1 tablespoon ginger, grated	

Method:

1) Heat the oil in a frying pan over a moderate heat and cook the onion until soft.

2) Add the carrots, cauliflower, chilli, garlic, ginger, spices and salt and cook for a further 3 minutes.

3) Pour in the stock, cover and cook for 5-10 minutes, until almost tender.

4) Add the peas and cook for a further couple of minutes until the vegetables are all tender.

5) Take the pan off the heat and stir in the yoghurt until the sauce has thickened.

Serve with brown rice, or brown basmati rice, or eat as an Indian dish on its own.

TIP 1 – You can use any Natural Live Yoghurt for Phase 1, as we don't worry about mixing for the first five days. If you want to avoid mixing then go for low fat yoghurt for a carb meal dish – the quantities are tiny though so really don't worry.

TIP 2 – Eat with meat for a fat meal or with vegetables for a carb meal.

Serves 4

Phase	Meal	V	C	H	Wheat free	Dairy free
1 & 2	Either	✓	✓	✓	✓	

Bean Paella

This dish has so many nutrients in it with a fantastic assortment of vegetables, pulses and whole-grains (rice). This is a cheaper alternative to the normal Spanish dish, which is full of seafood. The normal Paella also breaks the 'not mixing fats and carbs' rule, but this one doesn't.

Ingredients:

350g (dry weight) brown rice	2 'beef' tomatoes, chopped
2 tablespoons olive oil	100g button mushrooms
2 onions, finely chopped	100g tin red kidney beans, drained & rinsed
2 cloves garlic, crushed	
1 stick celery, finely chopped	Salt & ground black pepper
1 green pepper, deseeded & diced	½ teaspoon turmeric
	½ teaspoon oregano
1 aubergine, peeled & diced	2 tablespoons parsley, chopped
2 carrots, peeled & diced	

Method:

1) Cook the brown rice according to the directions on the packet.

2) While the rice is cooking, heat the oil in a large frying pan.

3) Stir-fry the onions, garlic, celery, pepper, aubergine and carrots for approximately 10 minutes, until the carrots are starting to soften.

4) Add the tomatoes and mushrooms and cook for a further 5 minutes.

5) Drain the rice and add it to the vegetable mixture. Add the kidney beans too and the seasoning, turmeric and oregano.

6) Cook on a very low heat for a further 15 minutes, stirring frequently.

7) Serve with the chopped Parsley on top as garnish.

TIP 1 – Leave out the kidney beans and mushrooms and this can be suitable for Phase 1 and Candida – great for vegetarians who struggle in Phase 1.

TIP 2 – For a Phase 1 dish, when mixing is allowed, you can replace the beans with 100-200g of mixed seafood. Add the seafood at step 5 instead of the beans.

Serves 4

Phase	Meal	V	C	H	Wheat free	Dairy free
(1 &) 2	Carb	✓	Can be	✓	✓	✓

Vegetable Hot Pot

This is a great carb dish, especially for the winter. Cook a batch at the weekend and then you can heat it up for main meals during the week. If you leave out the potatoes and nuts you can have this as a Phase 1 dish. Also leave out the potatoes if you have Hypoglycaemia.

Ingredients:

2 tablespoons olive oil	500ml water
1 onion, finely chopped	1 vegetable stock cube, crumbled
1 clove garlic, crushed	
1 tablespoon curry powder (mild or hot – as you like it)	2 carrots, peeled & chopped
	2 potatoes, peeled & chopped (optional)
1 teaspoon ground cumin	½ cauliflower, chopped
½ teaspoon ground cardamom	200g green beans, chopped
½ teaspoon ground nutmeg	200g Natural Live Yoghurt (low-fat)
½ teaspoon ground ginger	Salt & ground black pepper
½ teaspoon ground all spice	100g cashew nuts, chopped (optional)
1 chilli, finely chopped	
1 tablespoon corn flour (optional)	Fresh coriander to garnish

Method:

1) Heat the olive oil in a large saucepan over a moderate heat.

2) Add the onion, garlic, curry powder, spices and chilli and stir-fry until the onions and garlic are soft.

3) Stir in the corn flour (optional) for 1 minute. Remove from the heat.

4) Add approximately 500ml of boiling water to the stock cube, in a separate measuring jug and then add this to the saucepan.

5) Return to the heat and bring to the boil, stirring continuously until it thickens slightly.

6) Add all the vegetables, cover and leave everything to simmer until the vegetables are soft (chop the potatoes and carrots small enough so that they cook at the same time as the green beans).

7) Add the yoghurt a couple of minutes before serving – just long enough for it to warm through. Season to taste.

8) Sprinkle the nuts (not for Phase 1) and coriander on top.

TIP 1 – Nuts do have good amounts of both fat and carbohydrate. However, the quantities in this recipe, when mixed with all the other ingredients, are too small to make a difference.

Serves 4

Phase	Meal	V	C	H	Wheat free	Dairy free
(1 &) 2	Carb	✓	✓	Can be	✓	

Stuffed Peppers/Tomatoes

This can be done with either peppers or 'beef' tomatoes. The recipe below uses peppers as an example. Use multi-coloured peppers if you are cooking this for several people, so that you get a real assortment of colour.

Ingredients:

100g brown rice	1 clove garlic, crushed
1 litre vegetable stock	4 mushrooms, finely chopped
4 peppers (red, green or yellow)	1 teaspoon mixed herbs
1 tablespoon olive oil	Freshly ground black pepper
1 onion, finely chopped	

Method:

1) Preheat the oven to 350° F, 175° C, gas mark 4.

2) Cook the brown rice in the vegetable stock for approximately 30 minutes.

3) Meanwhile, prepare the peppers by slicing the tops off (keeping them intact) and scoop out the seeds from the middle. The idea is to make a 'bowl' with a 'lid', out of the peppers, to stuff the other ingredients into.

4) Approximately 5 minutes before the rice is cooked, gently fry the onion, garlic and mushrooms, in a frying pan, in the olive oil, until soft.

5) Add the herbs and stir in the cooked brown rice. Add some freshly ground black pepper and stuff the mixture into the prepared peppers.

6) Replace the top on the peppers and place them in an oven-proof dish. Bake for approximately 20-30 minutes.

TIP 1 – Leave out the mushrooms, or use another vegetable (e.g. courgettes) instead, and this can be suitable for Phase 1 and Candida.

Serves 4

Phase	Meal	V	C	H	Wheat free	Dairy free
(1 &) 2	Carb	✓	Can be	✓	✓	✓

Brown Rice Risotto Base

If you have the guest with 'everything' and they can't/won't eat meat/fish/wheat/dairy products and then some, you can't go wrong with risotto. This is a really useful risotto base recipe. You can use it to add your own vegetable combinations. For Phase 2 remember to keep the meat, fish and cheese away from risotto to separate your fats and carbs.

Ingredients:

2 tablespoons olive oil	1.5 litres vegetable stock, (you may not need all of this)
1 onion, finely chopped	
2 cloves garlic, finely chopped	1 teaspoon salt
400g short grain brown rice	Freshly ground black pepper
100ml dry white wine	

Method:

1) Warm the oil in a large frying pan over a medium heat. Gently fry the onion and garlic, for approximately 5 minutes, until soft.

2) Add the rice and stir constantly for approximately 3 minutes until the rice is just starting to 'toast'.

3) Add the wine and keep stirring until it has been absorbed by the rice.

4) Add 1-2 ladles of the stock and a pinch of salt. Keep the mixture simmering at a gentle boil and stir until the liquid is absorbed.

5) Turn the heat to low and set a timer for 5 minutes. Every 5 minutes or so add another 1-2 ladles of stock and a pinch of salt and stir the rice.

6) Continue this process until the rice is al dente (firm, but not hard). This will take approximately 45 minutes.

7) If you have liquid left in the pan when the rice is cooked, put a lid on the pan and let the rice sit covered for about 10 minutes. Drain away any liquid left after this.

8) Season to taste.

TIP 1 – Great carb options to add to this base recipe are:

- Butternut squash cubes (or pumpkin) and sage;

- Asparagus, peas and mint;

- Courgette and tomato.

TIP 2 – If you leave the wine out, and add the stock from step 3, this can be suitable for Phase 1.

TIP 3 – Risotto connoisseurs will only use Arborio rice. This recipe works perfectly by swapping the short grain brown rice for Arborio rice. You may need slightly less cooking and absorbing time with Arborio rice.

Serves 4

Phase	Meal	V	C	H	Wheat free	Dairy free
(1 &) 2	Carb	✓	✓	✓	✓	✓

Ginger Tofu & Okra

Tofu comes from the soybean as cheese comes from milk. It is a versatile and nutritious product and is an good source of vegetarian protein. In 100 grams of tofu there are eight grams of protein, four grams of fat and less than one gram of carbohydrate. Hence it is more fat than carb, but it is barely either. So it can be eaten with cheese as a fat meal or with vegetables and beans as a carb meal. It is a good source of calcium and has all eight essential amino acids.

Ingredients:

2 teaspoons peanut oil	1 tablespoon fresh ginger, grated
2 onions, sliced	60ml white wine (optional)
2 cloves garlic, crushed	
200g of okra, chopped into batons	2 tablespoons Tamari soy sauce (optional)
200g cabbage leaves, shredded (ideally white, green & red)	Salt & ground black pepper
400g firm tofu, diced	

Method:

1) Heat the oil in a large frying pan, over a moderate heat.

2) Add the onions and garlic and stir-fry until soft.

3) Add the okra (if this is not available then asparagus works really well, or broccoli florets) and the cabbage leaves. Cook for a minute.

4) Add the tofu cubes and stir occasionally and carefully, so that the tofu blackens but doesn't disintegrate.

5) Stir in the ginger, white wine and soy sauce.

6) Season to taste.

7) Cover the pan and simmer for 2 minutes.

TIP 1 – Take care with Food Intolerance with this dish as soy (from which soy sauce and tofu come) is one of the most common Food Intolerances.

TIP 2 – the Tamari version of soy sauce is invariably wheat/gluten free, unlike normal soy sauce. Check that the Tamari soy sauce that you buy is wheat-free. Typical ingredients will be water, soybeans, salt and distilled sake, which is rice based.

TIP 3 – If you are fine with wheat, this can be served with whole wheat noodles for a carb meal, or on its own as a wonderfully healthy stand-alone meal.

TIP 4 – Leave out the wine and this can be a Phase 1 dish.

Serves 4

Phase	Meal	V	C	H	Wheat free	Dairy free
(1 &) 2	Either	✓	✓	✓	✓	✓

PHASE 1 – FAT MAIN MEALS

Burmese Curry

This unusual curry can be made with either chicken or lamb, for a meat version, or with root vegetables, green beans and broccoli for a vegetarian version. It reheats really well.

Ingredients:

25g fresh ginger, chopped	2 tablespoons Tamari soy sauce
6 cloves garlic, roughly chopped	*600g chicken, diced* **OR**
	600g lamb, diced **OR**
2 onions, roughly chopped	*500g diced mixed vegetables*
5 tablespoons olive oil	500ml stock (meat or vegetable)
1 teaspoon paprika	
A generous pinch of saffron dissolved in 1 tablespoon of boiling water	Salt & ground black pepper
	A few sprigs of coriander
2 teaspoons chilli powder	

Method:

1) Place the ginger and garlic in a blender and blitz. When finely crushed, add the onions and blitz briefly until these are also finely crushed.

2) Heat 3 tablespoons of olive oil in a large, heavy-bottomed saucepan and, when very hot, stir in the onion mixture.

3) Reduce the heat and cook, stirring often, for 10-15 minutes until the mixture is dry, brown in patches and paste-like.

4) Add the paprika, saffron, chilli powder and soy sauce. Cook, stirring constantly, for approximately 30 seconds and then remove from the heat.

5) Brown the meat (or vegetables) in batches in the rest of the oil in a frying pan.

6) Add the meat (or vegetables) to the paste and then add the stock.

7) Bring to the boil, stirring frequently, and simmer for approximately 30 minutes until the meat (or vegetable selection) is tender.

8) Season to taste.

9) Serve with a few sprigs of coriander.

TIP 1 – Leave out the soy sauce if you are intolerant to soy products.

TIP 2 – The Tamari version of soy sauce is invariably wheat/gluten free, unlike normal soy sauce. Check that the Tamari soy sauce that you buy is wheat-free. Typical ingredients will be water, soybeans, salt and distilled sake, which is rice based.

Serves 4

Phase	Meal	V	C	H	Wheat free	Dairy free
1 & 2	Fat	Can be	✓	✓	✓	✓

Salade Niçoise/Salmon Niçoise

This is one of the healthiest and simplest main meals of all. It is a staple dish in France where it is served with delicious French dressing. You can select a dressing from our recipes and, if you select one without vinegar, this can be suitable for Phase 1 and Candida. The classic recipe has diced potatoes on top, but leave these out to keep the carbs away from this fat meal.

Ingredients:

150g green beans	4 char grilled tuna steaks or 400g tinned tuna (or salmon steaks or tinned salmon for Salmon Niçoise)
4 eggs	
1 iceberg lettuce	
24 cherry tomatoes	8 anchovy fillets
1 cucumber	100g black olives pitted
Olive oil or another dressing	Salt & ground black pepper

Method:

1) Chop the green beans into lengths of 3-4cm long. Cook them in boiling water until they are as soft or as crunchy as you like them. Strain them, dry them in kitchen paper and set them aside to cool.

2) Hard-boil the eggs (place them in a saucepan of boiling water for 5-10 minutes, depending on how hard you like the yolks).

3) Chop the lettuce up quite finely and cover 4 plates with it. Slice the cherry tomatoes in half and place them around the edge of each plate.

4) Dice the cucumber and sprinkle this over the lettuce; add the cooked and cooled green beans.

5) Quarter the hard-boiled eggs and arrange them on each plate.

6) Add dressing to taste – olive oil is perfect.

7) Place the char grilled tuna steaks (cook raw tuna on the barbecue, or in a frying pan, or just place it under a normal grill) or the tinned tuna in the middle of the plate.

8) Garnish with the anchovies and olives; season to taste.

TIP 1 – If you like anchovies, do take the trouble to add them to this dish. They bring great nutrition to a dish, already brimming with health. Anchovies are particularly good for B3 (Niacin) and are great all rounders for minerals from calcium to zinc.

Serves 4

Phase	Meal	V	C	H	Wheat free	Dairy free
1 & 2	Fat		✓	✓	✓	✓

Monkfish with Hoisin Sauce

This can be done using any white fish. Monkfish is chunky and has a unique taste, but this will work equally well with halibut or cod.

Hoisin sauce can be found in the oriental section in most supermarkets. It is sometimes called Peking sauce and is a thick, reddish-brown sauce. It is a sweet and sour sauce, used a lot in Chinese cooking. The natural 'sweet 'n sour' comes from the ingredients, which are a mixture of soy beans, garlic, chilli peppers and various spices.

Ingredients:

2 teaspoons olive oil	2 tablespoons Hoisin sauce
600g monkfish fillet, cut into 5cm chunks	½ teaspoon ground black pepper
1 red pepper, deseeded & sliced	120ml spring onions, thinly sliced
120ml water	

Method:

1) Place a large frying pan, over a medium-high heat. Once hot, add the olive oil and swirl to coat the pan. Add the (monk)fish chunks and fry for 2 minutes.

2) Add the red pepper slices and fry for a further minute. Add 120ml water, the Hoisin sauce and the black pepper and simmer for 3 minutes, until the fish is fork-tender.

3) Remove from the heat and add the sliced spring onions and serve immediately.

TIP 1 – To complement the Hoisin sauce, serve with pak choi, which is a member of the Brassica family. It has thick, creamy white stems and deeply crinkled, dark green leaves, which are similar to Swiss chard. It is a favourite in Chinese cuisine and is grown extensively in Asia.

Serves 4

Phase	Meal	V	C	H	Wheat free	Dairy free
1 & 2	Fat		✓	✓	✓	✓

Chicken Livers with Marsala & Sage

Marsala is a famous Italian wine from the Sicilian region. It is fortified with brandy to convert the sugar into a higher alcohol content. It has a rich flavour, sometimes described as 'smoky', which makes it a useful alcoholic ingredient in recipes. Since liver is also a strong flavour, these two go together really well.

Sage is a herb commonly used to accompany meat – especially red meat with its tasty fat content and stronger flavour. If you have ever had "stuffing" with roast dinners, you will be familiar with the distinctive aroma of sage. Sage and onion provide the flavouring for the most basic stuffing. Stuffing most likely originated as a way for using up stale bread – gain health and lose weight by using sage with liver instead.

Ingredients:

400g chicken livers	2 cloves garlic, crushed
6 sage leaves	2 tablespoons Marsala
2 tablespoons olive oil	Salt & ground black pepper
2 onions, finely chopped	

Method:

1) To prepare the chicken livers, discard any stringy bits and cut them into similar sizes. Pat them dry with kitchen paper.

2) Finely shred the sage leaves, cutting out the stalks if they seem tough. Put them to one side.

3) Heat the oil in a small frying pan, over a medium-low heat. Add the onions and garlic and cook until soft.

4) Add the Marsala and stir well.

5) Add the chicken livers to the pan, pushing aside the onions slightly so that the livers cook in the middle. Sprinkle over the sage and season to taste.

6) Cook the livers for a couple of minutes, flip them over and cook the other sides. Take care not to allow the livers to overcook – you want them brown all over but still pink and moist at their core and slightly wobbly to the touch.

7) Transfer to a warm plate, making sure to include all the delicious juices and eat immediately with a green salad.

Serves 4

Phase	Meal	V	C	H	Wheat free	Dairy free
1 & 2	Fat		✓	✓	✓	✓

Liver with Bacon & Onion

If you ever want to win a nutrition competition and have one food to choose – pick liver and you'll win hands down. It is simply the healthiest single food on earth. It is also one of the cheapest, so no excuses for not being able to afford optimum nutrition.

It is a little known fact that liver actually contains decent amounts of vitamin C, but you need to eat it raw to get the benefit. This is how the Eskimos get all the nutrients that they need. Andy tried it raw, in the interests of research and said it was perfectly palatable, but he'll get his vitamin C from vegetables as they're there.

Andy's recommendation for this recipe is lamb's liver, but you can use pig's liver, beef or calf, depending on your preference.

Ingredients:

4 fatty back bacon rashers, chopped into slices	2 onions, finely sliced 1kg liver, in slices as it comes from the butcher

Method:

1) Prewarm the oven to the lowest setting, ready to keep the bacon just warm.

2) Cook the bacon slices in a frying pan, in their own fat, until they are just browning and then transfer the bacon to a dish in the warm oven.

3) Fry the sliced onion in the fat from the bacon until the slices are just brown. Add them to the warm dish with the bacon.

4) Lightly fry the liver pieces on both sides, in the same frying pan. The liver should be nicely browned, but not burnt. The amount of frying will

depend on how well cooked you like your liver. Andy likes it pink on the inside, which takes about 3-4 minutes each side, so adjust the time as you like it.

5) Transfer the bacon and onions back to the frying pan and stir them around the liver for about 2 minutes until everything is thoroughly reheated.

6) Serve hot on a warmed plate with broccoli and you have the vitamin C back, which has likely been destroyed in cooking, and all the other vitamins and minerals vital for human health.

Serves 4

Phase	Meal	V	C	H	Wheat free	Dairy free
1 & 2	Fat		✓	✓	✓	✓

Hungarian Chicken

Paprika is a striking, red powder, with a sweet or lightly pungent flavour and a faint smoky after taste. Like cayenne, it is a spice deriving from the chilli family. Paprika is effectively the national taste of Hungary. It is the staple spice in goulash, paprikash and many other Hungarian and Balkan dishes. It is also widely used in Spain. Added to any dish Paprika gives the mildly spicy flavour of Eastern Europe. Our Hungarian chicken is a really tasty and creamy dish, but it is natural yoghurt that gives it the creamy texture so it is wonderfully healthy too.

Ingredients:

1 whole chicken	2 green peppers, deseeded & sliced
Salt & ground black pepper	4 'beef' tomatoes, chopped
1 tablespoon olive oil	
2 onions, chopped	240ml chicken stock
2 cloves garlic, crushed	1 tablespoon corn flour
1 tablespoon paprika	120ml Natural Live Yoghurt

Method:

1) Preheat the oven to 350° F, 175° C, gas mark 4.

2) Joint the chicken.

3) Season the chicken parts with salt and pepper and put it into a large oven-proof dish, ideally a casserole dish.

4) Heat the oil in a large frying pan, add the onions and garlic and fry until soft.

5) Add the paprika and stir for a few minutes and then add to the casserole dish.

6) Add the peppers and tomatoes and just enough of the chicken stock to cover them.

7) Cover and cook for approximately 60-90 minutes, or until the chicken is tender.

8) Before serving, mix the corn flour smoothly with the yoghurt and stir into the casserole and simmer for a few more minutes.

TIP 1 – The introduction to the Chicken Cacciatore recipe explains why a tiny amount of corn flour will be fine for Phase 1. It is a thickener, so you can always choose to leave it out.

Serves 4

Phase	Meal	V	C	H	Wheat free	Dairy free
1 & 2	Fat		✓	✓	✓	

Coconut Curry Chicken

This is a really light curry recipe. You can make it as mild or as spicy as you like by using different curry powders. Add a fresh chilli or two, at the time you fry the chicken, if you like spicy dishes. You can add more vegetables to the mixture, rather than serving them on the side, if you want a whole platter meal.

Ingredients:

150ml chicken stock	2 teaspoons curry powder
1 stalk fresh lemon grass, tough outer skin discarded and stalk crushed, or 2 teaspoons dried lemon grass	60ml unsweetened coconut milk
	100g sugar snap peas, ends trimmed (or mange tout)
4 chicken breasts, boneless & diced	Salt & ground black pepper

Method:

1) Put a large frying pan, on a medium-high heat. Once hot, add 1 tablespoon of the chicken stock and swirl to coat the pan.

2) Add the lemon grass and fry for 2 minutes.

3) Add the chicken cubes and fry for a further 3 minutes, until golden brown on all sides.

4) Add the curry powder and toss to coat.

5) Add the remaining chicken stock, coconut milk and snap peas and simmer for a few more minutes, until the chicken is cooked through and the liquid reduces slightly.

6) Season to taste.

Serve with okra, cauliflower and other vegetables that go well with curries.

TIP 1 – This is suitable for Phase 1, as coconut milk is non dairy and has anti-Candida properties.

Serves 4

Phase	Meal	V	C	H	Wheat free	Dairy free
1 & 2	Fat		✓	✓	✓	✓

Garden Chicken Supreme

The Herbes de Provence add such a great flavour, you will find it hard to believe this is suitable for Phase 1. Herbes de Provence is an aromatic mixture of dried herbs used in Southern France. If you don't have this mixture in the cupboard, you can mix your own using a selection of the following dried herbs: basil; bay leaves; chervil; cloves; fennel seed; marjoram; rosemary; sage; tarragon and thyme.

Ingredients:

4 chicken breasts, boneless	1 red, 1 green & 1 yellow pepper, deseeded & cut into strips
1 tablespoon Herbes de Provence	400g tin chopped tomatoes
6 tablespoons olive oil	
2 onions, chopped	Salt & ground black pepper
2 cloves garlic, chopped	2 tablespoons fresh parsley, chopped
2 courgettes, peeled & chopped	Basil leaves to garnish

Method:

1) Rub the chicken breasts with the herbs.

2) Heat 2 tablespoons of oil in a large pan, add the chicken (skin down) and fry for 8 minutes, then turn over and fry for another 5 minutes. Remove from the pan and keep warm.

3) Add the remaining oil, onions, garlic, courgettes and peppers to the pan. Cook stirring gently for 10 minutes.

4) Add the tomatoes (with the juice) and season.

5) Cover and simmer for 10 minutes.

6) Stir in the parsley and put the chicken on the top, cover and simmer for 10 minutes.

Serve with basil garnish.

Serves 4

Phase	Meal	V	C	H	Wheat free	Dairy free
1 & 2	Fat		✓	✓	✓	✓

Merguez Spiced Chicken

This comes from the South West region of France and is a simple and delicious chicken recipe. Merguez is a spicy sausage and this is what gives the flavour to the dish. Make sure you get the real Merguez as this is just meat, fat and spices and has no processed ingredients.

Ingredients:

4 chicken breasts, with the skin on	1 red pepper, deseeded & chopped
4 chicken thighs, with the skin on	400g tin chopped tomatoes
2 tablespoons olive oil	500ml vegetable or chicken stock
2 onions, finely chopped	
1 clove garlic, chopped	Tabasco
1 green pepper, deseeded & chopped	50g Merguez (or chorizo)

Method:

1) Preheat the oven to 325° F, 165° C, gas mark 3.

2) Put the chicken pieces in a large frying pan, skin down, and dry fry them on a moderate heat for 3-4 minutes. Turn over and cook the non skin side for 3-4 minutes (there will now be some natural fat in the pan to aid cooking). This should turn them lightly brown but, if not, cook for another couple of minutes until brown.

3) Transfer the chicken pieces to a large casserole dish.

4) Add the olive oil, onions, garlic and peppers to the frying pan and lightly fry until the onions are soft.

5) Add the tin of tomatoes and the stock to the frying pan with the onion and garlic mixture.

6) Add a healthy dash of Tabasco and simmer on a low heat for 5-10 minutes.

7) Slice the Merguez and sprinkle it over the chicken. Pour the saucepan mixture over the chicken and spicy sausage.

8) Put the lid on the casserole and cook it in the oven for 90 minutes.

TIP 1 – You can use chorizo instead of Merguez but, because this is processed, let it flavour the dish but leave the non-slimmers in the household to eat the actual chorizo itself.

Serves 4-6

Phase	Meal	V	C	H	Wheat free	Dairy free
1 & 2	Fat		✓	✓	✓	✓

Tandoori Chicken

This is a classic dish, which naturally meets Harcombe diet rules – even for Phase 1. The distinctive colour can be achieved by adding a dash of red food colouring to the marinade. However, unless you are sure of the origin of any food colouring that you find, leave this out.

Ingredients:

1 tablespoon ground cumin	2-3cm grated ginger
1 tablespoon garam masala	Juice of 1 lemon
1 teaspoon ground coriander	8 cloves garlic, crushed
1 teaspoon ground turmeric	500ml Natural Live Yoghurt
1 teaspoon chilli powder	4 chicken breasts
	1 lemon, quartered

Method:

1) Mix the spices, ginger, juice of 1 lemon and crushed garlic into a paste with a little water.

2) Stir the yoghurt into the mixture to make a tandoori marinade.

3) Slash knife marks in the flesh of the chicken. Coat the chicken with the marinade and leave to marinate for at least 2 hours.

4) Preheat the oven to 400° F, 200° C, gas mark 6.

5) For the authentic char grill markings, shake off the excess marinade and cook the chicken on the wire racks in the oven, turning half way through cooking. Alternatively place the chicken on a

baking tray, brushed with olive oil to avoid sticking, and again, turn half way through.

6) Cook for approximately 20 minutes – until the chicken juices run clear.

7) Serve with a lemon quarter on top.

TIP 1 – If you do find some natural red food colouring, you can add this to the paste mixture at step 1 of the process.

Serves 4

Phase	Meal	V	C	H	Wheat free	Dairy free
1 & 2	Fat		✓	✓	✓	

Spicy Moroccan Roast Chicken

Chicken is a low fat, high protein meat, so alternate it with red meat to get the great meat fats. Chicken is 75% water, 23% protein and barely 2% fat. The fat, interestingly, is equally balanced between saturated, monounsaturated and polyunsaturated.

Ingredients:

1 onion, finely chopped	1 teaspoon ground cumin
1 clove garlic, crushed	Large pinch of salt
1 teaspoon fresh parsley, chopped	1 tablespoon butter
1 teaspoon fresh coriander, chopped	Juice of ½ lemon
1 teaspoon paprika	2kg chicken or chicken joints (legs, breasts, wings)

Method:

1) Preheat the oven to 350° F, 175° C, gas mark 4.

2) Put the onion, garlic, herbs and spices in a bowl. Mix in the butter and lemon juice until it forms a smooth paste.

3) Rub the butter mix into the chicken and leave it to stand for an hour.

4) Roast the chicken for about 60 to 90 minutes, or until the chicken juices run clear.

Serves 4

Phase	Meal	V	C	H	Wheat free	Dairy free
1 & 2	Fat		✓	✓	✓	

Roast Chicken with Garlic & Lemon

Every recipe book should have a recipe for a really simple chicken dish and this is as simple as it gets. You can cook chicken in the oven, in its own juices, but it can be vastly enhanced by stuffing it with cloves of garlic and fresh lemons as follows.

Ingredients:

1 whole chicken	1 whole lemon
6-8 cloves garlic	Salt & ground black pepper

Method:

1) Preheat the oven to 350° F, 175° C, gas mark 4.

2) Allow 6-8 cloves of garlic and 1 whole lemon cut in quarters, for a medium sized chicken.

3) Remove the giblets and then stuff the garlic cloves and lemon quarters into the inside of the chicken, then season the outside of the chicken well with the salt and ground black pepper.

4) Cook 'up-side-down' for the first 30 minutes for the juices to penetrate the breast meat and then turn over.

5) Cook for a further 30-60 minutes.

Serve with a selection of vegetables in the winter or a mixed salad in the summer.

Serves 4

Phase	Meal	V	C	H	Wheat free	Dairy free
1 & 2	Fat		✓	✓	✓	✓

Thai Coconut Chicken Salad

Chicken can be quite a bland meat – breasts especially. This will spice up any chicken with an explosion of Thai flavours. This is especially handy for left over chicken pieces, which have been kept in the fridge overnight.

Ingredients:

120ml unsweetened coconut milk	2 jalapenos, finely chopped (optional)
4 tablespoons lime juice	4 chicken breasts, pre cooked & chilled
120ml olive oil	
2 tablespoons ginger (fresh, minced or ground)	Mixed oriental salad leaves (e.g. pak choi, Chinese cabbage)
2 cloves garlic, crushed	Sesame seeds (optional)
2 tablespoons coriander, finely chopped	

Method:

1) Blend the coconut milk, lime juice and olive oil together.

2) Add the ginger, garlic, coriander and jalapenos and give a quick blitz of the blender to mix everything together.

3) Coat the pre-cooked chicken breasts with the Thai mixture and then serve them on a bed of oriental salad leaves. Sprinkle with sesame seeds.

Serves 4

Phase	Meal	V	C	H	Wheat free	Dairy free
1 & 2	Fat		✓	✓	✓	✓

Minced Meat Stuffed Peppers

A great meat alternative to the classic vegetarian dish.

Ingredients:

3 tablespoons olive oil	1 teaspoon paprika
1 onion, finely chopped	Freshly ground black pepper
2 cloves garlic, crushed	
450g minced lamb or beef	4 red peppers, topped & deseeded

Method:

1) Preheat the oven to 350° F, 175° C, gas mark 4.

2) Lightly fry the onion and garlic in the olive oil for 3-4 minutes until transparent.

3) Add the minced meat and fry for 10-12 minutes until brown.

4) Add the paprika and pepper. Lower the heat and cook slowly for about 30 minutes. Add a small amount of water if the mixture starts to dry out.

5) Cut a small slice off the bottom of the pepper so that it will stand upright (keeping just enough of the bottom to keep the pepper closed). Stuff the minced meat mixture into each pepper. Place the stuffed peppers on a roasting disk. Pop the tops back on and cook for 30 minutes.

6) Remove from the oven and serve piping hot.

Serves 4

Phase	Meal	V	C	H	Wheat free	Dairy free
1 & 2	Fat		✓	✓	✓	✓

Meatballs

This is for any burger monsters who thought that Phase 1 would be an endurance test. Not so!

Ingredients:

1 onion, finely chopped	1 teaspoon mixed herbs
1 clove of garlic, crushed	400g tin of tomatoes
450g mince meat	Salt & ground black pepper
1 egg, beaten	

Method:

1) Preheat the oven to 400° F, 200° C, gas mark 6.

2) Mix the onion, garlic and mince in a bowl. Beat the egg in a separate bowl and add to the mixture. Add the mixed herbs and make sure that all the ingredients are mixed together well.

3) Take small handfuls of the mixture and form tight balls, about the size of golf balls. Place them on a flat baking tray and cook for about 15 minutes.

4) Remove the meatballs from the oven and transfer them to a casserole dish. Turn the oven down to a moderate heat (350° F, 175° C, gas mark 4).

5) Liquidise the tomatoes in a blender. Season them with freshly ground pepper and pour this over the meatballs in the casserole dish. Return the dish to the oven and cook for about 45 minutes.

Serves 4

Phase	Meal	V	C	H	Wheat free	Dairy free
1 & 2	Fat		✓	✓	✓	✓

Lamb with Oregano & Basil

Oregano and basil are two herbs commonly used in Italian cuisine, but they also feature in dishes from as far apart as Latin America and Palestine. Unusually, they go as well with spicy sauces as tomato sauces.

Ingredients:

1 clove of garlic, sliced	1 small bunch of basil, chopped
2 tablespoons olive oil	
1 small bunch of oregano, chopped	4 double lamb chops

Method:

1) Preheat the oven to 350° F, 175° C, gas mark 4.

2) Mix the garlic, olive oil, oregano and basil together.

3) Place the lamb chops on a plate and rub the mixture into them, turning the chops over to make sure that both sides are covered. Cover the chops with cling film and leave them to marinate for about an hour.

4) Pre-heat a grill and then grill the lamb chops for 2-3 minutes on each side, until brown. Transfer them to a roasting dish and cook for a further 20 minutes in the oven.

5) Serve the chops on individual plates and drizzle the juice from the roasting dish over them. Serve with a selection of fresh green vegetables.

Serves 4

Phase	Meal	V	C	H	Wheat free	Dairy free
1 & 2	Fat		✓	✓	✓	✓

Lamb Casserole

This is amazingly a Phase 1 recipe. There is only one vegetable to eat with a real lamb casserole, in the true French fashion, and that is haricot blanc. Haricot blanc would be mixing fats and carbs, however, so you should have French green beans to stick to the rules. You should also only have French green beans with this dish in Phase 1.

Ingredients:

2 tablespoons olive oil	200g broccoli florets
400g lamb, diced	½ teaspoon dried mint
2 red onions (or shallots for extra flavour), sliced	½ teaspoon dried rosemary
1 clove garlic, crushed	1 red pepper, deseeded & chopped
400g tin chopped tomatoes	8 black olives pitted

Method:

1) Heat the oil in a large frying pan. Fry the lamb until it is lightly brown and heated through (approximately 5-10 minutes).

2) Add the onions and continue to fry them for a couple of minutes before adding the garlic and frying for another couple of minutes.

3) Add the tinned tomatoes, broccoli, mint and rosemary. Simmer for 10 minutes.

4) Add the chopped pepper and olives and simmer for a further 10 minutes, or until the peppers have started to soften.

Serve with green beans in Phase 1, or haricot blanc in Phase 3.

Serves 4

Phase	Meal	V	C	H	Wheat free	Dairy free
1 & 2	Fat		✓	✓	✓	✓

Sunday Roast Lamb

You can have a Sunday roast dinner, served with parsnip chips and it would even meet Phase 1 rules.

Ingredients:

Boneless leg of lamb (approximately 2kg)	100g baby fennel, trimmed and cut in half lengthways
40g fresh mint	
1 clove garlic, crushed	110g baby leeks, trimmed
Salt & ground black pepper	200g courgettes, sliced lengthways
125ml olive oil	250g green beans, trimmed
250ml meat stock	150g asparagus, trimmed to 6cm lengths
225g baby carrots, tops trimmed	

Method:

1) Preheat the oven to 220°C, 425°F, gas mark 7.

2) Using a pestle and mortar, or in a food processor, pound or blend half the mint leaves with the garlic and seasoning until smooth. Slowly add the olive oil and continue to mix.

3) Score (slash with a knife) the lamb all over and smother the oil, garlic and mint mixture all over the lamb. Roast in the oven, brushing with the oil regularly until the lamb is cooked.

4) Cooking times for the lamb:

- Pink: 10 minutes for every 450g plus 20 minutes;

- Medium: 15 minutes for every 450g plus 20 minutes;

-   Well done: 20 minutes for every 450g plus 20 minutes.

    Remove from the oven, cover with tin foil and allow to rest on a plate for 10 minutes.

5) While the meat is resting, remove the fat from the roasting tin. Add the stock to the tin and make a light, tasty sauce by boiling and dissolving all the goodness at the bottom.

6) Cook the carrots and fennel in a large pan of boiling, salted water for 5 minutes. Add the rest of the vegetables and simmer for another 5 minutes.

7) Serve the vegetables in a shallow bowl with the lamb, sliced, on top and a little sauce and the rest of the fresh mint sprinkled over.

Serves 4

Phase	Meal	V	C	H	Wheat free	Dairy free
1 & 2	Fat		✓	✓	✓	✓

Parsnip Chips

TIP 1 – Here's how to make parsnip chips: Ideally use some small parsnips, or cut large parsnips into baton sizes. Wash the parsnips thoroughly, but keep the skins on. Brush a baking tray with olive oil and then place the parsnips/batons on the tray and bake in the oven for approximately 30-45 minutes at 400° F, 200° C, gas mark 6. Turn the 'chips' at least once during the cooking time, to brown them all over. To cook them in the same oven, at the same time as the lamb, put them on a lower shelf and bake for 30-45 minutes.

Lamb Kebabs

This marinade blend works especially well with lamb. However, it can be done with any meat that you like and it can also be done at any time of the year under a hot grill, or during the summer at barbecues.

Ingredients:

400g lamb, diced	1 tablespoon olive oil
150ml thick Greek yoghurt	12 cherry tomatoes
1 tablespoon ground coriander	200g mushrooms (or pepper strips or courgette slices)
1 teaspoon chilli powder	(& barbecue skewers)

Method:

1) Cut the meat into 2-3cm cubes.

2) Mix the yoghurt, coriander, chilli powder and olive oil.

3) Pour the mixture over the meat, cover and marinate for up to 4 hours.

4) Alternate the cherry tomatoes, mushrooms and meat cubes as you slide them onto the skewers.

5) Barbecue, or grill under a high flame, for 10 minutes.

Serve with grilled or barbecued aubergine slices or any other barbecued /grilled veg (courgettes work really well too).

TIP 1 – Use Natural Live Yoghurt, instead of Greek yoghurt, and this can be suitable for Phase 1.

Serves 4

With the mushrooms:

Phase	Meal	V	C	H	Wheat free	Dairy free
2	Fat			✓	✓	

Without the mushrooms:

Phase	Meal	V	C	H	Wheat free	Dairy free
1 & 2	Fat		✓	✓	✓	

Marinated Beef, Lamb or Pork

Please swap any red meat for another in our beef, lamb and pork recipes – try veal, venison – whatever is available at your butcher. In terms of micro nutrients (vitamins and minerals) there is not much difference between different red meats – they are all excellent sources of B vitamins and the minerals iron, magnesium and zinc.

In terms of macro nutrients (carbohydrate, fat and protein), taking beef, lamb and pork examples from the United States nutrition database we find that the main differences are in fat and water content. (There is no carbohydrate content in any real meat). Beef and lamb are approximately 60% water and pork is nearer 75%. Beef and lamb are higher in fat – at approximately 20% and 22% respectively; the pork example I looked at was 4% fat. The protein levels were 18%, 17% and 21% for the beef, lamb and pork examples respectively (the beef and lamb didn't quite add to 100% due to rounding). I chose cuts with up to ¼ inch fat trim to compare like with like. In all of the red meat examples, there is more unsaturated fat than saturated. So far, the only meat I can find on this planet with more saturated than unsaturated fat is venison. Ironically, a number of fat phobic people eat venison because it is low in fat overall.

All the fat that nature puts in food is vital, full of essentially fatty acids, full of vitamins A, D, E and K. We should ensure that we choose meat with excellent fat content, like lamb, regularly.

Ingredients:

4 large beef, lamb or pork steaks	1 tablespoon fresh basil, chopped
1 tablespoon fresh oregano, chopped	1 clove garlic, crushed
	Olive oil

Method:

1) To make the marinade: place the chopped oregano and basil in a mixing bowl with the crushed garlic. Sprinkle liberally with olive oil and stir the mixture together.

2) Place the meat steaks in a shallow dish and spoon half the marinade over them. Turn them over and spoon over the remaining marinade. Cover the dish in cling film and place it in the fridge.

3) The steaks are best left to marinate for about 8 hrs but if this is not practical, try to leave them for at least 2-4 hours for the flavours to fully infuse into the meat.

4) To cook the steaks, heat some olive oil in a frying pan and lightly fry the steaks to your liking.

5) Serve with a selection of green vegetables or a salad. Any yoghurt based accompaniment would also work well.

TIP 1 – Please note that the preparation time for this is only 15 minutes, but the marinating time is 2-8 hours and the cooking time is 20 minutes.

Serves 4

Phase	Meal	V	C	H	Wheat free	Dairy free
1 & 2	Fat		✓	✓	✓	✓

Farmhouse Hot Pot

This is a hot pot with just meat and vegetables – no potatoes – perfect for The Harcombe Diet. Bacon, beef and onions always makes for an irresistible combination. Think about all the B vitamins and iron in the beef and enjoy real food with real taste.

Ingredients:

100g streaky bacon, diced	1 tablespoon corn flour
1 tablespoon olive oil	1 beef stock cube
600g stewing steak, diced	350ml water
2 onions, chopped	1 sprig parsley
300g carrots, peeled & sliced	1 bay leaf
½ head of celery, chopped	1 clove garlic

Method:

1) Preheat the oven to 350° F, 175° C, gas mark 4.

2) Dice the bacon and fry it in its own fat in a frying pan. Transfer it to a casserole dish.

3) Add the oil to the bacon fat that has oozed out. Add the beef chunks and fry them until browned. Add them to the casserole dish.

4) Put the onions, carrots and celery in the pan with the remaining fat and cook for approximately 5 minutes. Add to the casserole dish.

5) Put the corn flour and crumbled stock cube in the same, well-used pan, and add the water and stir until boiling.

6) Add the parsley, bay leaf and garlic and then pour the whole mixture over the meat in the casserole.

7) Cover and cook for 2½ – 3 hours.

TIP 1 – Mushrooms also go really well with this dish. If Candida is not a problem for you, add 100g of button mushrooms to the pan at step 4 of the process for a Phase 2 variation.

TIP 2 – Just because carrots, onions and celery are classic hot pot vegetables doesn't mean that you can't add anything that you have available. Broccoli and cauliflower would also work well with this recipe.

Serves 4

Phase	Meal	V	C	H	Wheat free	Dairy free
1 & 2	Fat		✓	✓	✓	✓

Lamb Rogan Josh

We would like to thank one of our club members, Naomi, for this wonderfully rich Phase 1 recipe. Here we have a wonderful combination of well chosen ingredients.

Ingredients:

450g lamb, diced	¼ teaspoon ground cinnamon
1 onion, finely sliced	½ teaspoon cardamom pods, chopped
2 cloves garlic, crushed	
1 red chilli, finely chopped	400g tinned tomatoes, chopped
1 teaspoon cumin seeds	1 tablespoon tomato purée
½ teaspoon ground turmeric	3 teaspoon garam masala
1 teaspoon fresh or ground coriander	Salt & ground black pepper
1 teaspoon paprika	100ml Natural Live Yoghurt
1 teaspoon of finely sliced ginger	

Method:

1) Gently fry the lamb, onion, garlic and chilli on a medium heat (in a dash of olive oil).

2) Add the cumin seeds, turmeric, coriander, paprika, ginger, cinnamon and cardamom pods.

3) Cook for 1-2 minutes to work the spices into the lamb.

4) Add half the tinned tomatoes and tomato purée. Stir well for 1 minute.

5) Add the garam masala and stir well.

6) Add the remainder or the tin of tomatoes and some seasoning as desired.

7) Reduce the heat and simmer for 20-30 minutes.

8) Before serving, add the yoghurt for a richer, creamier sauce.

Serves 4

Phase	Meal	V	C	H	Wheat free	Dairy free
1 & 2	Fat		✓	✓	✓	

Pork, Chicken or Beef Kebabs

This can be done with any meat that you like. It can also be done any time of the year under a hot grill, or during the summer at barbecues. This is a great dish for children and it is also a perfect Phase 1 dish.

Ingredients:

400g meat, diced	¼ teaspoon chilli powder
4 tablespoons olive oil	2 cloves garlic, crushed
2 tablespoons lemon juice	1 red & 1 yellow pepper, deseeded
½ teaspoon cumin powder	200g mushrooms (or pepper strips or courgette slices)
½ teaspoon cardamom powder	(& barbecue skewers)
¼ teaspoon garam masala	

Method:

1) Cut the meat into 2-3cm cubes.

2) Mix the oil, lemon juice, spices and garlic.

3) Pour the mixture over the meat, cover and marinate for 60-90 minutes.

4) Chop the pepper into 2-3cm squares and alternate them with the meat cubes and whole mushrooms as you slide them onto the skewers.

5) Barbecue, or grill under a high flame, for 10 minutes.

Serve with grilled or barbecued aubergine slices or any other barbecued/ grilled veg (courgettes work really well too).

Serves 4

Without the mushrooms:

Phase	Meal	V	C	H	Wheat free	Dairy free
1 & 2	Fat		✓	✓	✓	✓

With the mushrooms:

Phase	Meal	V	C	H	Wheat free	Dairy free
2	Fat			✓	✓	✓

Roast Leg of Lamb with Rosemary

Lamb is such a tasty meat that it only needs to be cooked with garlic and rosemary and not much else.

Ingredients:

| 1 leg of lamb | Rosemary (fresh sprig if possible) |
| | 6-8 cloves garlic |

Method:

1) Preheat the oven to 400° F, 200° C, gas mark 6.

2) Place the leg of lamb in a large roasting dish and sprinkle with rosemary (fresh if possible).

3) Add a handful of garlic cloves (unpeeled) and pop the lot in the oven and roast until cooked to your liking.

4) As a guide, allow the following cooking times:

- Pink: 10 minutes for every 450g plus 20 minutes;

- Medium: 15 minutes for every 450g plus 20 minutes;

- Well done: 20 minutes for every 450g plus 20 minutes.

Serve with a selection of freshly cooked vegetables or stir-fried vegetables. The garlic cooked this way becomes sweet and can be eaten with the meat.

Serves 4

Phase	Meal	V	C	H	Wheat free	Dairy free
1 & 2	Fat		✓	✓	✓	✓

Cumin & Coriander Lamb

We have used lamb chops in this recipe, but any lamb works equally well with cumin and coriander. Rolled shoulder of lamb is a very tasty and good value cut. Follow the instructions for cooking Roast Leg of Lamb (previous recipe) if you select a joint.

Ingredients:

2 tablespoons ground cumin seeds 2 tablespoons ground coriander seeds 1 clove garlic, crushed	1 tablespoon olive oil 8 single or 4 double lamb chops Freshly ground black pepper

Method:

1) Place the cumin and coriander seeds in a pestle and mortar and coarsely crush them.

2) Mix the ground cumin, coriander, garlic and olive oil in a bowl.

3) Rub the mixture liberally into both sides of the chops (or around the joint). Cover and leave to marinate for approximately 30 minutes.

4) Place the chops on a roasting dish and cook under a hot grill for 3-4 minutes on each side, or until the chops are cooked to your liking.

5) Serve with a selection of fresh vegetables.

Serves 4

Phase	Meal	V	C	H	Wheat free	Dairy free
1 & 2	Fat		✓	✓	✓	✓

Steak au Poivre (Phase 1 version)

A simple grilled steak with a selection of lightly cooked green vegetables is just about the perfect meal. This is the Phase 1 version of Steak au Poivre.

Ingredients:

4 steaks (fillet, sirloin, entrecote – whatever you can buy)	1-2 tablespoons black peppercorns, crushed
	25g butter

Method:

1) Place the steaks on a chopping board and press fresh, coarsely ground, pepper into both sides.

2) Pre-heat a griddle pan until very hot – it's important to get it really hot as we want to quickly seal the steaks at this stage. Place the steaks on the griddle and cook for about a minute on each side.

3) When the steaks are cooking, preheat a frying pan and melt the knob of butter. When the steaks are sealed on the griddle, transfer them to the frying pan and cook for a further 1-2 minutes on each side in the butter.

4) Transfer the steaks to a warmed plate and pour the butter and juices from the frying pan over the steaks. Serve immediately.

Serves 4

Phase	Meal	V	C	H	Wheat free	Dairy free
1 & 2	Fat		✓	✓	✓	

Roast Rib of Beef

A rib of beef is perfect for families who like meat from rare to well done. The outside can be well cooked and the inside can be pink – it's up to you. Buy the best quality meat that you can afford – ideally grass grazed livestock from your local butcher. Choose a rib that's dark red in colour with a good marble of fat.

Ingredients:

1 rib of beef, at room temperature	2 large onions, chopped in half
Freshly ground pepper	12 cloves garlic, left in their skin

Method:

1) Preheat the oven to 425° F, 220° C, gas mark 7.

2) Season the beef well with black pepper. Grill the rib under a very hot grill for 5 minutes each side so that the flesh is dark brown. Remove from the grill and set aside.

3) Put the onions and garlic in a roasting dish and place the rib on top of them. Roast in the oven for 20 minutes. Reduce the heat to 325° F, 165° C, gas mark 3 and cook for a further 15 minutes per 450g of meat.

4) Remove the rib from the oven, cover with tin foil and leave to rest for 20 minutes before carving.

Phase	Meal	V	C	H	Wheat free	Dairy free
1 & 2	Fat		✓	✓	✓	✓

Chef's Salad

This is a base recipe – be your own chef and add in whatever you want – celeriac, beetroot, green beans – the more colour and vitamins the better.

Ingredients:

4 eggs (optional)	4 sticks celery
Diced cubes of ham, chicken & other cold meat	4 spring onions
	Red & green pepper strips
Diced cubes of hard cheese	1 carrot, grated
1 iceberg lettuce	Olive oil or another dressing
24 cherry tomatoes	Salt & ground black pepper
1 cucumber	

Method:

1) Boil the eggs (place them in a saucepan of boiling water for 5-10 minutes, depending on how hard you like the yolks).

2) Dice the meat and cheese.

3) Chop the lettuce up quite finely and cover 4 plates with it. Slice the cherry tomatoes in half and place them around the edge of each plate.

4) Slice the cucumber, celery, spring onions and sprinkle these over the lettuce; add the pepper strips and grated carrot.

5) Quarter the hard-boiled eggs and arrange them on each plate. Add the meat and cheese cubes.

6) Add dressing to taste – olive oil is perfect.

TIP 1 – Can be a Phase 1 dish, if you leave out the cheese. This also makes the dish dairy-free.

TIP 2 – Can be a vegetarian dish, if you leave out the meat.

Serves 4

Phase	Meal	V	C	H	Wheat free	Dairy free
(1 &) 2	Fat	Can be	✓	✓	✓	Can be

Thai Tuna Salad

This is one of the rare recipes to allow a pre-bought sauce. Thai sauces can be good staple ingredients for your kitchen cupboard. You should be able to find a sugar-free, wheat-free Thai fish sauce with anchovies and salt as the base ingredients. If you can't get a Thai fish sauce with only real ingredients, crumble a fish stock cube into a mug and half fill the mug with boiling water (to make a very concentrated stock). Use this with the lime juice and honey (optional) for the marinade.

Ingredients:

4 tablespoons Asian fish sauce	1 spring onion, finely chopped
4 tablespoons fresh lime juice	1 fresh red chilli pepper, deseeded and chopped
2 tablespoons honey (optional)	4 tablespoons fresh coriander, chopped
600g fresh tuna, diced	4 tablespoons fresh basil, chopped
4 tablespoons olive oil	
4 tomatoes, chopped	

Method:

1) In a small bowl, mix together the fish sauce (or stock), lime juice, and honey. Add the diced tuna, making sure that all sides have been coated. Cover the bowl with cling film and leave the tuna to marinade in the fridge for approximately 1 hour.

2) Heat the olive oil in a large frying pan over a high heat. When the oil is very hot, add the marinated tuna chunks and stir-fry them to your taste (a couple of minutes will just seal the flavour and

leave the tuna pinkish inside; longer will brown them inside and slightly char grill them on the outside).

3) Toss the warm fish cubes with the tomatoes, spring onion, red chilli pepper and herbs.

4) Serve in a small bowl, as the Thai people would, and even get your chopsticks out to savour the flavour.

TIP 1 – If you have to settle for fish stock, add a tablespoon of Tamari soy sauce to give the extra flavour needed.

TIP 2 – Make with fish stock and no soy sauce or honey to make this suitable for Phase 1.

TIP 3 – Don't worry about the tiny amount of honey for Phase 2 – by the time some has been left in the marinade bowl and some in the frying pan, you will just be left with the hint of honey.

Serves 4

Phase	Meal	V	C	H	Wheat free	Dairy free
(1 &) 2	Fat		✓	✓	✓	✓

Cod with Lemon & Coriander Relish

Cod is often chosen by people following low carb, low fat (and therefore high protein) diets. 100g of cod contains 81g water, 18g protein and 1g of fat. Cod is the fish equivalent of an egg white omelette in many ways (and white fish is often favoured by those who eat egg white omelettes). Any real fish is a welcome addition to your diet, but make sure you get plenty of oily fish and not just white fish, to get the best fats.

If you leave out the balsamic this works as a Phase 1 recipe. With or without the vinegar this is a wonderfully zesty and refreshing dish.

Ingredients:

2 tablespoons olive oil	1 teaspoon balsamic vinegar
4 x 200g cod fillets, boneless	Salt & ground black pepper
1 lemon	300g mange tout
1 red onion, finely chopped	Sprigs of coriander to garnish
25g fresh coriander, finely chopped	

Method:

1) Heat the oil in a large frying pan. Fry the fish fillets for 3 minutes on both sides; then remove them from the pan and keep them hot.

2) Cut half of the lemon into 4 wedges and sear on the hot pan for 5 minutes, turning occasionally. Remove and keep hot with the fish. These are your seared lemon wedges.

3) Squeeze the juice and grate the skin of the remaining lemon half into a bowl. Chop the red

onion and coriander, and then place them in the bowl with the balsamic vinegar. Season to taste and stir.

4) Steam the mange tout for 5 minutes and put this on 4 warmed plates and then lay each cod fillet on top.

5) Divide the lemon and coriander relish into 4 and serve on the side of each plate with a seared lemon wedge.

TIP 1 – Leave out the balsamic and this can be suitable for Phase 1 and Candida.

Serves 4

Phase	Meal	V	C	H	Wheat free	Dairy free
(1 &) 2	Fat		Can be	✓	✓	✓

Roasted Fish with Dill & Spinach

We've given you some flexibility to choose your own fish with this recipe. You may like to go for the fishmonger's "catch of the day", or anything on special offer, or something unusual for a change.

Our typical fish choices tend to be tuna and salmon. These fish are 60-70% protein and 30-40% fat – fish is always carb free, of course. Snapper can be up to 88% protein and 12% fat, so do vary the fish you eat as much as possible to get different nutrients.

It is a common misconception that food contains one type of fat only. Nature always delivers food with differing proportions of saturated, monounsaturated and polyunsaturated fat. The main fat in salmon is polyunsaturated, but it is monounsaturated in (blue fin) tuna. All fish also has saturated fat in it. This is why the good fats are the ones that nature provides and the bad fats are the ones that food manufacturers provide i.e. transfats.

So, what better excuse do you need to try these fish recipes? With the dill and spinach added to this one it could hardly be healthier.

Ingredients:

4 fish fillets (anything from salmon to tuna to snapper to sole)	1 tablespoon olive oil
	400g spinach leaves
1 tablespoon fresh lemon juice	1 clove garlic, crushed
4 tablespoons Dijon mustard	1 lemon, quartered lengthways
8 tablespoons fresh dill, finely chopped	

Method:

1) Preheat the oven to 400° F, 200° C, gas mark 6.

2) Brush an oven-proof dish with olive oil and place the fish inside.

3) Rub the lemon juice and mustard evenly over the fish.

4) Sprinkle 7 of the 8 tablespoons of dill over the fish.

5) Bake for approximately 10 minutes, or until the fish is just cooked.

6) Meanwhile, heat the olive oil in a pan. Add the spinach and garlic and stir for approximately 3 minutes, until the spinach reduces down.

7) Arrange the spinach on the serving plates. Place the fish on top. Garnish with the last tablespoon of dill and the lemon pieces.

TIP 1 – Leave out the Dijon mustard and this can be suitable for Phase 1 and Candida.

Serves 4

Phase	Meal	V	C	H	Wheat free	Dairy free
(1 &) 2	Fat		✓	✓	✓	✓

Seafood Curry

This is a really special meal – quick, nutritious and it can even be eaten in Phase 1 if you use stock instead of white wine and leave out the mushrooms. If you have it as a Phase 1 dish you can have rice with it, as we don't worry about mixing in Phase 1. If you have it as a Phase 2 meal, it is a fat meal so you should have it on its own and not with rice or any other carbohydrates.

Ingredients:

2 tablespoons olive oil	150g prawns
2 onions, chopped	1 teaspoon Worcestershire sauce
1 red pepper, deseeded & chopped	2 teaspoons tomato purée
2 celery sticks, chopped	6 tablespoons white wine
50g mushrooms, sliced	6 tablespoons water
1½ tablespoons curry powder	Salt & ground black pepper
½ teaspoon turmeric	2 tablespoons Natural Live Yoghurt (ideally low-fat)
½ teaspoon ground ginger	Juice of ½ lemon
250g haddock (or other white fish) skinned & diced	

Method:

1) Heat the oil in a large frying pan, and then fry the onions, pepper, celery and mushrooms in the olive oil until soft.

2) Add the curry powder, turmeric and ginger and cook for another couple of minutes.

3) Add the fish, Worcestershire sauce and tomato purée and stir well.

4) Stir in the wine, water and seasoning (use fish stock instead of wine for Phase 1).

5) Cover all and simmer gently for 10 minutes.

6) Just before serving, add the yoghurt and lemon juice.

TIP 1 – We have not ticked the Candida box with this recipe because of the tiny bit of vinegar in Worcestershire sauce. Unless your Candida is severe, you should be fine with a small amount of this sauce.

Serves 4

Phase	Meal	V	C	H	Wheat free	Dairy free
(1 &) 2	Fat		Can be	✓	✓	

Honey Scallop & Chilli Stir-fry

This takes approximately 3 minutes to cook – fantastic fast food. It is great served on a bed of bamboo shoots, water chestnuts and other oriental vegetables. There is a tablespoon of honey, which is strictly a refined food, but, as each serving gets just a quarter tablespoon of honey, this won't make any difference to your weight loss.

Ingredients:

3 teaspoons olive oil	100g snow peas
1 onion, chopped	200g scallops
2 red peppers, deseeded & chopped	1 tablespoon honey
	1 teaspoon chilli sauce
1 stick celery, chopped	2 teaspoons fresh mint

Method:

1) Heat the oil in a large frying pan.

2) Add the vegetables to the pan and stir-fry over a high heat for approximately 1 minute.

3) Add the scallops, honey, chilli sauce and mint to the pan. Fry for approximately 2 minutes, or until the scallops are tender.

TIP 1 – Leave out the honey and this can be suitable for Phase 1 and Candida.

Serves 4

Phase	Meal	V	C	H	Wheat free	Dairy free
(1 &) 2	Fat		Can be	✓	✓	✓

Red Pepper Chicken

Tasty dinners don't get much easier than this. This takes fewer than 10 minutes preparation time and then you have 30 minutes free-time while the chicken is in the oven.

Ingredients:

4 red peppers, deseeded & cut into large slices	4 cloves garlic, crushed
120ml water	Salt & ground black pepper
4 tablespoons Parmesan cheese, grated	4 whole skinless chicken breasts
2 tablespoons olive oil	

Method:

1) Pre-heat the oven to 350° F, 175° C, gas mark 4.

2) Put the peppers skin side-up, on a baking tray, and grill until charred.

3) Skin the peppers & then combine them with the water, cheese, olive oil, garlic cloves and seasoning together.

4) Place the chicken in a casserole dish and coat with the red pepper mixture. Cover and bake for 30 minutes. Serve with your choice of vegetables.

TIP 1 – Use Natural Live Yoghurt, instead of Parmesan, and this can be suitable for Phase 1.

Serves 4

Phase	Meal	V	C	H	Wheat free	Dairy free
(1 &) 2	Fat		✓	✓	✓	

Mexican Chicken

This is a really simple and delicious chicken recipe, which, with just one variation, is suitable for Phase 1. This can be done as a casserole or in a slow-cooker, as a meal prepared before work and then served when you get home. If done in a slow-cooker, just add everything in together and leave on the lowest setting possible to simmer for hours.

Ingredients:

1 whole chicken	1 teaspoon oregano
2 tablespoons olive oil	1 teaspoon mixed herbs
1 onion, chopped	1 teaspoon thyme
2 cloves garlic, crushed	2 teaspoons Tabasco sauce
200g mushrooms	
1 red & 1 green pepper, deseeded & chopped	Salt & ground black pepper
400g tin chopped tomatoes	100g of unsweetened sweet corn
4 tablespoons tomato purée	

Method:

1) Roast the chicken in its own juices. (See the simple recipe chicken in this book or buy a pre-roasted, hot, chicken).

2) Heat 2 tablespoons of olive oil in a large pan. Add the onion, garlic, mushrooms and peppers and stir-fry them until soft.

3) Stir in the tin of tomatoes and tomato purée.

4) Add the oregano, herbs, thyme, Tabasco, seasoning and simmer for 25-20 minutes.

5) Add the corn and then pour everything over the chicken and cook slowly until the chicken falls away from the bone when prodded with a fork.

TIP 1 – This doesn't have to be served with anything, as it has all the meat and vegetables in one meal.

TIP 2 – Leave out the mushrooms and this would be suitable for Phase 1 and Candida.

Serves 4

Phase	Meal	V	C	H	Wheat free	Dairy free
(1 &) 2	Fat		Can be	✓	✓	✓

Chicken Cacciatore

There is a tiny bit of corn flour in this recipe, and in many of the casserole recipes. Corn flour is recommended so that it is suitable for those with wheat intolerance. Flour is a carb, but the quantity used is so small as to make no difference to this fat meal. When we use corn flour in recipes it is either to lightly 'coat' meat or to thicken a sauce, but it is not essential and can easily be left out.

Ingredients:

1 whole chicken	1 clove garlic, crushed
Salt & ground black pepper	1 chicken stock cube
1 tablespoon corn flour	1 green pepper, deseeded & chopped
2 tablespoons olive oil	240ml water
1 onion, chopped	60ml dry white wine
400g tin chopped tomatoes	1 tablespoon parsley, chopped

Method:

1) Preheat the oven to 350° F, 175° C, gas mark 4.

2) Joint and skin the chicken.

3) Season the corn flour and coat the chicken well.

4) Heat the oil in a large frying pan, and brown the chicken joints. Put them into a large oven-proof dish, ideally a casserole dish.

5) Add the onion to the same pan. Fry until soft and then put these in the casserole dish.

6) Add any remaining corn flour to the pan and mix well. Add in the tomatoes, garlic, crumbled stock cube, green pepper and water.

7) Stir until boiling and then add the wine.

8) Pour everything over the meat in the casserole dish and cover.

9) Cook for approximately 1 hour, or until the chicken is tender.

10) Before serving, add a touch more black pepper and chopped parsley.

TIP 1 – Add an extra 60ml of water, instead of wine to make this suitable for Phase 1.

Serves 4

Phase	Meal	V	C	H	Wheat free	Dairy free
(1 &) 2	Fat		✓	✓	✓	✓

Ginger Spiced Pork

This dish can be thrown into a slow-cooker and cooked on the lowest setting to be ready to eat when you get home. Pork and ginger may sound like a strange combination but it works so well you will be amazed.

Ingredients:

1 tablespoon corn flour	For the sauce:
Salt & ground black pepper	¼ teaspoon Tabasco
1 level teaspoon ground ginger	400g tin chopped tomatoes
	100g mushrooms
600g casserole pork, diced	1 tablespoon Worcestershire sauce
1 tablespoon olive oil	2 tablespoons vinegar
	2 cloves garlic, crushed
	1 bay leaf

Method:

1) Preheat the oven to 325° F, 165° C, gas mark 3.

2) Mix the corn flour, salt, pepper and ginger in a mixing bowl.

3) Toss the pork cubes in the dry mixture to coat them.

4) Heat the oil in a frying pan.

5) Fry the pork quickly until browned, stirring frequently.

6) Transfer to a large oven-proof dish (ideally a casserole dish).

7) Combine the sauce ingredients and pour over the meat.

8) Cover and cook for approximately 2 hours, or until the meat is tender.

TIP 1 – We have not ticked the Candida box with this recipe because of the vinegar in the Worcestershire sauce and the mushrooms.

Serves 4

Phase	Meal	V	C	H	Wheat free	Dairy free
(1 &) 2	Fat		Can be	✓	✓	✓

Basque Pork Stew

The Basque region lies in between the South West part of France and the Northern Spanish border. It is a territory with a unique culture and with culture goes cuisine. The Basque cuisine draws heavily on hearty real food – meat, fish, vegetables, potatoes, breads and cheeses. This is a great Basque recipe for pork.

Ingredients:

2 tablespoons olive oil	5 garlic cloves, thinly sliced
1kg pork shoulder, diced	
2 onions, thickly sliced	1 teaspoon paprika
500ml meat stock	1 teaspoon dried thyme
2 tablespoons tomato paste	¼ teaspoon dried chilli (or an amount to suit your taste)
2 sweet red peppers, in strips	1 orange

Method:

1) Cut the meat into 2-3cm cubes.

2) Heat the olive oil, in a deep saucepan or large frying pan, over a medium heat.

3) Brown the pork in batches, adding more oil if necessary. Put the browned pork to one side.

4) Add the onions to the pan and cook over the medium heat, stirring occasionally, for 5 minutes.

5) Add the stock and tomato paste and bring to the boil.

6) Return the pork to the pan; stir in the red pepper strips, garlic, paprika, thyme and chilli.

7) Grate the rind from the orange and add it to the stew. Remove the pith from the orange and then chop the orange coarsely and stir it into the stew.

8) Transfer the stew to a casserole dish. Put on the cover; bring the mixture to the boil and then reduce the heat to simmer for approximately an hour, or until the pork is tender.

TIP 1 – Leave out the whole orange and this can be suitable for Phase 1. Adding the zest of the orange will be fine for Phase 1 – it's no different to a dash of lemon juice. You could also add the orange to the dish and give someone else your bits of orange if you are doing a strict Phase 1.

Serves 4

Phase	Meal	V	C	H	Wheat free	Dairy free
(1 &) 2	Fat		✓	✓	✓	✓

Beef à la Grecque

So many casseroles use wine as the added tasty ingredient; this one uses cider vinegar for a refreshing, tangy difference. This is a wonderfully simple casserole – just a few, well-chosen ingredients that blend so well together.

Ingredients:

3 tablespoons oil	75g tomato purée
600g stewing steak, diced	3 tablespoons cider vinegar
400g white onions, sliced	500ml water
1 onion, whole (peeled) and stuck with 4 cloves	Salt & ground black pepper
1 x 5cm stick of cinnamon	

Method:

1) Preheat the oven to 350° F, 175° C, gas mark 4.

2) Heat the oil in a large frying pan, and fry the meat cubes until brown.

3) Put the meat in a large oven-proof dish; ideally a casserole dish.

4) Add the white onions, the clove stuffed onion and the cinnamon.

5) Mix the tomato purée, vinegar and water together in a saucepan and bring to the boil.

6) Add the seasoning and then pour the whole mixture over the meat.

7) Cover and cook for approximately 2½ hours, or until the meat is tender.

TIP 1 – Leave out the vinegar, or use lemon juice instead, and this can be suitable for Phase 1 and Candida.

Serves 4

Phase	Meal	V	C	H	Wheat free	Dairy free
(1 &) 2	Fat		Can be	✓	✓	✓

Moroccan Beef

This is a really rich and luxurious meat dish. If you have a slow-cooker, you can add all the ingredients, except the corn flour, and leave it to cook itself. The corn flour can then be added to thicken the dish, minutes before it is served.

Ingredients:

1 tablespoon olive oil	400g tin chopped tomatoes
300g beef diced	
1 red onion, chopped	1 teaspoon coriander
1 onion, chopped	1 teaspoon cumin
2 cloves garlic, chopped	½ teaspoon cayenne pepper
3 carrots, grated	4 cardamom pods, crushed
2 tablespoons corn flour	
300ml beef stock	Juice & zest of 2 oranges

Method:

1) Heat the olive oil in a large frying pan, and fry the beef until it is brown.

2) Add the onions and garlic and cook until soft.

3) Add the grated carrot and mix well. Stir-fry for a further 5 minutes.

4) Add the corn flour and cook for 1 minute.

5) Then add the beef stock and mix well. Add the tinned tomatoes, coriander, cumin, cayenne pepper, cardamom pods, orange zest and orange juice and mix thoroughly.

6) Cover the pan and simmer for 40 minutes, or until the meat is tender.

Serve with broccoli, or cauliflower, or any 'chunky' vegetables.

TIP 1 – Substitute lemon zest and lemon juice for the orange zest and juice, and this can be suitable for Phase 1.

Serves 4

Phase	Meal	V	C	H	Wheat free	Dairy free
(1 &) 2	Fat		✓	✓	✓	✓

(Spaghetti) Bolognaise

This recipe can be adapted for any Phase of The Harcombe Diet. As written it is a Phase 2 recipe. TIP 1 below shows how to adapt it for Phase 1. Children can have this with (ideally whole wheat) spaghetti at any time for a Phase 3 meal and adults at their natural weight can join them in Phase 3.

Most Harcombe dieters report that 'not mixing' just becomes such second nature that they don't miss having classic sauces without the pasta that they used to have. They also don't miss the bloating either!

Ingredients:

1 tablespoon olive oil	100g rindless bacon, chopped
400g mince beef	
1 carrot, chopped	300ml red wine
2 onions, chopped	400g tin chopped tomatoes
1 stick celery, chopped	
2 cloves garlic, crushed	2 teaspoons oregano
50g button mushrooms	Salt & ground black pepper

Method:

1) Brown the mince in the olive oil, in a large frying pan, over a moderate heat.

2) Add the carrot, onions, celery, garlic, mushrooms and bacon and cook for another 5 minutes until these are soft too.

3) Pour in the wine and bring to the boil.

4) Add the tomatoes and oregano and season to taste. Simmer for approximately 45 minutes, stirring occasionally.

5) Cook the spaghetti approximately 10-15 minutes before serving.

Serve with freshly grated Parmesan.

TIP 1 – Substitute peppers for mushrooms, use vegetable stock instead of wine and this will be suitable for Phase 1.

TIP 2 – Substitute peppers for mushrooms and this is suitable for Candida.

TIP 3 – The reason for recommending whole wheat carbs, if you do have carbs, is because they are more filling and they are more nutritious. You will find you have more of a natural appetite limit with, say, brown rice than white rice. Non whole (refined) carbs have invariably had the most nutritious bits removed – the vitamins and minerals found in the whole grain. In terms of how whole or non whole carbs break down in the body – there is little difference. Starchy carbohydrates, like pasta, break down into glucose and the body needs to release insulin to return glucose levels to normal.

Serves 4

Phase	Meal	V	C	H	Wheat free	Dairy free
(1 &) 2	Fat		Can be	✓	Can be	Can be

Spiced Roast Lamb

This recipe works equally well with a good quality lamb joint or a cheaper shoulder cut; just cook a shoulder slower and longer than you would a quality leg joint.

Ingredients:

2.5kg leg of lamb	1 teaspoon fresh rosemary, chopped
4 cloves garlic, halved	4 tablespoons olive oil
2 teaspoons paprika	Juice of ½ lemon
2 teaspoons Dijon mustard (optional)	Freshly ground black pepper

Method:

1) Make deep incisions in the lamb and push the garlic halves into the holes.

2) Mix together the paprika, mustard, rosemary and olive oil and mix together thoroughly. Stir in the lemon juice to the mix.

3) Rub the mixture all over the lamb joint and then leave it to marinate for about 2 hours.

4) Preheat the oven to 375° F, 190° C, gas mark 5. Cook for approximately 2 hours, or to your liking, basting the joint with its own juices.

5) Carve and serve hot with a selection of vegetables.

TIP 1 – Leave out the mustard for Phase 1.

Serves 4

Phase	Meal	V	C	H	Wheat free	Dairy free
(1 &) 2	Fat		✓	✓	✓	✓

Lird Burgers

We would like to thank Lird for this recipe. These burgers are also known as "Turkish style feta stuffed Köfte". These are perfect barbecue burgers and the perfect accompaniment for them is Lird's Cacık recipe (see Phase 1 side dishes). Leave out the feta and these can be suitable for Phase 1.

Ingredients:

500g minced lamb	Approximately 1 teaspoon of each of the following spices & herbs: mixed spice; paprika; mint; cumin; black pepper
1 onion, finely chopped	
200g feta (crumbled)	
Half an egg, beaten	

Method:

1) Preheat the oven to 400° F, 200° C, gas mark 6 (there are other cooking options below).

2) Place all the prepared ingredients in a mixing bowl and mix thoroughly with your hands.

3) Take a handful of the mixture and form a small but tight ball with your hands. Place the meat ball on a baking tray and lightly pat down to make a burger shape. Repeat until all the mixture is used up.

4) Bake in the oven for approximately 15-30 minutes, depending on the size of the burgers. The cooking options for Andy's Cheese Burgers also work with Lird Burgers.

Makes approx 4-6 burgers, depending on their size

Phase	Meal	V	C	H	Wheat free	Dairy free
(1 &) 2	Fat		✓	✓	✓	Can be

Meat Ball Kebabs

Just leave out the mustard to make this a Phase 1 dish.

Ingredients:

450g minced lamb	1 teaspoon paprika
450g minced beef	1 egg, beaten
1 onion, finely chopped	Freshly ground black pepper
2 cloves garlic, crushed	
1 teaspoon Dijon mustard (optional)	Slices of red & green peppers, courgettes & red onions

Method:

1) In a large bowl, mix the minced meat, onion and garlic until the onion and garlic are evenly distributed. Then mix in the mustard and paprika.

2) Whisk the egg in a separate bowl and then add it and the pepper to the minced meat mix. Knead the mixture for about 2 minutes, until it forms a constant consistency.

3) Take small handfuls of the mixture and squeeze it into balls, slightly smaller than golf balls. Skewer the balls, squeezing them around the skewer so that they don't fall off. Alternate meat balls with vegetable slices. Aim for 3-4 balls per skewer.

4) Grill the skewers under a very hot grill, or barbecue them, for 4-5 minutes each side until nicely brown.

Serves 4-6

Phase	Meal	V	C	H	Wheat free	Dairy free
(1 &) 2	Fat		✓	✓	✓	✓

Warm Chicken Salad

Warm salads are a great way to get the goodness of meat and greens all year round.

Ingredients:

10 tablespoons olive oil	2 garlic cloves, crushed
4 chicken breasts, skin on, cut into strips	600g mixed salad leaves
2 tablespoon white wine vinegar (or lemon juice)	300g cherry tomatoes, halved
2 tablespoon freshly chopped herbs (coriander, basil, oregano ideally)	Freshly ground black pepper

Method:

1) Heat 4 tablespoons of the oil in a frying pan and fry the chicken strips until cooked through and golden brown. Turn off the heat and leave the chicken in the pan to keep warm.

2) Mix together the remaining oil, white wine vinegar, herbs and garlic to make the salad dressing.

3) Place the mixed salad leaves and cherry tomatoes in a salad bowl and add the warm chicken pieces.

4) Pour the freshly made dressing over the chicken and salad. Season and serve immediately.

TIP 1 – Just use lemon juice instead of vinegar to make this suitable for Phase 1 and Candida.

Serves 4

Phase	Meal	V	C	H	Wheat free	Dairy free
(1 &) 2	Fat		Can be	✓	✓	✓

Special Fried Rice

This is our only Phase 1 mix recipe, although the Bean Paella can be made with seafood as a Phase 1 mix option. If you stay on Phase 1 for a while it is best to adopt the no mixing rule after a week or so. If you are just doing the standard 5-day Phase 1, you may really enjoy paella, meat curries with brown rice and this simple and delicious recipe.

Ingredients:

200g brown rice	1 chilli, chopped (optional)
1 stock cube (vegetable, meat or fish – as you like)	3 spring onions, thinly sliced
25g of butter	100g cooked chicken, diced
1 egg, beaten	100g cooked prawns
2 tablespoons of olive oil	1 tablespoon Tamari soy sauce (optional)
1 onion, finely sliced	
1 clove garlic, crushed	

Method:

1) Cook the rice in a saucepan with the crumbled stock cube and boiling water so that the rice absorbs the stock flavours. 10-15 minutes before the rice is cooked, you can start on the rest of the dish:

2) Heat the butter in a small frying pan.

3) Add the beaten egg and slosh it around the pan to cover the base of the pan evenly. Cook for 1-2 minutes until it turns into a golden omelette. Slide the omelette out onto another plate, cut into strips and keep warm.

4) Heat the oil in a large frying pan. Add the onion, garlic, chilli and spring onions and stir-fry for a couple of minutes.

5) Add the rice, which should be cooked by now, and the chicken and prawns and fry for approximately 5 minutes – until the meat and fish are well heated through.

6) Stir in the soy sauce at the end for an added 'kick'.

7) Arrange the omelette strips on top of the dish when it is served.

TIP 1 – Use more olive oil instead of the butter and this can be dairy-free.

TIP 2 – Leave out the soy sauce if you are intolerant to soy products.

TIP 3 – The Tamari version of soy sauce is invariably wheat/gluten free, unlike normal soy sauce. Check that the Tamari soy sauce that you buy is wheat-free. Typical ingredients will be water, soybeans, salt and distilled sake, which is rice based.

TIP 4 – In Phase 3 (or for the natural weight people eating with you), this can be served with poppadoms (also known as pappadums, puppodums and about a dozen other names). Poppadoms are invariably made from lentil flour, and/or rice flour with vegetable oil and salt – all acceptable ingredients.

Serves 4

Phase	Meal	V	C	H	Wheat free	Dairy free
1 & 3	Mixes		✓	✓	✓	Can be

PHASE 1 – SIDE DISHES & SAUCES

This is one of the most valuable sections of this book. Base sauces can be used to make meat, fish or vegetarian dishes and the favourites that you discover here can be used with many different staple meal ingredients – chicken, diced pork, chunks of fish, rice pasta, mixed vegetables and so on.

We start with the essential base recipes for curry – one of the most popular take-away meals world-wide. You'll know exactly what's gone into your curry. You can keep tubs of the base recipe in the freezer to defrost whenever you fancy a curry – just add the different curry flavours on the night with your chosen meat, fish, quorn or vegetables. The Bhuna Masala is easily adaptable for Phase 1 and the Korma is a Phase 2 recipe (with cream), but we have kept them all together in this section, as the ultimate suite of curry base recipes.

This section also has some of our favourite vegetable accompaniments – from simple asparagus cooked in butter to the exquisite celeriac chips.

We have recipes for beef, chicken and vegetable stock, so that you can use leftovers to make real stock rather than relying on stock cubes.

Our famous 15 minute tomato sauce is also in this section – the perfect pasta sauce for rice pasta in Phase 1. Use a concentrated (less water) version of this and/or the tomato salsa recipe in this section to have Harcombe friendly chips and tomato sauce in Phase 2.

Finally, we have the classic dressings from French vinaigrette to mayonnaise, with some wonderful variations of all of these.

Indian Curry Sauce Base Recipe

This is the base recipe for the four curry variations to follow. We highly recommend keeping a tub of this in the freezer and then you just need to make the variation when you are cooking your meat or vegetables.

Ingredients: (makes approximately 750ml of sauce)

1 tablespoon olive oil	450ml cold water
2 onions, sliced	400g tin tomatoes
2 cloves garlic, crushed	1 teaspoon turmeric
25g root ginger, sliced	1 teaspoon paprika

Method:

1) Heat the olive oil in a saucepan and lightly cook the onion, garlic and ginger. Remove from the heat and add the cold water. Blend this mixture, with a hand held blender in the pan, until completely smooth.

2) Blend the tinned tomatoes, until they are completely smooth, and add them to the saucepan.

3) Stir in the turmeric and paprika, bring the whole mixture to the boil then turn down and simmer for 15 minutes.

4) Skim off and discard any froth that forms. Use the sauce immediately or chill/freeze for later use.

Serves 4

Phase	Meal	V	C	H	Wheat free	Dairy free
1 & 2	Either	Can be	✓	✓	✓	✓

Indian Curry

This is the simplest curry dish to make, building on the basic recipe. You can make this as hot as you like by adding an extra teaspoon or two of chilli powder.

Ingredients:

400ml curry sauce base recipe	1 teaspoon garam masala
450g cooked meat, fish, quorn or vegetable chunks	½ teaspoon ground cumin
	1 tomato, sliced
½ teaspoon chilli powder	1 tablespoon coriander, finely chopped

Method:

1) In a large saucepan, bring the curry sauce base to the boil. Add your cooked meat, fish or vegetable chunks and the chilli powder. Reduce the heat and simmer for 5 minutes.

2) Stir in the garam masala and ground cumin and simmer for a further 5 minutes.

3) Add the sliced tomato and half the coriander and cook for a further 2-3 minutes.

4) Serve immediately using the remainder of the coriander as garnish.

TIP 1 – Stir-fry your meat, fish or vegetable chunks in olive oil while you are bringing the base sauce to the boil. The same applies for any of the curry recipes.

Serves 4

Phase	Meal	V	C	H	Wheat free	Dairy free
1 & 2	Either	Can be	✓	✓	✓	✓

Bhuna Masala Curry

This is a classic favourite on every Indian restaurant menu – a deliciously spicy use of the base curry recipe.

Ingredients:

1 tablespoon olive oil	450g cooked meat, fish, quorn or vegetable chunks
50g mushrooms	1½ teaspoons garam masala
1 green pepper, thinly sliced	1 teaspoon ground cumin
400ml curry sauce base recipe	½ teaspoon dried fenugreek
½ teaspoon chilli powder	1 tablespoon coriander, finely chopped
1 green chilli, finely chopped	

Method:

1) Heat the oil in a large saucepan and lightly fry the mushrooms and pepper. Add the curry sauce base, chilli powder, chopped chilli and your meat, fish or vegetable chunks and bring to the boil. Reduce the heat and simmer for 10 minutes.

2) Stir in the garam masala, ground cumin and fenugreek and simmer for a further 10 minutes.

3) Serve immediately and garnish with the coriander.

TIP 1 – Leave out the mushrooms to be suitable for Phase 1 and Candida.

Serves 4

Phase	Meal	V	C	H	Wheat free	Dairy free
(1 &) 2	Either	Can be	Can be	✓	✓	✓

Korma Curry

This is the mild, creamy version of curry for those who don't want the roof of their mouth blown off. This goes particularly well with chicken or quorn.

Ingredients:

1 tablespoon olive oil	½ teaspoons garam masala
400ml curry sauce base recipe	1 teaspoon ground cumin
450g cooked meat, quorn or vegetable chunks	150ml single cream
2 tablespoons cashew nuts, chopped	1 tablespoon coriander, finely chopped

Method:

1) Heat the oil in a large saucepan, add the curry sauce base and bring to the boil. Add the chicken or quorn, or similar, and cashew nuts. Reduce the heat and simmer for 10 minutes.

2) Stir in the garam masala and ground cumin and simmer for a further 5 minutes.

3) Stir in the cream and half the chopped coriander and heat gently for a further 2 minutes.

4) Serve immediately using the remainder of the coriander as garnish.

Serves 4

Phase	Meal	V	C	H	Wheat free	Dairy free
2	Fat	Can be	✓	✓	✓	

Dhansak Curry

This is a hot and sour dish, which goes particularly well with lamb. You can use any cut of pre-cooked lamb.

Ingredients:

2 tablespoons olive oil	1½ teaspoons garam masala
400ml curry sauce base recipe	1 teaspoon ground cumin
450g cooked meat, fish or vegetable chunks	2 tablespoons lemon juice
1 teaspoon chilli powder	1 tablespoon coriander, finely chopped
1 green chilli, finely chopped	

Method:

1) Heat the oil in a large saucepan, add the curry sauce base and bring to the boil. Add the lamb, or chosen substance, chilli powder and chopped chilli. Reduce the heat and simmer for 10 minutes.

2) Stir in the garam masala, ground cumin and lemon juice and simmer for a further 5 minutes.

3) Stir in half the chopped coriander and heat gently for a further 2 minutes.

4) Sprinkle with the remainder of the coriander and serve immediately.

Serves 4

Phase	Meal	V	C	H	Wheat free	Dairy free
1 & 2	Either	Can be	✓	✓	✓	✓

Stir-fry Vegetables

Stir-frying vegetables seals in their flavour and goodness. This makes a delicious meal in itself or it can be served as an accompaniment to other dishes. The amount of vegetables can be varied to suit but, as a guide, allow approximately 200g of uncooked vegetables per person. Don't worry if this looks too much, the vegetables will reduce in volume as you cook them.

Ingredients:

Sesame seed oil (or other flavoured oil)	Cauliflower florets;
2 onions, roughly chopped	Carrot batons;
	Chillies (add sparingly to taste);
1 clove garlic, chopped	Green beans in 3-4cm lengths;
Mixture of cleaned & peeled vegetables, chopped into bite size pieces:	Mange tout pieces;
	3-4cm strips of coloured peppers;
(Baby) sweet corn cut in two;	Water chestnuts etc
Bean sprouts;	and anything else that you like
Broccoli florets;	
Cabbage strips (white, red and green);	

Method:

1) Heat the oil, in a large frying pan, over a high heat. Fry the onions, garlic and chillies (if you opted for these) and the vegetables that take longer to cook e.g. broccoli, carrots, cauliflower, corn, peppers from the above list for 4-5 minutes.

2) Add the other vegetables and fry everything, stirring regularly, for another 2-3 minutes.

3) When the vegetables start to soften, add a soup ladle full of tap water, continuing to stir the vegetables. Cook until the water is evaporated and serve. This final step seals in the flavour and the goodness of the vegetables.

4) Add freshly ground black pepper to taste and a dash of Tabasco if you like a bite to your dishes.

Serve with brown rice, quinoa or tofu.

TIP 1 – For a variation on the above recipe, experiment with different oils (olive oil, groundnut oil) or add a handful of nuts with the water.

Serves 4

Phase	Meal	V	C	H	Wheat free	Dairy free
1 & 2	Either	✓	✓	✓	✓	✓

Sprout Salad

This is a simple and extremely nutritious salad. The definition of a sprout is a vegetable seed that just starts growing. Sprouts grow from the seeds of vegetables, grains and various beans and are the first edible shoots. Let us look at some of the key ingredients in this recipe:

- Alfalfa has been used by the Chinese since the sixth century to treat kidney stones and to relieve fluid retention and swelling. In addition to these medicinal properties alfalfa is also an anti-Candida agent and it detoxifies the body. It has a nutty taste that goes well with cheese.

- Lentil sprouts can come in many different colours. They have a peppery flavour and are often used in soups and casseroles. We use them in this recipe for their added spice.

- There are many variations of cress, but garden cress is the most common and the one most likely to be available in supermarkets. It is often grown by children, at school, as their first introduction to plant biology and it can grow up to 3cm tall. It has been a favourite in English cooking since the sixteenth century thanks to its pleasantly spicy, peppery taste, similar to watercress, but more pungent.

- If you can get hold of mustard sprouts this will add even greater spice to this salad. Mustard has many medicinal properties and is a staple of Chinese medicine – used for everything from colds to stomach disorders, with rheumatism and toothache in between.

Ingredients:

	For the dressing:
½ lettuce, shredded	150ml olive oil
1 leek, finely sliced	Zest & juice of 1 lime
75g alfalfa sprouts	4 tablespoons lemon juice
75g lentil sprouts	
1 carton of cress and/or mustard	Salt & ground black pepper

Method:

1) Shred the lettuce and finely slice the leek. Mix with the sprouts.

2) Whisk the dressing ingredients together.

3) Pour the dressing over the salad ingredients. Toss well and season to taste.

Serves 4

Phase	Meal	V	C	H	Wheat free	Dairy free
1 & 2	Either	✓	✓	✓	✓	✓

Ratatouille

This recipe is great with meat, fish or vegetarian protein alternatives for a fat meal. Or it can make a perfect carb meal with pasta or a crispy baked potato.

Ingredients:

6 tablespoons olive oil	1 green pepper, deseeded & chopped
2 aubergines, diced in 2cm squares	1 clove garlic, finely chopped
2 courgettes, cut into batons	400g tin chopped tomatoes
2 onions, finely sliced	1 teaspoon mixed herbs
1 red pepper, deseeded & chopped	Salt & ground black pepper

We have two methods below – a long version, which makes a rich, soft and perfectly blended ratatouille and a quicker version, which can be knocked up at any time.

Method:

1) Preheat the oven to 325° F, 165° C, gas mark 3.

2) Warm the olive oil in a large frying pan.

3) Cook the aubergines until they are browned, stirring regularly to brown them all over. Transfer them to a casserole dish.

4) Cook the courgette batons in the pan until they are browned, stirring regularly to brown them all over. Transfer them to the casserole dish.

5) Cook the onions in the pan for 2-3 minutes.

6) Add the peppers and garlic and cook for a further 3-4 minutes, until soft.

7) Transfer the onions, peppers and garlic to the casserole dish with the aubergines and courgettes.

8) Pour the tin of chopped tomatoes and sprinkle the mixed herbs over the ingredients. Season to taste.

9) Put a lid on the casserole dish and cook the ingredients in a low oven 325° F, 165° C, gas mark 3 for approximately 45 minutes.

Quick Method:

1) Warm the olive oil in a large casserole dish.

2) Add the onion, garlic, peppers, courgettes and aubergine and cook for 2-3 minutes.

3) Pour in the tin of tomatoes. Add the mixed herbs and seasoning. Put the lid on. Bring to the boil and simmer for 20-30 minutes.

Serves 4

Phase	Meal	V	C	H	Wheat free	Dairy free
1 & 2	Either	✓	✓	✓	✓	✓

Bubble & Squeak

This is a great way to use up left over vegetables to make a delicious side dish. It works with any mixture of leftover vegetables. Just keep them in the fridge overnight and use them the following day in this dish.

Ingredients:

2 tablespoons olive oil 1 onion, finely chopped 1 clove of garlic, crushed Dash of Tabasco (optional) Freshly ground black pepper	This works well with any vegetables e.g. broccoli, Brussels sprouts cabbage, carrots, cauliflower, leeks, parsnips, swede, etc

Method:

1) Lightly fry the onion and garlic in the olive oil for 2-3 minutes until transparent, but not browned.

2) Add all the other vegetables to the frying pan and cook slowly until thoroughly warmed through, stirring frequently.

3) Add a dash of Tabasco (optional) and season with freshly ground pepper. Serve immediately as a side dish.

TIP 1 – The ingredients in Tabasco are white distilled vinegar, red pepper and salt, but a dash will be fine for Phase 1. It can be left out if you prefer.

Add fresh vegetables to meet the required servings.

Phase	Meal	V	C	H	Wheat free	Dairy free
1 & 2	Either	✓	✓	✓	✓	✓

Marinated Olives

You can buy marinated olive in any delicatessen, but you can't always be sure what has been used in the marinade. This recipe is delicious, simple and guaranteed to be free of unnecessary ingredients.

Ingredients:

For the marinade:	The olives:
6 tablespoons freshly chopped herbs (parsley, coriander, rosemary etc)	450g unpitted green olives
1 clove garlic, thinly sliced	
Pinch of cumin seeds	
2 tablespoons olive oil	
Juice of ½ lemon	

Method:

1) Put all the ingredients for the marinade together in a bowl and mix thoroughly.

2) Add the olives and stir well so that they are well covered by the mixture.

3) Cover and leave to marinade in the fridge for a few days and then transfer to smaller dishes for serving.

Serves 4

Phase	Meal	V	C	H	Wheat free	Dairy free
1 & 2	Either	✓	✓	✓	✓	✓

French Green Beans

One of the best ways to do fat meals is to go for plain and perfectly cooked meat or fish served with special accompaniments or to go for simple side dishes served with our spicier meat and fish dishes. You may choose only to mix rich main meals with rich accompaniments for dinner parties. This is a simple and yet extravagant side dish from Provence – a great accompaniment to a plain main meal.

Ingredients:

2 tablespoons olive oil	50g of black olives (stoned)
1 onion, sliced	
1 clove garlic, sliced	250ml cold water
6 'beef' tomatoes, coarsely chopped	Salt & ground black pepper
450g French beans	

Method:

1) Heat the oil in a deep frying pan and lightly fry the onion and garlic for about 5 minutes until transparent.

2) Add the tomatoes, beans, olives and water to the pan. Bring everything to the boil. Turn the heat down and lightly simmer, stirring occasionally, for approximately 15 minutes.

3) Season to taste and serve hot.

Serves 4

Phase	Meal	V	C	H	Wheat free	Dairy free
1 & 2	Either	✓	✓	✓	✓	✓

Celeriac Chips

These are quite extraordinary and a great way to get an unusual vegetable into your diet. Celeriac is a good source of the version of vitamin K provided by plants (K1). It is also useful for many minerals from calcium to zinc, with magnesium and manganese in between.

Ingredients:

1 celeriac	½ teaspoon black mustard seeds
75g butter	½ teaspoon black onion seeds
1 level tablespoon curry powder	
½ teaspoon fenugreek seeds	

Method:

1) Preheat the oven to 350° F, 175° C, gas mark 4.

2) Peel, or cut away, the outer skin of the celeriac and cut into "chips". Place them on a baking tray.

3) Melt the butter in a saucepan. Add the curry powder and seeds and heat to release the flavour for approximately 30 seconds. Don't allow to burn.

4) Pour the butter over the celeriac and mix the chips in the butter until they are fully coated.

5) Cook the chips for 45-60 minutes, turning occasionally. The chips will not be crisp; they remain deliciously chewy.

Serves 4

Phase	Meal	V	C	H	Wheat free	Dairy free
1 & 2	Either	✓	✓	✓	✓	

Lird's Cacık

This is the perfect accompaniment to the Lird Burgers, which are in the Phase 1 fat main meal section (1 &) 2.

Ingredients:

250g Greek Natural Live Yoghurt	Leaves from 2 sprigs of mint, finely chopped
¼ cucumber, finely diced	Salt & ground black pepper
Juice of ½ lemon	
1 or 2 cloves garlic, crushed	

Method:

1) Mix all the ingredients together in a bowl.

2) Keep chilled in the fridge until needed – especially on warm barbecue days.

TIP 1 – Use low fat Natural Live Yoghurt to accompany a carb meal and whatever you prefer to accompany a fat meal.

Phase	Meal	V	C	H	Wheat free	Dairy free
1 & 2	Either	✓	✓	✓	✓	

Herb & Peppercorn Sauce

This simple and delicious sauce is perfect for any meat or fish 'steaks' – beef, pork or lamb steaks or fillets of salmon or tuna or aubergine slices.

Ingredients:

1 teaspoon cumin seeds	coriander, chives, oregano works well)
2 tablespoons mixed peppercorns (black, white, green)	2 tablespoons olive oil
	Juice of ½ lemon
3 bunches of fresh herbs, finely chopped (any combination of parsley,	Pinch of salt

Method:

1) Put the cumin and peppercorns in a pestle and mortar and coarsely crush them together.

2) Place the chopped mixed herbs in a mixing bowl. Add the crushed cumin and peppercorns, olive oil, lemon juice and a pinch of salt and stir well.

3) Cover the bowl with cling film and place it in the fridge until you are ready to use it.

4) Cook your meat or fish steaks on a hot griddle to seal in their natural flavour.

5) In parallel, gently warm the sauce in a small pan until the olive oil begins to bubble and then pour the sauce over your meat/fish when serving.

Phase	Meal	V	C	H	Wheat free	Dairy free
1 & 2	Either	✓	✓	✓	✓	✓

Cajun Seasoning

This is great rubbed onto meat, fish or vegetables before they are grilled or barbecued. We have included below some interesting factoids about some of the base spices in this fabulous recipe:

Cardamom – is one of the oldest and most treasured spices in the world. It is the third most expensive, after saffron and vanilla. In India it is second only to pepper in the list of important spices. Its key therapeutic benefit is as a breath cleanser, which happens when you chew the seeds.

Coriander – this spice originated in the Mediterranean region but is now cultivated world-wide. Its medicinal properties include indigestion and migraine cures.

Cumin – this spice gives a distinctive warm flavour to an enormous range of savoury dishes in India, North Africa, the Middle East, Mexico and America. It is used less so in Europe. Its medicinal properties are interesting – it is taken in India as a remedy for diarrhoea, flatulence and indigestion.

Fennel – this spice has long been used in India and China, where the seeds were taken as a remedy for scorpion and snake bites, and has spread in popularity across the rest of the world. Fennel can also be used to ease breathing problems, stomach complaints and toothache.

Peppercorns – black peppercorns are made from green peppercorns, which are pickled, left to ferment and then sun-dried. For centuries pepper was used as currency in the East and West, as it was considered such a precious commodity. Pepper is said to help relieve flatulence and to have diuretic properties (relieves water retention).

We hope that these notes inspire you to use the following blend as a wonderful enhancement to any meat or fish:

Ingredients:

½ teaspoon cardamom seeds	2 teaspoons dried oregano
1 teaspoon coriander seeds	1 teaspoon dried basil
1 teaspoon cumin seeds	1 teaspoon paprika
1 teaspoon fennel seeds	½ teaspoon chilli powder
1 teaspoon black peppercorns	½ teaspoon garlic salt

Method:

1) Put the coriander, cumin, fennel and cardamom seeds together with the black peppercorns in a pestle and mortar and crush them well.

2) Transfer the crushed seeds and peppercorns to a mixing bowl and add the remaining ingredients. Mix everything together thoroughly.

3) Rub the mixture into steak, lamb, pork, chicken, fish, aubergine steaks, vegetables and anything else that you would barbecue or grill. Cook the meat, fish or vegetables as you would normally.

Phase	Meal	V	C	H	Wheat free	Dairy free
1 & 2	Either	✓	✓	✓	✓	✓

Gravy

We have included a number of options for gravy recipes here, as the most basic recipe is suitable for Phase 1. Every time you roast meat (beef, lamb, pork or poultry), put onions and garlic cloves in the roasting tray. When the meat is roasted, these vegetables and the meat juices ensure that you have the base ingredients that you need for the perfect gravy.

Ingredients:

2 large onions, chopped in half	½ glass wine (white or red) (optional)
12 cloves garlic, left in their skin	300ml stock (to complement your dish)
1 tablespoon corn flour (optional)	

Method:

1) As with the Rib of Beef recipe, every time you roast a chicken or meat joint put the onions and garlic cloves in the bottom of the roasting tray and place the meat on top.

2) A few minutes before you plan to serve the meat, warm some home-made stock, or boil some water and make some stock with a stock cube.

3) Remove the meat from the roasting tray leaving the onion, garlic and other juices in the dish.

4) Place the roasting tray on the stove over a medium to high heat. Add the corn flour (optional) and stir until it starts to thicken.

5) Mash the vegetables in the tray with a potato masher (or scrape out the vegetables and solid bits and blend them and return them to the tray).

6) Add the wine at this stage (optional) and let the mixture boil for a few minutes to cook the alcohol away.

7) Pour approximately 300ml of warm stock into the tray. Bring everything to the boil; continue stirring, scraping the bits from the base of the tin as you go.

8) Reduce the heat and simmer the mixture until the volume is reduced by a half.

9) You can either serve as is, or pass the mixture through a sieve to remove any lumps.

TIP 1 – Try to match your stock to your meat: beef stock for Rib of Beef, chicken stock for roast chicken etc.

TIP 2 – White wine may go better with white meat and red wine with red. Red wine does also go well with chicken, however, so you can't go wrong with red wine.

TIP 3 – The simplest gravy recipe just needs the roasting tray vegetables and juices and stock. The tiny amount of corn flour will also be fine for Phase 1 and does help to make thicker gravy,

TIP 4 – The wine is for a Phase 2 recipe. This will make wonderfully rich gravy – a perfect accompaniment to a simple roast joint. Try sherry instead of wine for a variation.

Phase	Meal	V	C	H	Wheat free	Dairy free
1 & 2	Either		✓	✓	✓	✓

Vegetarian Stock

Leftovers are meant to be used for stock – not thrown away with so many nutrients in the skin and peel. Make a batch of stock for the freezer if you have leftovers and no immediate need for stock.

Ingredients:

Any leftover vegetables (You can use carrot tops, or peel, - anything you would normally throw away)	1 bouquet garni sachet A few peppercorns 1-2 cloves

Method:

1) Put the vegetables in a saucepan.

2) Add boiling water to come three quarters of the way up the vegetables.

3) Add the bouquet garni, peppercorns and cloves.

4) Cover and boil for 20-30 minutes.

5) Pour the contents through a sieve and the liquid is your vegetable stock.

TIP 1 – Use the liquid from any boiled vegetables as a stock base.

TIP 2 – Juice from sugar-free/salt free canned vegetables can also be used as a stock base. You can add the bouquet garni sachet, peppercorns and cloves to either of these natural juices, bring to the boil and there is a quick stock.

Phase	Meal	V	C	H	Wheat free	Dairy free
1 & 2	Either	✓	✓	✓	✓	✓

Chicken Stock

The healthiest cultures use every part of the animal to ensure that none of the nutrients are wasted. Every time you roast and eat a free range chicken you should make stock as a matter of course.

Ingredients:

1 chicken carcass, including giblets if available	1 stick of celery
	1 carrot
	1 teaspoon peppercorns
1 onion, quartered	1 bay leaf
1 clove garlic, peeled & left whole	1½ litres water

Method:

1) Put all the ingredients in a large casserole dish or saucepan.

2) Add the water, making sure that it is sufficient to cover the ingredients, and bring everything to the boil. Reduce the heat and simmer for 20 minutes. Remove from the heat and allow it to cool.

3) Pour the contents through a sieve into a jug (throw away the carcass and vegetables) and this stock can be used immediately or frozen in batches for use as required.

TIP 1 – Add any fat and liquids from the bottom of the roasting tray to the stock ingredients for extra flavour and nutrition.

Phase	Meal	V	C	H	Wheat free	Dairy free
1 & 2	Either		✓	✓	✓	✓

Beef Stock

This takes a bit more work than the chicken stock but the flavour compared to stock cubes is so superior that you'll never use beef stock cubes again. This is a must as the base for the French Onion soup recipe.

Ingredients:

2-3kg beef bones	1 carrot
2 onions, quartered	1 teaspoon peppercorns
2 cloves garlic, peeled & left whole	1 bay leaf
	2 litres water

Method:

1) Preheat the oven to 375° F, 190° C, gas mark 5.

2) Place the bones in a roasting dish and roast them for 20-30 minutes until nicely browned.

3) Put the bones and any scraps from the roasting dish into a large saucepan. Add the vegetables and the water and bring everything to the boil. Reduce the heat so that it's barely simmering and cook for 1 hour or 2 – more if possible. Then remove from the heat and allow it to cool.

4) Before the fat forms on the top of the stock, scoop out the bones and vegetables and pass the stock through a fine sieve.

TIP 1 – The stock will have a layer of fat on top when it cools. You can remove this, to use for cooking, or leave it to give the stock a fuller flavour. Don't waste it!

Phase	Meal	V	C	H	Wheat free	Dairy free
1 & 2	Either		✓	✓	✓	✓

Thai Inspired Stir-Fry Sauce

After much experimenting with stir-fries and being disappointed, one of our club members, Helen (Fidget) came up with this delicacy. Helen would like to dedicate this recipe to her lovely husband who always appreciates her culinary efforts. We are not surprised!

Ingredients:

2 teaspoons sesame oil	2 tablespoons Tamari soy sauce
2 tablespoons sunflower oil	2 tablespoons creamed coconut, grated
4 cloves garlic, crushed	4 spring onions, chopped
½ teaspoon dried chilli	4 tomatoes, chopped
Fresh ginger, chopped, quantity equivalent to garlic	A little water/stock to thin (optional - depends how juicy the tomatoes are)
2 teaspoons lemon or lime juice	

Method:

1) Heat the 2 oils in a frying pan. Add all the other ingredients and gently fry until the tomatoes have softened and the flavours have combined.

2) Leave the sauce chunky, or let it cool slightly, blend it and return it to the pan. You can then add prawns or diced fish or meat and vegetables for a main meal.

Phase	Meal	V	C	H	Wheat free	Dairy free
1 & 2	Either	✓	✓	✓	✓	✓

15 Minute Tomato Sauce

This is such a versatile sauce. It goes with meat, fish, pasta, spaghetti, quinoa, quorn, vegetables and tofu, or just about anything else you can think of.

Ingredients:

2 tablespoons olive oil	2 teaspoons of basil (ideally fresh)
1 onion, finely chopped	
1 clove garlic, crushed	Salt & ground black pepper
400g tin chopped tomatoes	

Method:

1) Heat the olive oil in a large frying pan, until it is sizzling.

2) Fry the onion and garlic until soft (2-3 minutes) and then add the chopped tomatoes. These will take approximately 2 minutes to warm through.

3) Add the basil, salt & pepper and you can then serve immediately or leave the sauce to simmer until some pasta is cooked (10-15 minutes).

TIP 1 – This freezes well, so make a big batch and keep the extra in portion size tubs in the freezer.

TIP 2 – This also re-heats well, so you can have it with pasta one night and meat or fish the next.

TIP 3 – If wheat is a problem for you, you can get rice pasta and corn pasta from health food shops and many supermarkets, which look and taste just like wheat but without the side effects.

TIP 4 – This recipe is a great base pasta sauce – add courgettes and/or peppers to make it more substantial.

TIP 5 – To make this a hot and spicy pasta sauce just buy some spicy olive oil and use this for cooking instead. Or, add a finely chopped chilli or some Tabasco sauce.

TIP 6 – As mentioned in the introduction to "Phase 1 Side Dishes & Sauces", you can drain/boil off the liquid in this sauce to make a more concentrated version of tomato 'ketchup'.

Serves 2-4

Phase	Meal	V	C	H	Wheat free	Dairy free
1 & 2	Either	✓	✓	✓	✓	✓

Perfectly Cooked Vegetables

The best fast food is a simple piece of meat or fish with some well cooked vegetables – natural taste and nutrition with no fuss. Pan fry a salmon steak in 25g of butter; grill a tuna steak or a chicken breast; grill or fry a steak or chop and add one, or more, of the following vegetables to make the perfect fat meal. Finish off with strawberries and cream/yoghurt, or a cheese platter, and you will hardly believe that you are 'on a diet'.

For vegetarians – any of these vegetables can be eaten with omelettes or vegetarian alternative proteins – the stir-fry vegetables are particularly good with stir-fried tofu or chunks of quorn.

Spinach

Wash approximately 500g of spinach. Put 25g of butter in a medium saucepan and place the spinach on top. Cook on a medium heat, stirring occasionally, until the spinach reduces to about one quarter of the volume that it was. Turn the heat right down to low and simmer for 2-3 minutes. This gives perfectly cooked and delicious buttery spinach – to go with fat meals.

Green beans

Top and tail the green beans, wash them thoroughly and chop them into 3-4cm lengths. Either place in a saucepan of boiling water for a few minutes until just soft to a fork touch, or, for a great microwave version – put them in a microwaveable bowl; cover them with a piece of dampened kitchen paper (or microwave safe cling film) and then microwave for 2 minutes.

Brussels Sprouts

Carefully split the stem with a knife and place the sprouts in a saucepan of boiling water. Cook for approximately 5 minutes – until the sprouts are just soft to a fork touch. Don't overcook sprouts, as they are best firm and not mushy.

Asparagus

This is a wonderful vegetable – expensive, but worth it for special occasions. Either pan fry it in butter, turning regularly, until the bottom of the stalk is soft to a fork touch (approximately 5 minutes). Or, cook it in the microwave as per the green beans recipe above.

Mushrooms

For those who have managed to get Candida nicely under control, there is nothing like mushrooms as an accompaniment to steak or chops. Melt a knob of butter in a frying pan over a medium heat and fry the mushrooms, stirring regularly, until slightly blackened all over.

Root vegetables option 1

Wash the carrots, parsnips and/or turnips thoroughly; top and tail them but don't peel them – to keep all the goodness in the whole vegetable. Cut them into same sized batons, so that they cook evenly. Place them in a saucepan of boiling water and cook for approximately 5-10 minutes – until they are soft to a fork touch.

Root vegetables option 2

Wash the carrots, parsnips and/or turnips thoroughly; top and tail them but don't peel them. Cut them into same sized batons. Brush a baking tray with olive oil and then place the batons on the tray and bake in the oven for approximately 30 minutes at 400° F, 200° C, gas mark 6. Turn the batons at least once during the cooking time, to brown them all over.

Phase	Meal	V	C	H	Wheat free	Dairy free
1 & 2	Either	✓	Can be	✓	✓	Can be

Tapenade

Tapenade is a classic dish from the Provençal region of France. Its name comes from the Provençal word for capers – tapenas. The classic ingredients are olives, capers, anchovies and olive oil. We have added a lemon twist. This is a delicious accompaniment to any main meal, or it can be served as a starter on a bed of rocket or other strongly flavoured greens.

Ingredients:

200g pitted black olives	Zest of 1 lemon
50g tin anchovies	Freshly ground black pepper
2 tablespoons capers	
150ml olive oil	

Method:

1) Coarsely chop the olives, anchovies and capers and mix them together in a bowl with the olive oil.

2) Add the grated lemon rind to the mixture and stir well.

3) Season with pepper, cover and leave to stand for at least 30 minutes.

4) Serve at room temperature.

TIP 1 – This is also great served as a dip with crudités or served as Hors D'oeuvres on mini oat cakes.

Serves 4

Phase	Meal	V	C	H	Wheat free	Dairy free
1 & 2	Fat		✓	✓	✓	✓

Aioli – Garlic Mayonnaise

Aioli is a classic recipe from Provence in France. It is made by mixing garlic, eggs, lemon and olive oil making it a great alternative to vinegar based dressings.

Ingredients:

4 cloves of garlic, crushed Pinch of salt 2 egg yolks	250ml extra virgin olive oil Juice of ½ lemon

Method:

1) Put the crushed garlic and pinch of salt in a blender.

2) Add the egg yolks and whisk vigorously until the mixture is smooth, which will take about 30 seconds.

3) Very slowly, add the olive oil, a small amount at a time, continuing to blend until all the oil is added and the mixture is thick and creamy.

4) Add the lemon juice. Give a final quick blend and serve immediately.

TIP 1 – Lemon juice is fine for Phase 1. It is used in such tiny quantities because of its strong flavour. "Stop Counting Calories" lists olive oil and lemon juice as the simplest vinegar-free salad dressing for Phase 1.

Phase	Meal	V	C	H	Wheat free	Dairy free
1 & 2	Either	✓	✓	✓	✓	✓

Herb Aioli

This is a variation of the classic Aioli. The lemon juice is replaced with a selection of fresh herbs, which will give the dressing a lovely yellow and green appearance and make it perfect for Phase 1.

Ingredients:

4 cloves of garlic, crushed	4 tablespoons freshly chopped herbs (parsley, coriander, sage, rosemary etc)
Pinch of salt	
2 egg yolks	
250ml extra virgin olive oil	Freshly ground black pepper

Method:

1) Put the crushed garlic and pinch of salt in a blender.

2) Add the egg yolks and whisk vigorously until the mixture is smooth, which will take about 30 seconds.

3) Very slowly, add the olive oil, a small amount at a time, continuing to blend until all the oil is added and the mixture is thick and creamy.

4) Stir in the chopped herbs and the ground pepper. Cover and leave to stand for at least 30 minutes.

TIP 1 – This recipe can be chilled and served as required but you will need to let it return to room temperature and give it a little whisk before serving.

Phase	Meal	V	C	H	Wheat free	Dairy free
1 & 2	Either	✓	✓	✓	✓	✓

Tomato Salsa

This salsa is the perfect accompaniment to steak, lamb, pork, tuna, white fish, cheese... anything really. We recommend multiplying the quantities to make a large batch, which you can freeze and reheat as required.

Ingredients:

2 tablespoons olive oil	8 'beef' tomatoes, roughly chopped
4 spring onions or 1 regular onion, finely chopped	1 tablespoon of balsamic vinegar (optional)
2 cloves garlic, crushed	Freshly ground black pepper

Method:

1) Heat the olive oil in a frying pan and lightly fry the onions and garlic for about 2 minutes.

2) Add the tomatoes and cook on a lower heat for a further 3-4 minutes, stirring frequently, until the tomatoes are soft.

3) Allow the mixture to cool slightly and then stir in the balsamic vinegar.

4) Serve warm with any meat or chill and serve cold with cold meats or cheese.

TIP 1 – Leave out the balsamic to make this suitable for Phase 1 and for Candida.

Serves 4

Phase	Meal	V	C	H	Wheat free	Dairy free
(1 &) 2	Either	✓	Can be	✓	✓	✓

Roasted Peppers

Peppers are one of the most nutritious and versatile salad/vegetables. They can be used hot or cold and as part of salad or vegetable dishes. They provide a useful amount of the minerals calcium, magnesium, phosphorus and potassium. Peppers are particularly good for vitamin C – 100 grams of yellow, red and green peppers provide 183mg, 128mg and 80mg of vitamin C respectively.

Ingredients:

4 red peppers	1 clove garlic, sliced
2 green peppers	Freshly ground black pepper
2 yellow peppers	
5 tablespoons olive oil	200g tin artichoke hearts, drained
1 tablespoon balsamic vinegar (optional)	50g sun dried tomatoes

Method:

1) Slice the peppers in half, lengthways. Remove the seeds and place them on a baking tray. Roast in a hot oven (400° F, 200° C, gas mark 6), for 30-45 minutes until they begin to blacken. Remove the peppers from the oven and set them aside to cool.

2) Mix the olive oil and balsamic vinegar, add the sliced garlic and season with the black pepper.

3) Trim the stalks from the peppers and slice them thickly. Cut the artichoke hearts in half and thinly slice the sun dried tomatoes.

4) Add the sliced peppers, sun dried tomatoes and artichokes to the olive oil mix and stir. Serve immediately or chill and use as required.

TIP 1 – Leave out the balsamic to make this suitable for Phase 1 and for Candida.

Serves 4

Phase	Meal	V	C	H	Wheat free	Dairy free
(1 &) 2	Either	✓	Can be	✓	✓	✓

Crunchy Coleslaw

As Harcombe diet club members will know, five-a-day was started as a marketing campaign by fruit and vegetable companies. It has no scientific basis and yet it has become the most widely known 'nutritional' message in over 20 countries across three continents. Fruit, whilst very enjoyable, is not needed in our diets and can be quite *unhelpful* for weight loss. Vegetables can be useful providers of vitamins and minerals, especially when eaten raw (but always a poor second to animal foods for anything other than vitamin C). Coleslaw is quite a useful side serving, therefore and is also really tasty and versatile.

Ingredients:

300g mixed cabbage, finely sliced (white/red/green – whatever you fancy)	For the dressing:
	4 tablespoons sunflower oil
150g carrots, grated	2 tablespoons wine vinegar
1 red & 1 green pepper, deseeded & finely chopped	2 teaspoons Dijon mustard
1 onion, finely chopped	Salt & ground black pepper
30g sunflower seeds (optional)	
60g dates, chopped (optional)	

Method:

1) If you have a food processor you can throw in the cabbage, carrots, peppers and onion and shred/chop/grate them automatically. Without a

processor you need a grater, a sharp knife and some elbow power.

2) Put all the vegetables into a salad bowl. Add the seeds and dates if desired.

3) Mix the dressing in a small bowl and then pour on top of the coleslaw. Mix thoroughly.

TIP 1 – Substitute lemon juice for vinegar and leave out the seeds and dates and this can be suitable for Phase 1.

TIP 2 – Leave out the chopped dates, even in Phase 2, for Candida or Hypoglycaemia.

TIP 3 – Put the coleslaw in a fun little pot, with a spoon, for a (school) lunchbox.

Serves 4

Phase	Meal	V	C	H	Wheat free	Dairy free
(1 &) 2	Either	✓	Can be	Can be	✓	✓

163

Char Grilled Vegetables

If you leave out the balsamic, this makes a great Phase 1 recipe – a real bonus for vegetarians, who can struggle in Phase 1.

Ingredients:

Olive oil for brushing a baking tray	Broccoli florets
	Peppers, any colours, sliced
1kg of mixed vegetables. The following work really well:	Carrots, peeled & sliced
	Parsnips, peeled & sliced
Aubergine, sliced with skin on	Butternut squash, sliced with skin left on
Courgette, sliced with skin on	Balsamic vinegar (optional)
Onions, sliced with skin on	Pine nuts & Parmesan (optional)

Method:

1) Preheat the oven to 350° F, 175° C, gas mark 4.

2) Brush a baking tray with olive oil.

3) Place the sliced vegetables on the baking tray and brush the vegetables with olive oil.

4) Roast them in the oven until the vegetables are charred around the edges and soft to a fork touch (approximately 30 minutes). (Note the parsnips and butternut squash will be soft in the middle but very crispy on the outside – you have just made healthy chips).

5) Flavour with balsamic vinegar (not in Phase 1, or if you have Candida) or extra olive oil if desired.

6) Add a few pine nuts and/or a small grating of Parmesan cheese for extra taste.

TIP 1 – Vegetable kebabs can be done with the same vegetables on a skewer, on a barbecue, or roasted in the oven.

TIP 2 – Go easy on, or leave out, the butternut squash if you are very carbohydrate sensitive.

Serves 4

Phase	Meal	V	C	H	Wheat free	Dairy free
(1 &) 2	Either	✓	Can be	✓	✓	✓

PHASE 1 – SOUPS, STARTERS & LITE BITES

Gazpacho Soup

This is such an easy recipe for this classic summer soup and it offers all the benefits of raw food. This will be like having a health boosting smoothie for a starter, as it is packed with vitamin C and has useful amounts of other vitamins and minerals from vitamin K to copper.

Ingredients:

1 cucumber, peeled, deseeded & chopped	1 litre of tomato juice, chilled
1 onion, chopped	1 tablespoon of sunflower or olive oil
1 red pepper & 1 green pepper, deseeded & chopped	Salt & ground black pepper
Juice of 1 lemon	

Method:

1) Put all the ingredients in a blender and blend until smooth. You will likely need to do this in batches. Season to taste.

2) Chill in the fridge for 2 hours before serving.

TIP 1 – Peel the cucumber whole; cut lengthways into quarters; slice out the seeds in one knife action and you have a peeled and deseeded cucumber.

TIP 2 – Add a clove of garlic for extra kick and anti-Candida properties.

Serves 4-6

Phase	Meal	V	C	H	Wheat free	Dairy free
1 & 2	Either	✓	✓	✓	✓	✓

Pea Soup

The only vitamin that we really need to eat vegetables for is vitamin C (and that's if we don't eat raw liver or chestnuts). Peas are a great source of vitamin C and this soup must be one of the nicest ways to eat them.

Ingredients:

450g frozen peas	700ml of vegetable stock (home-made or from a stock cube)
2 onions, chopped	
A handful of mint leaves	50g butter
A handful of parsley, not stalks	Salt & ground black pepper

Method:

1) Place the peas, onions, mint, parsley and stock in a large saucepan and boil for approximately 20 minutes.

2) Just before serving, add the butter and seasoning and then blend in the pan with a hand held blender until smooth.

TIP 1 – Serve with a circle of Natural Live Yoghurt on top for garnish and added creaminess.

TIP 2 – Use petit pois (little peas) for added sweetness.

TIP 3 – This works really well with chicken stock, but would not then be vegetarian.

Serves 4

Phase	Meal	V	C	H	Wheat free	Dairy free
1 & 2	Either	✓	✓	✓	✓	

Grilled Tomato Soup

It takes a bit of time to pre-grill the tomatoes in this recipe, but it really is worth it. The taste of the slightly charred vegetables makes the whole soup really special.

Ingredients:

Olive oil for brushing baking trays	3 cloves garlic, crushed
1.3kg of tomatoes (yes 1.3kg)!	1 fennel bulb, sliced
	2 sticks celery, chopped
2 tablespoons olive oil	Salt & ground black pepper
2 onions, sliced	

Method:

1) Preheat the oven to 350° F, 175° C, gas mark 4.

2) Cut the tomatoes in half and put them on baking trays, which have been lightly brushed with olive oil.

3) Place the tomatoes under a very hot grill for 10 minutes. (You may need to do them in batches if you don't have lots of baking trays and a large grill).

4) Transfer them all to a large saucepan once they have been grilled.

5) Put 2 tablespoons of olive oil into a large frying pan and gently fry the onions, garlic, fennel and celery, until the onions begin to soften.

6) Then, transfer all the fried ingredients onto a baking dish and place them at the top of the oven for 30 minutes.

7) Pour all the fried & oven baked vegetables onto the grilled tomatoes in the saucepan and mix well.

8) Use a hand held blender to blend the mixture until smooth.

9) Warm everything in the saucepan (not quite to boiling point); season to taste and then serve immediately.

TIP 1 – Add some shavings of fresh ginger or 1 teaspoon of ground ginger for a quite extraordinary taste variation.

Serves 4-6

Phase	Meal	V	C	H	Wheat free	Dairy free
1 & 2	Either	✓	✓	✓	✓	✓

Sam's Spicy Soup

Spicy food can be a great way to clear the nasal passages if you are unfortunate enough to pick up a winter cold. This one will have you reaching for the tissues and have the germs running for their lives.

Ingredients:

4 tablespoons olive oil	1 onion, chopped
1 teaspoon hot paprika	2-4 fresh chillies, chopped (to taste)
½ teaspoon chilli powder	
½ teaspoon cumin seeds	700ml of vegetable stock (home-made or from a stock cube)
4 cloves garlic, crushed	
3 bay leaves	A few drops of Tabasco (optional, to taste)
1 butternut squash, peeled, deseeded & diced	
2 carrots, peeled & diced	Cream or Natural Live Yoghurt (for decoration - optional)
2 sticks of celery, cut into chunks	

Method:

1) Heat the olive oil in a large frying pan. Add the paprika, chilli powder, cumin seeds, garlic and bay leaves and cook for 45 seconds, ensuring that the ingredients do not burn.

2) Add the chopped vegetables and chillies and stir until they are coated in the spices.

3) Add the stock (and Tabasco if desired) and simmer for 30-40 minutes until the vegetables are soft.

4) Remove the bay leaves and liquidise the mixture in a blender.

5) You may like to serve this with a circle of Natural Live Yoghurt in the middle of each bowl – this provides a wonderful cool contrast to the spicy soup.

TIP 1 – For a Phase 2 variation you can add approximately 100ml of double cream to the soup just before serving. Make sure that the soup is piping hot before you do this, as the cream will cool everything a little. Or you can serve the soup with cream decoration instead of NLY.

TIP 2 – For a non-vegetarian version, you can add 2 slices of bacon, thinly sliced, at step (2) of the method and gently fry these with the vegetables and spices until they are cooked. Set the cooked bacon pieces aside, before the stock is added, and keep them warm. Then add them to the soup as a topping before serving – with or without the cream or NLY.

Serves 4

Phase	Meal	V	C	H	Wheat free	Dairy free
1 & 2	Either	✓	✓	✓	✓	Can be

Root Vegetable Soup

This is a real winter warming soup and it feels hearty and filling. Root vegetables have had a bad press with Atkins and other very low-carb diets. They are higher in carbohydrate than green vegetables, but you only need to avoid them if highly carbohydrate sensitive. Turnips are a surprisingly good source of vitamin C. Two of the fat soluble vitamins, A and K, have one form that comes from animal foods and one form that comes from vegetation. Carrots are rich in carotene (which can be converted to vitamin A by most people) and K1. A bowl of this will easily keep you going until the next meal.

Ingredients:

2 tablespoons olive oil	700ml of vegetable stock (home-made or from a stock cube)
1 onion, finely chopped	
1 clove garlic, finely chopped	Salt & ground black pepper
1kg of root vegetables, peeled & diced (carrots, parsnips, swede and turnips are all ideal)	Dash of Tabasco (optional)

Method:

1) Heat the olive oil in a large pan.

2) Fry the onion and garlic until soft.

3) Add all the vegetables and give them a good stir.

4) Add the vegetable stock and bring everything to the boil.

5) Reduce the heat and simmer gently for approximately 30 minutes, or until the vegetables are cooked. Season to taste.

6) Turn off the heat and allow to cool for 5 minutes before serving.

7) Leave chunky, or use a hand held blender to blend the mixture until smooth.

TIP 1 – This soup can be eaten with either fat or carb meals, as it is just vegetables. However, it is better with carb meals, as the vegetables are all high carb content ones.

TIP 2 – We put a bracket around (H) for Hypoglycaemia, as some very carbohydrate sensitive people may find the root vegetables too starchy to keep their blood glucose levels nicely stable.

TIP 3 – Squashes also work well with this soup. Try seasonal mixed squashes, pumpkins and/or butternut squash.

TIP 4 – This soup will naturally be quite orange in colour. To turn this soup the most amazing pink colour, add fresh beetroot as one of the vegetables. Drain some of the liquid off before blending and you end up with a pink purée, which can also be served as a vegetable accompaniment.

Serves 4

Phase	Meal	V	C	H	Wheat free	Dairy free
1 & 2	Carb	✓	✓	(✓)	✓	✓

Roast Butternut Squash Soup

Butternut squash is one of our favourite vegetables. The taste and texture appeal to Andy, as the chef and the nutrition appeals to Zoë. Butternut squash has almost unparalleled levels of vitamin A. Remember, however, that the body needs vitamin A in the form of retinol. Only animal foods contain retinol. Vegetables contain carotene and this needs to be converted by the body into retinol. The conversion is not very efficient (one to six has been calculated in a scientific study) and some people (diabetics, for example) struggle to be able to convert carotene to retinol at all. For this reason, don't rely on orange vegetables, such as butternut squash and carrots, for vitamin A – we need animal foods in our diet.

Ingredients:

1 butternut squash, peeled, deseeded & diced	1 teaspoon coriander seeds, crushed
4-5 cloves garlic (left in their skins)	1 litre chicken stock
5 tablespoons olive oil	2-3 tablespoons fresh oregano, finely chopped
1 onion, chopped	

Method:

1) Preheat the oven to 375° F, 190° C, gas mark 5.

2) Place the butternut squash and garlic on a roasting dish. Drizzle with half the olive oil and roast in the oven for 30-40 minutes, until the squash flesh is soft.

3) Heat the remaining oil in a saucepan and lightly fry the onion and coriander for 3-4 minutes.

4) Squeeze the roast garlic flesh out of their skins and add to the pan with the onion and coriander.

5) Add the roast squash and chicken stock and bring to the boil. Reduce and simmer for 10 minutes.

6) Remove the soup from the heat and allow it to cool for a few minutes. Add half the oregano and blend the mixture until it's completely smooth.

7) Serve the soup immediately with the remaining fresh oregano sprinkled on top for garnish.

TIP 1 – This soup can be eaten with either fat or carb meals, as it is just vegetables. However, it is better with carb meals, as butternut squash is quite high in carbohydrate.

TIP 2 – You can use vegetable stock with this but we always do it with our home-made chicken stock. It just adds a bit more flavour (and nutrition) to the dish. You are not mixing here – as you are having chicken flavour, not chicken.

Serves 4

Phase	Meal	V	C	H	Wheat free	Dairy free
1 & 2	Either	✓	✓	✓	✓	✓

Red Pepper & Tomato Soup

Peppers and tomatoes were made to go together.

Ingredients:

50g butter and a little olive oil	2 tablespoons parsley, chopped
2 onions, chopped	1 bay leaf
2 cloves garlic, crushed	¼ teaspoon basil
3 red peppers, deseeded & chopped	¼ teaspoon oregano
400g tin chopped tomatoes	700ml stock (using one of our recipes or use 2 stock cubes)
2 tablespoons tomato purée	Salt & ground black pepper

Method:

1) Heat the butter and olive oil in a frying pan. Fry the onions, garlic and peppers until soft.

2) Add the rest of the ingredients, bring to the boil and then simmer for approximately 30 minutes.

3) Blend the mixture with a hand held blender until smooth; adjust the seasoning if necessary.

TIP 1 – This looks particularly attractive served with a circle topping of Natural Live Yoghurt.

Serves 4

Phase	Meal	V	C	H	Wheat free	Dairy free
1 & 2	Either	✓	✓	✓	✓	

Coriander Marinated Salmon & Lime

This can be done with smoked salmon, but fresh is always best. This is also known as Carpaccio of salmon – thinly sliced raw salmon.

Ingredients:

450g fresh salmon fillets, thinly sliced	Freshly ground pepper
	Fresh coriander, chopped
4-5 tablespoons olive oil	Juice of 1 lime

Method:

1) Place a thin slice of salmon on a plate and then drizzle some olive oil over the salmon, then some black pepper and chopped coriander.

2) Place a second layer of sliced salmon on top of the first and repeat step 1 until all the salmon is dressed. Finish with a drizzle of olive oil

3) Cover with cling film and leave in the fridge for at least 24 hours.

4) To serve, share the slices of salmon amongst 4 plates, squeeze a small amount of the lime juice over the salmon and sprinkle some freshly chopped coriander to garnish.

TIP 1 – If you are short of time, you can use smoked salmon instead of fresh. Simply follow the same steps as above, allowing 1 hour for the smoked salmon to marinate.

Serves 4

Phase	Meal	V	C	H	Wheat free	Dairy free
1 & 2	Fat		✓	✓	✓	✓

Hot Sizzling Prawns

Do try to add seafood to your diet when possible. A couple of prawns with any fish dish, or with steak for 'surf 'n turf' – there are invaluable and unique nutrients to be found in food from the sea. Prawns are good sources of the fat soluble vitamins A, D and E and seafood generally is a valuable source of the mineral zinc, which is often difficult to get in our diets.

Ingredients:

2 tablespoons olive oil 2 chillies, deseeded & chopped (more if you like food really spicy)	2 cloves of garlic, finely sliced 16 large prawns Juice of 1 lemon

Method:

1) Heat the olive oil in a frying pan and, when the oil is hot, add the chillies and garlic and fry for 1 minute.

2) Add the prawns and fry for a further 4-5 minutes, turning regularly, until the prawn shells are lightly burnt.

3) Transfer the prawns to a warmed dish and pour the oil from the frying pan over the prawns.

4) Squeeze the juice of the lemon over the prawns and serve immediately. Eat with your fingers.

Serves 4 as a starter or 2 as a lite bite

Phase	Meal	V	C	H	Wheat free	Dairy free
1 & 2	Fat		✓	✓	✓	✓

Egg & Bacon Salad

This would make the perfect 'brunch'.

Ingredients:

500g mixed salad leaves	1 tablespoon olive oil
4 tablespoons of one of our aioli dressings (Phase 1)	4 eggs
4 fatty bacon rashers, chopped	Freshly ground black pepper

Method:

1) Place the salad leaves in a large mixing bowl and toss them in the salad dressing. Divide them between 4 plates.

2) Fry the bacon in its own fat, in a frying pan, until nicely brown. Transfer it to a warmed dish and keep it warm.

3) Heat the oil in the same pan and fry the eggs.

4) Just before the eggs are cooked, divide the warm bacon between the 4 plates and then pop an egg on top of each one.

5) Season and serve immediately.

TIP 1 - As a variation, you could try making this dish with poached or boiled eggs.

Serves 4

Phase	Meal	V	C	H	Wheat free	Dairy free
1 & 2	Fat		✓	✓	✓	✓

Carpaccio of Beef

The secret to success with this dish is the quality of the beef and the sharpness of your carving knife – you want the beef sliced as thinly as you can manage. This is a luxurious fat starter to serve dinner party guests.

Ingredients:

500g fillet steak	Juice of 1 lemon
1 teaspoon of sea salt	Shavings of parmesan (or parmaggio)
4 tablespoons olive oil	
½ teaspoon cracked black pepper	

Method:

1) Rub the salt into the beef and then wrap it tightly in tin foil and chill for 2 hours in the fridge (getting the beef really cold will make it easier to slice).

2) Mix together all the other ingredients in a bowl.

3) Arrange the beef on a large platter so that it is well spread out with little overlap. Pour the olive oil mix over the slices and decorate with the parmesan shavings.

4) Serve immediately, or cover with cling film and keep cool until serving later that day.

Serves 4

Phase	Meal	V	C	H	Wheat free	Dairy free
1 & 2	Fat		✓	✓	✓	

Tzatziki – Greek Dip

This is such an easy starter to make and it can be served with a delicious assortment of crudités – batons of carrots, cucumber, celery sticks, slices of peppers and so on.

Ingredients:

½ cucumber, peeled & grated	2 tablespoons fresh mint, finely chopped
1 clove garlic, crushed	Salt & ground black pepper
240ml Greek yoghurt	

Method:

1) Mix the cucumber, garlic, yoghurt, mint, salt & pepper together in a bowl.

2) Chill in the fridge for at least an hour.

TIP 1 – Use Natural Live Yoghurt, instead of Greek yoghurt, and this can be suitable for Phase 1.

TIP 2 – Use low fat yoghurt and you can serve this with pita bread, as a Phase 2 carb meal, if you are OK with wheat.

Serves 4

Phase	Meal	V	C	H	Wheat free	Dairy free
(1 &) 2	Fat	✓	✓	✓	✓	

Cauliflower Vichyssoise with Chive Cream

This is a wonderful chilled soup, absolutely delicious at any time of the day in the summer. It will impress at a dinner party, or be a great starter to a summer salad, if you just fancy a special meal for dinner one night.

Ingredients:

1 head of cauliflower	240ml single cream
1 litre of water	Salt & ground black pepper
½ teaspoon sea salt	
1 large bunch chives (with chive flowers attached, if possible)	

Method:

1) Trim the base of the cauliflower; remove the leaves and any dark spots and break into florets. Put the florets into a medium saucepan. Add 1 litre of water and ½ teaspoon sea salt (the water won't cover the cauliflower).

2) Cut half the chives into ½ cm lengths and add them to the cauliflower. Set the rest aside.

3) Bring the cauliflower mixture to a boil. Lower the heat, cover the pan, and cook for 25 minutes or until the cauliflower is very soft.

4) Transfer the cauliflower mixture to a food processor or blender. Add the cream and blend until smooth.

5) Season the soup with salt and pepper to taste. Allow it to cool.

6) In a small saucepan, bring the remaining cream and chives to the boil. Add 2 tablespoons water

and a pinch of salt. Lower the heat and simmer for
1 minute.

7) Transfer to a blender; purée until smooth and then
add this to the cauliflower mixture and let it cool.
Cover and refrigerate until cold.

8) Serve with chive flowers or chopped chives as
garnish.

TIP 1 – Replace the cream with Natural Live Yoghurt
and this can be suitable for Phase 1. This will make it
quite sharp, however.

Serves 4

Phase	Meal	V	C	H	Wheat free	Dairy free
(1 &) 2	Fat	✓	✓	✓	✓	

Spinach Paté

This is such a simple starter. It can be made a day ahead, so it makes a great dish when entertaining, if you want to save time on the day. This is a fat starter so no bread with it – serve it with crudités instead.

Ingredients:

60ml water	1 teaspoon corn flour
1 vegetable stock cube	30g butter
1 teaspoon ground nutmeg	1 onion, finely chopped
	2 cloves garlic, crushed
200g spinach (pre-cooked weight)	120ml double cream

Method:

1) Put the water in the bottom of a large saucepan, crumble in the stock cube and add the nutmeg.

2) Stuff the spinach on top. Bring everything to the boil; reduce the heat; simmer, uncovered, for approximately 5-10 minutes, stirring every now and again, until the spinach has reduced to the bottom of the saucepan.

3) Mix the corn flour with a teaspoon of water into a paste. Add this to the saucepan and stir over a moderate heat until the spinach mixture boils. Remove from the heat and leave to one side.

4) Melt the butter in a medium saucepan, add the onion and garlic and cook over a moderate heat until they are soft.

5) Put the spinach mixture and onion mixture together in a blender and add the cream.

6) Blend everything until smooth and then transfer to a serving dish and leave in the fridge for several hours, or until firm.

Serve with a selection of crudités as a dip. Good options would be strips of coloured peppers, carrots, celery sticks, cucumber etc.

TIP 1 – Use Natural Live Yoghurt, instead of cream to make this suitable for Phase 1. This will make the paté quite sharp, however.

Serves 4 (starter size portions)

Phase	Meal	V	C	H	Wheat free	Dairy free
(1 &) 2	Fat	✓	✓	✓	✓	

Salmon Mousse with Lemon & Chives

Salmon is a classic starter base and this is a really impressive alternative to the standard smoked salmon appetiser. Fresh salmon is also better than smoked salmon for Candida. Finally, this dish can be prepared in advance, leaving you free to welcome the guests.

Ingredients:

200g flaked, poached salmon OR 200g tin of red salmon, drained	3 teaspoons gelatine
	2 tablespoons boiling water
1 stick celery, chopped	60ml double cream
2 teaspoons lemon juice	1 egg white
2 teaspoons Natural Live Yoghurt	4 sprigs of parsley
1 tablespoon fresh chives, chopped	

Method:

1) Put the salmon, celery, lemon juice and yoghurt in a blender and mix up until smooth.

2) Place the mixture into a bowl and stir in the chives.

3) Dissolve the gelatine in the 2 tablespoons of boiling water.

4) Stir into the salmon mixture.

5) Stir the cream into the salmon mixture.

6) Whisk the egg white until firm peaks appear and then fold it into the salmon mixture.

7) Divide the mixture into 4 small serving bowls and chill in the fridge for at least 2 hours.

8) Serve with a garnish of parsley.

TIP 1 – Use extra Natural Live Yoghurt, instead of cream, to make this suitable for Phase 1.

Serves 4

Phase	Meal	V	C	H	Wheat free	Dairy free
(1 &) 2	Fat		✓	✓	✓	

Prawn & Cucumber Soup

This is a delicious chilled soup, fat starter. It makes a refreshing alternative to prawn cocktail.

Ingredients:

1 cucumber, grated whole	250ml single cream
½ teaspoon sea salt	2 tablespoons chives, chopped
300ml Natural Live Yoghurt	150g prawns, shelled & peeled
6 tablespoons lemon juice	

Method:

1) Grate the unpeeled cucumber into a bowl. Sprinkle with the sea salt and set aside.

2) Mix the yoghurt, lemon juice and cream in a separate bowl. Add this to the cucumber.

3) Stir in the chives and prawns.

4) Either leave as is for a coarse soup, or blend with a hand held blender until smooth.

5) Chill in the fridge for at least an hour before serving.

TIP 1 – Use only Natural Live Yoghurt (550ml), and no cream and this can be suitable for Phase 1.

Serves 4

Phase	Meal	V	C	H	Wheat free	Dairy free
(1 &) 2	Fat		✓	✓	✓	

Phase 2

(P190) Breakfasts

(P202) Carb Main Meals (all vegetarian)

(P222) Fat Main Meals

(P289) Side dishes & sauces

(P303) Soups, Starters & Lite Bites

(P330) Desserts

PHASE 2 – BREAKFASTS

Fruit Platters

We have seen children who swear that they hate fruit dive into a fruit platter as if they haven't eaten for a week. There are two things going on here:

1) As soon as you put one platter in between two or more children, the scarcity principle kicks in and they grab at the food regardless.

2) Fruit is naturally sweet and delicious and children think they don't like it because they get bored with eating a whole apple or can't be bothered to peel an orange. If you have chopped up all the fruit and removed the inedible skins for them, they will really enjoy the different flavours.

Ingredients:

A good selection of ripe, fresh, fruit in season e.g.: apples; grapes; melon; nectarines; oranges; peaches; pears	Low-fat Natural Live Yoghurt (optional) Low-fat cottage cheese (optional)

Method:

1) Use the largest plate you have.

2) Get peeling, chopping and slicing. Leave any edible skins on and chop all the fruit so that you just have to dive in with fingers and enjoy. This is a really satisfying meal and seems a lot more filling than when you just eat pieces of fruit on their own. You can add a couple of spoonfuls of low-fat cottage cheese or low-fat Natural Live Yoghurt in the middle of the platter for a filling dip.

Tropical Fruit Platter:

Pineapple, mango, melon, papaya, banana, sharon fruit, star fruit, kiwi fruit and grapes – whatever you can find in the supermarket.

Berry Fruit Platter:

Strawberries, raspberries, blueberries and blackberries – again whatever you can find.

Stone Fruit Platter:

Nectarines, peaches, plums and apricots.

Citrus Fruit Platter:

Orange segments, grapefruit segments, kumquats, satsumas and clementines.

Staple Fruit Platter:

Available all year round – sliced apples, sliced pears, grapes and bananas.

TIP 1 – We have put brackets round Candida and Hypoglycaemia, in the table below, as too much fruit and particularly tropical fruits, can be bad for both conditions. Please use your judgement – if your conditions are not too severe then the refreshing enjoyment of a fruit platter may outweigh the dis-benefits.

Phase	Meal	V	C	H	Wheat free	Dairy free
2	Carb	✓	(✓)	(✓)	✓	Can be

The Perfect 'Carb' Breakfast

The traditional start to most people's days is cereal with milk. This feeds the most common Food Intolerances – milk, wheat and sugar – as soon as you wake up. Not the ideal way to start the day. Almost every pre-packaged cereal is at least 20% sugar (even adult bran cereals are at least 18% sugar, so imagine how much sugar there is in the cereals that are advertised to children). There are now some excellent alternatives to the processed cereal box. Here are a few suggestions:

For adults who are OK with wheat and milk (and most, if not all, children):

1) Shredded wheat (100% whole wheat and nothing else) or bite sized shredded wheat.

2) Home-made muesli – you can buy bags of different grains from a health food shop or good supermarkets. You can then mix and match combinations until you get a cereal that you really enjoy. Choose from: oat flakes; wheat flakes; millet flakes; barley flakes; rye flakes. Adults can mix a few nuts and sunflower seeds with the mixture; children can have more nuts, sunflower seeds and even some dried fruit (sultanas, raisins, chopped dates etc).

3) Porridge oats.

4) Puffed rice cereal (tastes like sugar puffs, but without any sugar).

All of these can be eaten with skimmed, or semi-skimmed, milk for adults and any milk for children.

Anyone with just milk intolerance should try real (unpasteurised) milk before trying milk made from carbs, like soya milk or rice milk. The latter are not natural products. Cooking porridge oats with boiling water, rather than milk, is one of the easiest and healthiest breakfasts you can have. You can also get used to having cereal dry – the puffed rice cereal is especially delicious dry, as it retains its crunch and is like rice cakes, but with a lower glycaemic index.

For anyone with just wheat intolerance – you can have options 3 and 4 with no problem (porridge and puffed rice). You can also make home-made muesli with no wheat flakes – just oat, millet and barley flakes. You can add in nuts and seeds too for added crunch and flavour. You just need to avoid option 1 – the wheat cereals. Wheat based cereals are also best avoided by those suffering from Candida.

For those of you who are fine with milk, one of the quickest and simplest ways to make porridge is to put the amount of milk you want in a cereal bowl and microwave it on high for 2-3 minutes until boiling. Take the bowl out of the microwave; add the oats, stirring constantly, and eat as soon as it reaches the consistency that you like. You could boil the milk in a small saucepan as an alternative starting point.

For anyone unfortunate enough to have milk and wheat intolerance, the perfect carb breakfasts are either porridge, made with hot water, or dry puffed rice cereal. The most basic way to make porridge with water is to put the desired quantity of oats in a breakfast bowl and pour kettle boiled water on top. Stir well as you add the water and stop adding the water when it ends up the consistency that you like it. With 'just enough' water you end up with quite a sticky consistency. If you keep adding water, it will become more soft and runny.

For anyone with Hypoglycaemia, take care with the puffed rice cereal as this does have quite a high glycaemic index and will make your blood sugar levels rise more than porridge. Hypoglycaemics are well advised to have porridge for breakfast each day, or to alternate fat breakfasts with porridge on a regular basis.

For breakfast on the run, health food shops do have cereal bars that contain no sugar and some that also have no wheat. If you really don't have time to sit down to a fat or carb breakfast then one or two of these will keep you going until lunchtime.

Key things to avoid are:

- Any sugared, processed cereals;

- Cereal bars – especially the 'breakfast' cereal bars that have sprung up recently. They are invariably full of sugar, wheat and additives and will not start the day in an ideal way;

- Cereals and cereal bars that claim to be sugar-free but have very high dried fruit or fruit juice content, to give them sweetness.

Phase	Meal	V	C	H	Wheat free	Dairy free
2	Carb	✓	✓	Can be	Can be	Can be

Berry/Fruit Compote

This is a lovely mix of fruit, which is great for breakfast either by itself, or with yoghurt. It also works well as a dessert. This does have a bit of honey, which is fine for children. Adults can leave out the honey and it will still taste great. Children can also have full fat yoghurt with this (they play with it and make it change colour) as they are fine mixing fats and carbs. Adults should stick to (very) low-fat yoghurt as this is a carb dish.

Ingredients:

1 nectarine, stoned & sliced 1 apple, cored & sliced 1 pear, cored & sliced 4 tablespoons blueberries 4 tablespoons blackberries	4 tablespoons raspberries 4 tablespoons strawberries, quartered 1 tablespoon honey (optional)

Method:

1) Gently heat the fruit and honey in a pan over a low heat for approximately 15 minutes.

2) Allow to cool or refrigerate before use.

TIP 1 – This has too much fruit to be suitable for Candida sufferers.

Serves 4

Phase	Meal	V	C	H	Wheat free	Dairy free
2	Carb	✓		✓	✓	✓

Smoothies

Keep tubs full of frozen fruit in the freezer and then these delicious smoothies can be made, in a couple of minutes, at any time.

The base of all smoothies is banana, so peel some ripe bananas (even slightly overripe is fine) and then chop them into slices no more than 2cm thick and put them in a tub in the freezer. Bananas can be too high in carbohydrate for adults with Hypoglycaemia, so we haven't ticked the "H" box for this recipe.

For a variety of recipes you can also freeze tubs of hulled raspberries, strawberries and blackberries and any other fruit you fancy.

Fruit juice is the usual liquid in smoothies, so we offer this as a Phase 3 option below (since fruit juice is refined fruit). We also have a Phase 2 option based on milk and/or a low fat runny Natural Live Yoghurt.

Strawberry and/or Raspberry Smoothie

Ingredients:

Fruit base:	Liquid:
Approximately 100g frozen banana chunks	Phase 3 – Approximately 200ml unsweetened orange juice
Approximately 100g frozen strawberry chunks or raspberries	Phase 2 – Approximately 100ml Low fat (runny) Natural Live Yoghurt and 100ml skimmed milk (or 200ml of either milk or yoghurt)

Method:

1) Take a few pieces of frozen banana and put them at the bottom of a blender/liquidiser.

2) Add some frozen strawberries and/or raspberries on top (play with the ratio to suit your taste – more banana will give a thicker texture; more berries will give more flavour. Start with an equal volume of each and then try different variations in the future).

3) Pour the liquid option on top of the fruit to leave a few pieces sticking out above the liquid line. (Add in more liquid if you are struggling to get it to blend).

4) Blend, shaking the fruit around to get it well blended in.

Blackberry & Cranberry Smoothie

This is made in exactly the same way as the recipe above except that you use blackberries instead of strawberries or raspberries and you use cranberry juice instead of orange juice. Blackberries and natural yoghurt, with no fruit juice, makes a really tangy Phase 2 smoothie.

Tropical Smoothie

This is made in exactly the same way as the strawberry /raspberry smoothie except that you use frozen mango or pineapple chunks instead of strawberries or raspberries and you use tropical fruit juice instead of orange juice. Again – go for the tropical fruit and milk and/or NLY for a Phase 2 version.

TIP 1 – Squeeze your own oranges and keep the pulp and bits to make the juice as unrefined as possible and hence a good carbohydrate.

TIP 2 – You can opt for a mixture of juice and Natural Live Yoghurt/milk for Phase 3. This gives a thick creamy texture and a bit of a tang – especially nice in the blackberry and cranberry smoothie. If you add Natural Live Yoghurt to this smoothie, you will be getting a double therapeutic blend of cranberry as a natural remedy for cystitis and the yoghurt as a natural balance against Candida.

TIP 3 – Candida sufferers should only have the version that uses cranberry juice, berries and/or Natural Live Yoghurt.

TIP 4 – If you do add normal yoghurt the recipe becomes a "mixes" dish, rather than a carb dish, as you will be having fats (yoghurt) with carbs (fruit and fruit juice). The low-fat Natural Live Yoghurt avoids the mixing.

Serves 2-4

Phase	Meal	V	C	H	Wheat free	Dairy free
2 or 3	Carb	✓	Can be		✓	Can be

Salmon & Chive Omelette

Omelettes are delicious, nutritious and, when made with salmon and cream, form the basis for an extravagant breakfast or a quick meal at any other time of the day.

Ingredients (per person):

3 eggs 50ml double cream Knob of butter	1 teaspoon fresh chives, chopped 50g smoked salmon, chopped

Method:

1) Crack the eggs into a mixing bowl. Add the cream and then beat together until you have a smooth, creamy consistency.

2) Warm a frying pan and melt the butter. When the butter begins to bubble, add the egg mixture and cook on a medium heat for about 3 minutes, drawing the egg from the edge of the pan towards the middle as it becomes solid.

3) Sprinkle the chopped chives and salmon over the cooking omelette mix and cook for a further 3-4 minutes until the omelette is firm.

4) Fold one half of the omelette over the other to make a semi-circle and then slide it onto a warmed plate. Serve immediately.

Phase	Meal	V	C	H	Wheat free	Dairy free
2	Fat		✓	✓	✓	

Tuna & Broccoli Frittata

Mat, our most active club member, is also one of our best recipe inventors. We would like to thank Mat for this great Phase 2 fat breakfast or brunch, which is also ideal to pop in the fridge at work for a cold fat lunch.

Ingredients:

6 eggs	200g tin of tuna, drained of oil or brine
180ml double cream	A handful of broccoli florets
250g cottage cheese	

Method:

1) Preheat the oven to 375° F, 190° C, gas mark 5.

2) Either use leftover cooked broccoli, or put your broccoli florets in a saucepan of boiling water and boil them for approximately 5 minutes, until soft.

3) Meanwhile, crack the eggs into a mixing bowl. Add the cream and cottage cheese and then beat together until a smooth and creamy consistency.

4) Fold the tuna and broccoli into the egg mixture.

5) Grease a small quiche tin with butter and pour the mixture in.

6) Cook in the oven for 35-40 minutes. Check after 30 minutes; the edges should be golden by this time. If this is the case; turn the oven down a notch and cook until the middle is just firmed up.

Serves 2-4

Phase	Meal	V	C	H	Wheat free	Dairy free
2	Fat		✓	✓	✓	

Crustless Quiche

We would like to thank Splodge, another of our club members, for this creative Harcombe friendly alternative to quiche. This is perfect for a weekend breakfast, or to take to work for a cold fat lunch.

Ingredients:

Olive oil for cooking	2 tablespoons fresh chives, finely chopped
2 onions, finely chopped	100g cheddar cheese, grated
125g bacon, chopped	
8 eggs	Salt & ground black pepper
300ml single cream	2 tomatoes, thinly sliced

Method:

1) Preheat the oven to 350° F, 175° C, gas mark 4.

2) Grease a round oven-proof dish (approximately 25cm in diameter) with some olive oil.

3) Warm a dash of olive oil in a frying pan and fry the onions and bacon until the onions are soft and transparent. Spread the cooked onions and bacon over the base of the greased dish.

4) Whisk the eggs, cream, chives and cheese in a bowl until all the ingredients are combined. Season to taste. Pour this mixture over the onions and bacon and then arrange the tomato slices on top.

5) Bake for 40 minutes or until it is set and golden.

Serves 4

Phase	Meal	V	C	H	Wheat free	Dairy free
2	Fat		✓	✓	✓	

PHASE 2 – CARB MAIN MEALS

Spinach, Bean & Tarragon Pasta

This is a really unusual pasta dish, with a great selection of nutritious vegetables. Tarragon, the key herb in this dish, is a favourite with French cuisine. It has a slightly bittersweet flavour and an aroma similar to anise (aniseed).

Ingredients:

1 teaspoon olive oil	1 bunch spring onions, finely sliced
225g fresh baby spinach	
500g broad beans, shelled	1 tablespoon tarragon, finely chopped
250g asparagus	Salt & ground black pepper
500g fresh peas	300-400g (dry weight) whole wheat or rice pasta
125g green beans, halved	
6 tablespoons Natural Live Yoghurt (low-fat)	

Method:

1) Heat the oil in a saucepan, add the spinach, cover and cook for 5 minutes.

2) Cook the broad beans and asparagus in a little boiling water for 3 minutes, then add the peas and green beans and cook for another 2 minutes. Drain and set aside.

3) Blend the spinach and low-fat yoghurt to a purée in a blender.

4) Combine the purée with the drained vegetables, mix in the spring onions and tarragon.

5) Season to taste. Keep warm on a low heat.

6) Cook the pasta according to the directions on the packet.

7) Toss with the vegetable/purée mix and garnish with extra tarragon.

TIP 1 – Use rice pasta to make the recipe wheat-free.

TIP 2 – Use kidney beans or black eyed beans for tasty variations.

Serves 4

Phase	Meal	V	C	H	Wheat free	Dairy free
2	Carb	✓	✓	✓	Can be	

Vegetable & Pulse Chilli

This is a simple and yet very tasty vegetarian chilli recipe. The chickpeas *and* kidney beans give a good variety of pulse nutrients. You can leave out either pulse and double up on the other and it will not affect the recipe. Serve with brown rice or a crispy baked potato.

Ingredients:

300-400g (dry weight) brown rice	400g tin kidney beans, drained & rinsed
1 tablespoon of olive oil	400g tin chickpeas, drained
1 red onion, finely chopped	400g tin chopped tomatoes
1 onion, finely chopped	75g tomato purée
2 cloves garlic, crushed	2 teaspoons mixed herbs
3 carrots, chopped	2 teaspoons chilli powder
1 red & 1 green pepper, deseeded & diced	150-300ml vegetable stock
50g mushrooms, chopped	

Method:

1) Cook the rice so that it is ready for when the sauce is done

2) Heat the oil in a large frying pan. Add the 2 varieties of onions and cook until soft. Add the garlic and continue to cook for approximately 2 minutes.

3) Add the chopped carrots, peppers and mushrooms and cook for approximately 3-4 minutes.

4) Add the kidney beans, chickpeas, tomatoes, herbs, chilli powder and vegetable stock. Continue to simmer until the carrots are tender.

5) Make an attractive 'bed' with the rice on the plate and then arrange the vegetables on top.

TIP 1 – Leave out the mushrooms and this can be suitable for Candida.

TIP 2 – If you use 150ml of stock, the recipe will be quite thick and 'tomatoey' and this works really well if you eat the chilli with baked potatoes. If you use closer to 300ml of stock, the recipe will be runnier and this soaks into the rice better – it's up to you depending on your serving choice.

Serves 4

Phase	Meal	V	C	H	Wheat free	Dairy free
2	Carb	✓	Can be	✓	✓	✓

Asparagus & Basil Pasta

Asparagus is quite simply one of the best vegetables to come out of the ground – in terms of taste and nutrition. It has one of the highest concentrations of folic acid of any vegetable. This is important for women – pregnant women in particular. It also has good quantities of vitamin C and the vegetation forms of vitamins A and K (K1). For minerals, asparagus is a good source of iron and copper. It has one of the highest overall food nutrition scores on the United States all-food database (94 out of 100).

Ingredients:

| The following vegetables, cut into batons:

- 2 carrots, peeled

- 400g asparagus

- 1 red pepper, deseeded

- 1 courgette

100g fresh or frozen green peas

6 cloves garlic, crushed | 2 teaspoons olive oil

400g tin chopped tomatoes

60ml dry white wine

50g fresh basil leaves, sliced

1 red onion, thinly sliced

Salt & ground black pepper

300-400g (dry weight) whole wheat or rice pasta |

Method:

1) Fill a big saucepan with water and bring it to the boil. Prepare the vegetables while it is warming up.

2) Add the carrots first to the boiling water. After a couple of minutes add the asparagus and pepper. After another couple of minutes add the courgette and peas.

3) Meanwhile fry the garlic and oil in a saucepan for approximately 2 minutes. Add the tomatoes and wine and cook on a moderate heat for approximately 5 minutes. Add the basil and red onion and stir well.

4) When the carrots are just slightly soft to the touch, add all the vegetables to the tomato saucepan and stir them in well. Season to taste. Cover and leave to simmer gently.

5) Keep the pot of boiling water for cooking the pasta. Cook the pasta according to the directions on the packet.

6) Top with the tomato vegetable sauce and serve immediately.

TIP 1 – Use rice pasta to make this a wheat-free dish.

Serves 4

Phase	Meal	V	C	H	Wheat free	Dairy free
2	Carb	✓	✓	✓	Can be	✓

Chickpea Burgers with Chive Relish

Chickpeas are one of the most complete sources of amino acids for people who don't consume animal foods. They have good amounts of the minerals iron, magnesium, copper and zinc and have almost the entire daily need for manganese in one good serving. This is a great alternative burger base for vegetarians.

Ingredients:

For the burgers:	For the relish:
60g bulghar wheat	150g Natural Live Yoghurt, low-fat
400g tin chickpeas, drained	2 spring onions, thinly sliced
250g carrot, grated	2 tablespoons fresh chives, finely chopped
1 clove garlic, crushed	Freshly ground black pepper
1 large handful coriander, chopped	
2 tablespoons lemon juice	For cooking:
1 level teaspoon ground cumin	1 tablespoon olive oil
75g whole wheat bread crumbs	
Salt & ground black pepper	

Method:

1) Put the bulghar wheat in a bowl, cover with boiling water and leave to stand for 20 minutes; then drain off the water.

2) Then put the bulghar wheat, chickpeas, carrot, garlic, coriander, lemon juice and cumin into a blender and blend until smooth.

3) Transfer the mixture to a bowl. Add the breadcrumbs and season to taste. The mixture should be slightly soft, but not sticky. Adjust with a few more breadcrumbs as necessary.

4) Divide the mixture into 4 portions and shape them into burgers. Put them in the fridge to chill.

5) Make the relish by mixing the yoghurt, spring onions, chives and black pepper in a bowl. Mix well and leave to stand while you make the burgers.

6) Heat the oil in a non-stick frying pan. Cook the burgers over a moderate heat for approximately 5 minutes on each side until golden brown and slightly crispy.

7) Serve in wholemeal baps lined with iceberg lettuce and relish.

TIP 1 – Swap brown rice for the bread crumbs to make the burgers wheat-free. Cook approximately 40-50g (dry weight) brown rice to give you 75g of cooked brown rice to replace the breadcrumbs.

Serves 4

Phase	Meal	V	C	H	Wheat free	Dairy free
2	Carb	✓		✓		

Baked Potatoes

Let's hear it for the fabulous baked potato. The poor spud has been beaten back into the ground by Atkins, but there is nothing like this staple food for a cheap, nutritious and versatile dish. AND you can get them in sandwich shops and special spud kiosks in many towns, so it is a great lunch food for people away from home.

The potato has been attacked because it has a high glycaemic index. This means it is not a great dish for people with Hypoglycaemia.

Any time you put the oven on, put in a handful of potatoes and bake them until lightly brown. Then, all you need to do is put them back in the oven for 10-15 minutes and you have a speedy main meal, any time during the week.

Don't forget that this is a carb meal and you must keep the skin on the potato, otherwise you are not eating the whole food. The fillings must also be carb fillings therefore, and have little, or no, fat in them. Here are some options:

Great fillings for baked potatoes:

- Low-fat/very low-fat cottage cheese;
- Low-fat/very low-fat natural yoghurt (ideally live);
- Ratatouille (recipe in this book);
- Any tin of sugar-free/artificial ingredient-free baked beans (from health food shops);
- Any mixture of beans (kidney beans, black beans, chickpeas etc) in a tin of chopped tomatoes – makes your own version of baked beans;
- Vegetarian chilli (recipe in this book);
- Butternut squash curry (recipe in this book).

Method:

1) Preheat the oven to 350° F, 175° C, gas mark 4.

2) Stab the potatoes in random places with a fork to stop the skins bursting. Bake them for at least an hour until you can prod a knife in them easily and until they are how you like them outside.

Phase	Meal	V	C	H	Wheat free	Dairy free
2	Carb	✓	✓		✓	Can be

Harcombe Friendly Chips

For a carb lite bite meal, you could have chips and tomato sauce. Use the 15 minute tomato sauce recipe and drain off the liquid to make a concentrated 'ketchup'. For the chips:

- Preheat the oven to 400° F, 200° C, gas mark 6.

- Wash the potatoes thoroughly. Keeping the skins on, cut the potatoes into the size chips that you like.

- Brush a baking tray with olive oil and then place the chips on the tray and bake in the oven for approximately 30-45 minutes. Turn the 'chips' at least once during the cooking time, to brown them all over.

Phase	Meal	V	C	H	Wheat free	Dairy free
2	Carb	✓	✓		✓	✓

Lentil Moussaka

This dish is well worth the effort. It is tasty and impressive enough to serve when entertaining and it is great to cook at the weekend and to take into work for lunches during the week (either cold or re-heated in a microwave). It can be served with roasted vegetables in the winter or with a Greek salad in the summer. Use low-fat ingredients, where practical, in the topping so that this remains a carbohydrate meal.

Ingredients:

2-4 tablespoons olive oil	For the topping:
2 onions, finely chopped	250ml low-fat milk
1 red pepper, deseeded & chopped into 1cm pieces	50g of butter
2 cloves garlic, crushed	1 egg
2 aubergines, diced	250ml of low-fat ricotta cheese
2 x 400g tins of chopped tomatoes	Some grated Parmesan or "Grana Padano" cheese
3 tablespoons of tomato purée	
100g lentils (half green & half red)	
500ml vegetable stock	

Method:

1) Preheat the oven to 375° F, 190° C, gas mark 5.

2) Put 2 tablespoons of the olive oil in a large frying pan, and gently fry the onions for 3-4 minutes, until soft.

3) Add the chopped pepper and stir-fry for a further 5 minutes.

4) Then add the garlic and stir-fry for a further 2-3 minutes.

5) Transfer the mixture to a plate and leave to one side.

6) Add the rest of the olive oil to the same pan, and fry the aubergines until brown all over.

7) Add back the fried onion, pepper and garlic and then add the tin of tomatoes, tomato purée, lentils and stock and give the mixture a good stir.

8) Bring the whole mixture to boiling point and then reduce the heat to simmer for 10 minutes.

9) Transfer the mixture to a large oven-proof dish; add the topping (see below) and then sprinkle with grated Parmesan cheese.

10) Cook in the oven for 45 minutes, when the topping and Parmesan will be a golden brown. Allow to cool for 10 minutes before serving.

For the topping:

1) Bring the milk and butter to the boil in a saucepan and then allow them to cool for 5 minutes.

2) Add a whisked egg.

3) Whisk the whole mixture and then whisk in the ricotta cheese. Add some freshly ground black pepper to taste.

Serves 6

Phase	Meal	V	C	H	Wheat free	Dairy free
2	Carb	✓	✓	✓	✓	

Whole Wheat Couscous & Chickpeas in Coriander Sauce

For another Phase 2 carb meal you can use our char grilled vegetables recipe and the couscous instructions below to make couscous with char grilled vegetables.

Ingredients:

2 tablespoons olive oil	2 teaspoons ginger, finely chopped
1 onion, finely chopped	A handful of fresh coriander (or 2 tablespoons of dried)
1 clove garlic, crushed	
400g tin chopped tomatoes	350g couscous
400g tin chickpeas, drained	600ml vegetable stock

Method:

1) In a large saucepan, heat the oil over a moderate heat and add the onion and garlic and gently fry until the onion is soft.

2) Add the tin of tomatoes and chickpeas and stir well.

3) Add the ginger and coriander, put on the lid and simmer for 20-30 minutes.

4) Meanwhile, put the couscous in a bowl and pour the vegetable stock over it. Cover with cling film and leave to stand for approximately 20-30 minutes. (This is the easiest way to make couscous).

5) To serve, make a couscous 'bed' on a plate and then spoon on the sauce. Garnish with some freshly chopped coriander.

TIP 1 – We put brackets around the 'wheat-free' tick below because couscous is strictly in the wheat family. However, as with bulghar wheat, many people find they can tolerate couscous on occasions whereas they can't cope with pure wheat.

Serves 4

Phase	Meal	V	C	H	Wheat free	Dairy free
2	Carb	✓	✓	✓	(✓)	✓

Vegetarian Chilli

Vegetarian chilli is another classic recipe that every household cook should be able to dish up at any time. This is a really filling dish and great for re-heating for quick meals. As the beans provide protein, this can be eaten as a meal in itself, if you don't have time to do rice or a baked potato to go with it.

Ingredients:

2 tablespoons olive oil	400g tin of unsweetened kidney beans, drained & rinsed
2 onions, finely chopped	
1 red pepper, deseeded & chopped	400g tin chopped tomatoes
1 clove garlic, crushed	2 chillies, deseeded & sliced
1.5kg of mixed vegetables, peeled & diced (use carrots, courgette, cauliflower, broccoli, leeks – anything you like)	Chilli powder to taste (somewhere between 2 and 4 teaspoons)

Method:

1) In a large saucepan or frying pan, heat the oil and gently fry the onions until soft.

2) Add the pepper and garlic and fry for a further 3-4 minutes.

3) Then add all the mixed vegetables, including the kidney beans, tinned tomatoes and chillies and give it all a good stir.

4) Stir in the chilli powder and then put the lid on the pan. Bring to the boil and then reduce to simmering point and cook for 20-30 minutes, or until the vegetables are cooked to your liking.

Serve with brown rice, or a crispy baked potato.

TIP 1 – Avoid mushrooms to make this recipe suitable for Candida.

Serves 4-6

Phase	Meal	V	C	H	Wheat free	Dairy free
2	Carb	✓	✓	✓	✓	✓

Aubergine Pasta

Tomato and aubergine make a wonderful combination. This is not a five minute pasta dish but, every now and again, this slightly more involved recipe is worth all the effort.

Ingredients:

Olive oil for brushing a baking tray	3 cloves garlic, crushed
2 aubergines, sliced	400g tin chopped tomatoes
Sprinkling of sea salt	1 tablespoon dried basil
1 tablespoon olive oil	300-400g pasta (dry weight)
3 onions, chopped	

Method:

1) Preheat the oven to 350° F, 175° C, gas mark 4. Brush a baking tray with olive oil.

2) Slice the aubergine crossways into 2cm thick slices. Lightly salt each slice. Place the slices on the baking tray and put them in the oven. Flip the aubergine slices over after approximately 15 minutes and cook the other side.

3) In a large saucepan, on a low heat, fry the onions and garlic in the oil until soft.

4) Add the tin of tomatoes to the saucepan. Add the basil and continue to cook, stirring occasionally, until the sauce begins to thicken.

5) Approximately 5 minutes before the aubergine finishes baking, bring a large covered pot of water to the boil.

6) When the aubergine slices are tender and browned, remove them from the oven, allow them

to cool slightly, and then cut them into strips. Stir the aubergine into the tomato sauce and cook for approximately 10 more minutes.

7) When the water boils, stir in the pasta, cover and return to the boil. Cook the pasta according to the directions on the packet. Drain and serve immediately topped with the tomato-aubergine sauce.

TIP 1 – Use rice pasta to make this wheat-free.

Serves 4

Phase	Meal	V	C	H	Wheat free	Dairy free
2	Carb	✓	✓	✓	Can be	✓

Bean & Tomato Chilli

This is a great variation to traditional vegetarian chilli. It can be an invaluable dish for vegetarians in Phase 2, as the beans deliver good protein variation.

Ingredients:

2 tablespoons olive oil	200g tin chickpeas, drained
1 onion, finely chopped	
1 clove of garlic, crushed	400g tin tomatoes, chopped
200g tin butter beans or flageolet beans, drained	1 small red chilli, deseeded & finely sliced
200g tin red kidney beans, drained	

Method:

1) Heat the oil in a large frying pan. Lightly fry the onion and garlic for 2-3 minutes until transparent, but not browned.

2) Add the beans, chickpeas, tomatoes and chilli to the frying pan.

3) Bring the whole mixture to the boil and then lightly simmer for 10 minutes.

4) Serve with brown rice, wholemeal pita bread or a crispy baked potato.

Serves 4

Phase	Meal	V	C	H	Wheat free	Dairy free
2	Carb	✓	✓	✓	✓	✓

Quinoa Chilli with Walnuts & Beans

Don't worry about the small amount of nuts in this Phase 2 dish – the added nutrition and taste more than compensates for the small amount of mixing.

Ingredients:

1 tablespoon olive oil	500ml tomato juice
1 onion, chopped	200g quinoa
1 clove garlic, chopped	100g walnuts, crushed
1 carrot, peeled & sliced	200g tin kidney beans, drained & rinsed
2 sticks celery, chopped	1 teaspoon mixed herbs
1 red pepper, chopped	1 teaspoon chilli powder
1 courgette, chopped	

Method:

1) Warm the olive oil in a large saucepan and then fry the onion, garlic, carrot and celery until soft.

2) Add the pepper and courgette to the pan and continue to fry until they are soft.

3) Add the tomato juice, quinoa, walnuts, beans, herbs and chilli powder. Simmer everything for approximately 30 minutes.

TIP 1 – You can cook the quinoa separately to serve with the chilli, but it tastes better cooked in the juices.

Serves 4

Phase	Meal	V	C	H	Wheat free	Dairy free
2	Carb	✓	✓	✓	✓	✓

PHASE 2 – FAT MEALS

Four Cheese Salad

We recommend eating salads almost every day, even in the winter, as vegetables and salads are always more nutritious eaten raw. In the winter eat a salad together with a warm soup and you will find this compensates for the chill of the salad.

Ingredients:

1 iceberg lettuce	200g cottage cheese
24 cherry tomatoes	50-75g per person of various cheese options, diced (Cheddar, Edam, Emmental and Feta all work well)
1 cucumber, diced	
4 sticks celery, diced	
1 red pepper, deseeded & diced	
Sprinkling of pine nuts (optional)	Salt & ground black pepper
Olive oil, or balsamic, or our French salad dressing	

Method:

1) Chop the lettuce up quite finely and cover 4 plates with it.

2) Slice the cherry tomatoes in half and place them around the edge of each plate.

3) Dice the cucumber, celery and pepper and sprinkle this over the lettuce (sprinkle a few pine nuts on too if you like these).

4) Add your chosen dressing over the salad base.

5) Place 50g, or so, of cottage cheese in the middle of each plate.

6) Add the cubes of cheese to taste around the cottage cheese. Feta with balsamic and cottage cheese goes really well together, so do Cheddar, Emmental and cottage cheese.

Serves 4

Phase	Meal	V	C	H	Wheat free	Dairy free
2	Fat	✓	✓	✓	✓	

Aubergine Bake

Aubergine is a coloured vegetable so it does have a higher carbohydrate content than green vegetables. However, this still counts as a fat meal because of all the cheese.

Ingredients:

1 red onion, sliced into rings	Pine nut kernels
2 courgettes, sliced	2 tablespoons olive oil
1 aubergine, sliced	250g mozzarella, sliced
1 clove garlic, finely chopped	1 red pepper, deseeded & sliced
2 tablespoons tomato purée (dissolved in 500ml, of vegetable stock)	100g Emmental (or other hard cheese like Edam or Cheddar)

Method:

1) Preheat the oven to 350° F, 175° C, gas mark 4.

2) Place 1 layer of vegetables in a baking dish (approximately 20 x 30 cm): first the red onion; then the courgettes and then the aubergine.

3) Sprinkle the garlic on before adding further layers, in the above order, until all the vegetables are in the dish.

4) Pour the tomato purée and vegetable stock over the vegetables and sprinkle a handful of pine nut kernels over everything.

5) Cover the top layer of vegetables with a drizzle of olive oil.

6) Slice the Mozzarella on top of the vegetables.

7) Cut the red pepper into strips and lay it on top of the mozzarella.

8) Grate the Emmental on top of everything.

9) Bake in the oven for approximately an hour, or until the cheese topping is crisp and brown.

Serves 4

Phase	Meal	V	C	H	Wheat free	Dairy free
2	Fat	✓	✓	✓	✓	

Aubergine Boats

These look fabulous – definitely impressive enough for a dinner party. Each person gets one boat and they can be served on a bed of spinach or stir-fried vegetables. Aubergines are often called the 'steak' of the vegetarian world as they are so 'meaty'.

Aubergines are good sources of vitamins K & B6, folic acid and the mineral Manganese. Manganese is not widely talked about, but it is crucial for everything from bone formation to thyroid function to calcium absorption to blood glucose regulation and then the immune system and fat and carbohydrate metabolism on top. Vitamins and minerals are collectively called micro nutrients – because we need them in small amounts. The amounts can still be difficult to get unless we eat a real food diet and the consequences of not getting them are health, and sometimes life, threatening.

Ingredients:

1 aubergine	2 tomatoes, finely chopped
1 onion, finely chopped	Salt & ground black pepper
1 clove garlic, crushed	100g Emmental (or other hard cheese like Edam or Cheddar)
4 button mushrooms, finely chopped	
2 tablespoons olive oil	

Method:

1) Preheat the oven to 350° F, 175° C, gas mark 4.

2) Cut the aubergine in half lengthways. Scoop out the flesh of the aubergine to leave two 'boats' made from the outside.

3) Chop the aubergine flesh finely and chop the other vegetables – onion, garlic, mushrooms and tomatoes.

4) Heat the oil in a large frying pan, until the olive oil is sizzling.

5) Stir-fry the onion and garlic for a couple of minutes alone before adding the mushrooms, aubergine and tomatoes. Season and then stir-fry everything until the vegetables are soft.

6) Pour the stir-fried vegetables into the aubergine boats.

7) Grate the Emmental on top.

8) Bake in the oven, for approximately an hour, or until the cheese topping is crisp and brown.

TIP 1 – Leave out the mushrooms to make this recipe suitable for Candida.

Serves 2 – 1 boat each

Phase	Meal	V	C	H	Wheat free	Dairy free
2	Fat	✓	Can be	✓	✓	

Mushroom Stroganoff

Once you've got Candida under control, being able to enjoy mushrooms again is a real treat. This is a fat dish, because of the cream and butter, so it can be served as a cream sauce, with meat, to make it a fat meal. For those lucky people at their natural weight, who can mix fats and carbs, it can be served with brown rice.

Ingredients:

50g butter	½ teaspoon thyme or tarragon
1 onion, sliced	
4 celery sticks, sliced	1 bay leaf, ground or ½ teaspoon dried bay
350g mushrooms, sliced	150ml single cream
1 tablespoon corn flour	Salt & ground black pepper
150ml water	
1 teaspoon yeast extract	Chopped parsley to garnish

Method:

1) Melt half the butter in a large frying pan, and gently fry the onion and celery until soft.

2) Add the rest of the butter and the mushrooms and gently fry for 2-3 minutes.

3) Stir in the corn flour, and then add the water, yeast extract and herbs.

4) Bring to the boil, reduce the heat and simmer, uncovered, for 2-3 minutes.

5) Off the heat, stir in the cream and season to taste.

6) Heat very gently to serving temperature.

Serve with meat for people watching their weight (to keep it as a fat meal) and with brown rice for children. Sprinkle with parsley for both.

TIP 1 – Experiment with different mushrooms to add different flavours. Shitake mushrooms are especially spectacular or use a few different varieties to mix flavours. Sprinkle in a few dried mushrooms too as they add another taste experience.

TIP 2 – To make this a meat stroganoff, allow approximately 150g of frying steak (cut into bite size strips) per person and fry the steak at stage 2 of the method – instead of the mushrooms, or as well as.

Serves 4

Phase	Meal	V	C	H	Wheat free	Dairy free
2	Fat	✓		✓	✓	

Egg & Asparagus Bake

Use green beans or broccoli, instead of asparagus, if the latter is out of season.

Ingredients:

24 asparagus spears 4 tablespoons unsalted butter, melted 4 eggs	100g grated Parmesan cheese Salt & ground black pepper

Method:

1) Pre-heat the oven to 400° F, 200° C, gas mark 6.

2) Steam the asparagus until tender and place evenly across the bottom of an oven-proof dish.

3) Whisk, or hand-beat, the eggs with the melted butter and pour the mixture over the asparagus.

4) Sprinkle the grated cheese over everything evenly and season with a dash of salt and freshly ground black pepper.

5) Bake in the oven until the eggs are set and the cheese is golden brown – about 10-15 minutes.

Serves 4

Phase	Meal	V	C	H	Wheat free	Dairy free
2	Fat	✓	✓	✓	✓	

Cauliflower & Courgette Bake

Another 'Bake' variation will hopefully inspire you to use up any vegetables in this simple, healthy and delicious way. Any bake also makes a great cold lunch.

Ingredients:

1 head of cauliflower, broken into florets	150ml milk
1 tablespoon olive oil	2 tablespoons corn flour
2 courgettes, sliced	4 eggs, separated
1 tablespoon Dijon mustard	Salt & ground black pepper

Method:

1) Pre-heat the oven to 400° F, 200° C, gas mark 6.

2) Cook the cauliflower in boiling water until tender.

3) Fry the courgettes in the olive oil until soft.

4) Bring the mustard, milk and corn flour to the boil in a pan and simmer for a minute until thick.

5) Blend the cauliflower, egg yolks and white sauce.

6) Whisk the egg whites until stiff and fold them into the cauliflower mixture. Season to taste.

7) Pour the cauliflower mixture into a greased oven-proof dish. Place the courgette slices on top.

8) Bake in the oven until the eggs are set and the topping is golden brown – about 10-15 minutes.

Serves 4

Phase	Meal	V	C	H	Wheat free	Dairy free
2	Fat	✓	✓	✓	✓	

Creamy Fish in Sherry Sauce

You can use any chunky white fish for this recipe. Cod and haddock work really well as do monkfish, halibut and the more unusual fishes. You can also use salmon, but don't venture into the oily fish category any further than this or the fish flavour will compete with, rather than enhance the rest of the dish.

Ingredients:

4 x 150g fish fillets	150ml fish stock
Salt & ground black pepper	100ml sherry or Madeira
2 leeks, thinly sliced	150ml single cream
2 sticks celery, thinly sliced	25g butter (optional)
2 carrots, peeled & thinly sliced	Fresh parsley to garnish

Method:

1) Season the fish fillets and place them in a non-stick pan on a low heat.

2) Pile the leeks, celery and carrots on top and pour in the fish stock and sherry or Madeira.

3) Bring everything to the boil, reduce the heat and simmer for approximately 10 minutes.

4) Scoop out the vegetables with a slotted spoon, to leave the liquid in the pan. Arrange them on pre-warmed plates. Scoop out the whole fish fillets and place these on top of the vegetables. Keep the plates warm under a low grill or in a cool oven.

5) Bring the liquid in the pan back to the boil and cook, uncovered, until the volume reduces by about half.

6) Add the cream and simmer for approximately 2 minutes, stirring all the time until the sauce thickens.

7) Add in the butter, if desired, for an extra rich and creamy sauce.

8) Season to taste and then pour the sauce over the fish, garnish with parsley and serve immediately.

Serves 4

Phase	Meal	V	C	H	Wheat free	Dairy free
2	Fat		✓	✓	✓	

Halibut in Cheese Sauce

Do try this, as fish and cheese seems an unusual mixture but this is a quick and delicious dish. Halibut is a thick white fish, generally seen as more filling than the flat white fishes like plaice. Nutritionally, it is rich in the minerals magnesium, selenium, phosphorus and potassium. It is also good for the B vitamins niacin (B3) and B12.

Ingredients:

4 halibut steaks (or any other white fish)	1 teaspoon tarragon
50g butter	1 tablespoon lemon juice
1 onion, chopped	100g cheddar cheese, grated
100g mushrooms, finely chopped	

Method:

1) Put the fish pieces on a tin foil lined grill pan.

2) Brush them with half the butter, melted.

3) Grill the fish under a moderate heat for 4-5 minutes.

4) Meanwhile gently fry the onion and mushrooms in the rest of the butter.

5) Add the tarragon and lemon juice.

6) Turn the steaks and pour the onion & mushroom mix onto them.

7) Sprinkle the grated cheese over them and grill for another 4-5 minutes.

Garnish with lemon slices and serve with fresh vegetables or a side salad.

TIP 1 – Use cauliflower florets, instead of mushrooms, and this can be suitable for Candida.

Serves 4

Phase	Meal	V	C	H	Wheat free	Dairy free
2	Fat		Can be	✓	✓	

Cod with White Wine Sauce

This works well with any white fish – cod, haddock, halibut, swordfish, whiting and so on. The key thing is to choose a chunky fillet of fish to have a substantial main meal.

Ingredients:

4 fillets of cod, or other white fish	1 tablespoon corn flour
Freshly ground black pepper	240ml milk
	6 tablespoons white wine
Garlic salt	1 tablespoon parsley, chopped
30g butter	
1 onion, finely chopped	

Method:

1) Preheat the oven to 350° F, 175° C, gas mark 4.

2) Arrange the fish pieces in an oven-proof dish.

3) Sprinkle with pepper and garlic salt.

4) Heat the butter in a frying pan and gently fry the onion until soft.

5) Add the corn flour and mix well.

6) Add the milk, stir until boiling and simmer for 3 minutes.

7) Gradually stir in the wine and add more pepper and garlic salt as desired and then pour this over the fish.

8) Cook in a moderate oven for approximately 30 minutes.

9) Sprinkle with parsley before serving.

TIP 1 – Always allow approximately 200g of fish for each person. This is a main meal, intended to be filling enough to keep hunger away until the next main meal, so our dishes need to be substantial.

TIP 2 – Coloured vegetables work particularly well with white fish: a) they provide colour to the plate and b) white fish is naturally low fat, so you can go for the higher carb vegetables.

Serves 4

Phase	Meal	V	C	H	Wheat free	Dairy free
2	Fat		✓	✓	✓	

Tuna with Crème Fraîche & Asparagus

This will also work well with salmon, but the unique taste of tuna is unbeatable in this simple recipe.

Ingredients:

4 tablespoons crème fraîche	600g fresh tuna, diced
4 tablespoons fresh basil, finely chopped	200g asparagus, cut into 2-3cm lengths
Juice of 1 lemon	100g cherry tomatoes, halved
Salt & ground black pepper	100g black olives, stones removed
Knob of butter	

Method:

1) Mix the crème fraîche, basil, lemon juice and seasoning in a cup.

2) Melt the butter in a large frying pan and lightly fry the tuna and asparagus for a few minutes, until they start to blacken.

3) Add the tomatoes and olives to the frying pan and stir gently until they are just warmed through (or cook a bit longer to char the tomatoes slightly).

4) Just before serving, stir in the crème fraîche mix. Can be served alone, or with salad or vegetables.

Serves 4

Phase	Meal	V	C	H	Wheat free	Dairy free
2	Fat		✓	✓	✓	

Cheese on Cod

You simply must try this. You will not be able to believe that something so quick and easy is so absolutely delicious.

Ingredients:

4 fillets of cod, or other white fish. Allow a good 200g per person Knob of butter	200g cherry tomatoes, halved 200g cheddar cheese, grated

Method:

1) Preheat the oven to 350° F, 175° C, gas mark 4.

2) Melt the butter in a large frying pan and lightly fry the cod on both sides to seal.

3) Transfer the cod to a baking dish and pour the butter from the frying pan over the fish.

4) Sprinkle the chopped cherry tomatoes first and then the grated cheddar over the pieces of cod.

5) Cook in a moderate oven for approximately 15-20 minutes, until the cheese is turning golden and bubbling.

6) Can be served alone, or with a selection of vegetables.

Serves 4

Phase	Meal	V	C	H	Wheat free	Dairy free
2	Fat		✓	✓	✓	

Creole Fish Casserole

This works well with any white fish – haddock, halibut, plaice, swordfish, whiting and so on. The simplicity of the white fish with the bite of the spicy sauce makes for a wonderful combination. This could be served when entertaining, or as a main meal at any time.

Ingredients:

4 fillets of cod or other white fish	For the sauce:
Salt & ground black pepper	30g butter
	1 tablespoon corn flour
Lemon juice	360ml water
1 bay leaf	¼ teaspoon anchovy essence
30g butter, melted	2-3 cloves
	A pinch of mixed spice
	½ teaspoon chilli sauce
	200g tomatoes, peeled & chopped
	A few drops of Tabasco sauce
	1 teaspoon parsley, finely chopped
	A pinch of paprika

Method:

1) Preheat the oven to 350° F, 175° C, gas mark 4.

2) Arrange the fish pieces in an oven-proof dish.

3) Sprinkle with salt, pepper and lemon juice. Add the bay leaf and brush with butter.

4) Cover the dish with tin foil and cook for approximately 30 minutes.

5) While the fish is cooking make the sauce – melt the butter in a saucepan or frying pan, add the corn flour and cook for a few minutes.

6) Add the water, stir until boiling and boil for 1 minute.

7) Add the anchovy essence and all the other ingredients except the paprika.

8) Simmer for approximately 20 minutes.

9) Pour over the fish and continue cooking for approximately 15 minutes.

10) Sprinkle with paprika before serving.

Serves 4

Phase	Meal	V	C	H	Wheat free	Dairy free
2	Fat		✓	✓	✓	

Mackerel with Basil

Mackerel is part of the oily fish family and is therefore packed full of nature's real fats to make your skin, hair and nails healthy and strong. Mackerel also has a great meaty texture and a unique taste. Either fry it gently in butter, or grill it, turning regularly to cook right through. After 10-15 minutes the fish should be cooked. It needs no garnish at all but you can squeeze lemon juice on it. For a more adventurous mackerel dish, try this one:

Ingredients:

4 whole mackerel fillets, beheaded	6 tablespoons red wine
Salt & ground black pepper	½ teaspoon oregano
3-4 'beef' tomatoes, sliced	2 teaspoons basil, chopped
1 tablespoon corn flour	2 tablespoons chives, finely chopped
250ml fish stock	

Method:

1) Preheat the oven to 350° F, 175° C, gas mark 4.

2) Arrange the mackerel fillets in an oven-proof dish, skin side up.

3) Sprinkle with salt and pepper and arrange the tomato slices on top.

4) Bring the red wine and stock to boiling point in a pan. Mix the corn flour with a little cold water and then add to the stock. Simmer for 2-3 minutes.

5) Add the oregano and basil to the sauce and pour over the fish. Sprinkle with chives.

6) Cover and cook for approximately 15 minutes.

TIP 1 – Mackerel recipes also work well with trout. Trout tends to have a milder flavour than mackerel.

Serves 4

Phase	Meal	V	C	H	Wheat free	Dairy free
2	Fat		✓	✓	✓	✓

Marinated & Grilled Mackerel

This works equally well with any oily fish – trout would be a good alternative to try. We do laugh when diet advisors tell people to eat oily fish three times a week and avoid fat. Mackerel has 14g of fat per 100g of fish – that's over three times the amount in a boneless pork chop and it also has twice the saturated fat as the same amount of the pork. Don't fear any real fat – it is absolutely essential for optimal health. The only fat to fear is the stuff that man has managed to invent. The vitamin A and D content is particularly valuable in mackerel and other oily fish.

Ingredients:

4 whole mackerel fillets, beheaded	For the marinade:
	150ml olive oil
	75ml white wine or cider
	A few drops of Tabasco sauce (optional)
	Salt & ground black pepper
	Juice & zest of 1 orange

Method:

1) Mix all the marinade ingredients together in a jug.

2) Make 2 incisions across both sides of the fish and place them on a baking tray.

3) Spoon the marinade over the fish and marinate for up to 2 hours, turning the fish half-way through.

4) Cook the marinated fish under a hot, preheated grill, for 5-8 minutes on each side. (Warm the plates below the grill).

5) Transfer the mackerel to warm plates and pour the marinade over the fish.

6) Serve hot with a selection of vegetables.

Serves 4

Phase	Meal	V	C	H	Wheat free	Dairy free
2	Fat		✓	✓	✓	✓

Parmesan & Garlic Fish Fillets

This is a wonderfully tasty and nutritious meal. The fish provides essential fatty acids, the spinach is packed with iron and the yoghurt provides calcium and B vitamins. This is a fat meal so enjoy real, full-fat, Greek yoghurt for extra flavour.

Ingredients:

1 teaspoon olive oil	50g Parmesan cheese, grated
4 onions, sliced	
4 cod fillets	2 tablespoons Worcestershire sauce
120ml Greek yoghurt	2 tablespoons lemon juice
1-2 cloves garlic, crushed	
A handful of thyme, finely chopped	200g spinach
	30g butter

Method:

1) Preheat the oven to 375° F, 190° C, gas mark 5.

2) Coat an oven-proof dish with 1 teaspoon of olive oil.

3) Arrange the onions on the bottom of the dish and place the fish pieces on top.

4) In a small bowl, combine the Greek yoghurt, garlic, thyme, Parmesan cheese, Worcestershire sauce, and lemon juice and mix until blended.

5) Spread this mixture over the fish pieces and bake in the oven for 30 minutes or until the fish flakes easily.

6) Approximately 5 minutes before the fish is ready, put the spinach and butter in a saucepan. Put the

lid on and cook until the spinach reduces down to a soft, dark mush.

7) Put a dollop of buttery spinach next to each cod fillet to serve.

TIP 1 – We have not ticked the Candida box with this recipe because of the tiny bit of vinegar in Worcestershire sauce. Unless your Candida is severe, you should be fine with a small amount of this sauce.

Serves 4

Phase	Meal	V	C	H	Wheat free	Dairy free
2	Fat			✓	✓	

Mussels in Cider

Andy lived in France for three years and was taught that this is the only way to prepare mussels. The two goals of preparing mussels are 1) to clean them and 2) to fatten them up, to make them tasty.

Mussels are notoriously 'dirty', living on rocks and feeding on plankton and they needed to be flushed out. In the method below, the salt in the water keeps the mussels alive until they are cooked. The mussels gorge on the flour and release waste products, so this cleans them and fattens them at the same time. The second salted bucket completes the cleaning process and the mussels are perfectly ready for cooking.

The Belgians apparently have mussels with chips (and mayonnaise). The French have mussels with more mussels!

Ingredients:

1kg fresh mussels	1 onion, finely sliced
2 tablespoons salt	1 stick of celery, chunked
1 tablespoon flour	500ml cider
Knob of butter	Freshly ground pepper

Method:

1) To prepare the mussels:

- Place the fresh (live) mussels in a bucket of cold water with a tablespoon of salt and a tablespoon of flour and leave for approximately 1 hour;

- Drain and discard the water and refill the bucket with fresh water and sprinkle with a tablespoon of salt and leave for another hour;

- Finally, drain the water and remove the 'beards' from the mussels and discard any that remain open.

2) In a large saucepan, melt the butter then add the sliced onion and celery. Cook on a low heat for 2-3 minutes then add the cider and bring to the boil.

3) Add the mussels to the pan, put on the lid and cook for about 5 minutes, occasionally shaking the pan to mix up the mussels.

4) Line a sieve with kitchen paper and drain the mussels through the sieve, collecting the juice in a clean saucepan. Discard any mussels that have remained closed and the celery stick.

5) Transfer the mussels to 2 serving dishes and pour the strained stock over the muscles. Serve immediately.

Serves 2

Phase	Meal	V	C	H	Wheat free	Dairy free
2	Fat		✓	✓	✓	

Seafood Chowder

This is a wonderful member recipe – full marks to Kimberley (DiscoSmurfette) for inventing this one. She says if you love seafood, you will love this. We tried it and agree.

A possible origin for the term "Chowder" is the French word Chaudière – a cooking pot into which stew type ingredients are put. Chowder is a name mainly used to describe fish and seafood based dishes. Some versions also have bacon. The dish probably started with fishermen throwing the catch of the day and anything else they could find into the Chaudière

Ingredients:

2 carrots, roughly chopped	500g marinara mix (mixed seafood)
2-3 sticks celery, sliced	1 salmon fillet
2 parsnips roughly chopped	200ml double cream
1 litre chicken or vegetable stock	Salt & ground black pepper
1 tablespoon olive oil	2 tablespoons fresh parsley, chopped
2 cloves garlic, chopped	

Method:

1) Put the carrots, celery, parsnip and stock in a large saucepan. Cover and bring to the boil. Reduce heat and simmer for about 10 minutes, or until the vegetables are tender.

2) Blend the mixture until smooth. (Using a hand held blender in the pan or move the stock and vegetables to a liquidiser and then return them to the pan when blended). Keep this warm.

3) Warm the olive oil in a separate frying pan. Add the garlic, marinara mix and the salmon. Lightly fry these ingredients until the salmon is cooked.

4) Add the fish mix and cream to the pan containing the blended vegetable mix. Stir, without boiling, until the chowder is hot. Season to taste.

5) Stir in the chopped parsley and serve immediately

Serves 4

Phase	Meal	V	C	H	Wheat free	Dairy free
2	Fat		✓	✓	✓	

Salmon with Mediterranean Vegetables

There are some great vegetable nutrients in this dish – tomatoes, onions, garlic, mushrooms and spinach are all good sources of vitamins and minerals. Salmon is approximately 60% protein and 40% fat and a good proportion of this fat is omega-3. Omega-3 and omega-6 fats are called "Essential Fatty Acids" because the body cannot make them, so it is essential that they are consumed.

Please note that this dish does also have meat in it – which is why it is the first of the meat dishes and the last of the fish dishes.

Ingredients:

3 tablespoons olive oil	200g spinach leaves, chopped
50g prosciutto, diced	
3 cloves garlic, chopped	1 torn fresh basil leaf (or ¼ teaspoon dried basil)
2 red onions, chopped	4 salmon fillets
250g button mushrooms, stems removed, caps thinly sliced	Salt & ground black pepper
4 plum tomatoes, cored & diced	

Method:

1) Heat ½ tablespoon of oil in a small non-stick pan over a low heat.

2) Add the prosciutto and fry for 5 minutes, or until crispy. Stir in the garlic and turn off the heat.

3) Heat 2 tablespoons of oil in a large non-stick pan over a moderate-high heat. Add the onions and mushrooms and fry for 3-5 minutes, or until they are soft.

4) Stir in the tomatoes and cook for a further 3 minutes. Add the spinach and basil and cook for 3 more minutes. Stir in the prosciutto-garlic mixture. Cover and keep warm.

5) Season the salmon fillets with salt and pepper.

6) Heat the remaining ½ tablespoon oil (in the same pan used to cook the prosciutto) over a moderate heat.

7) Add the salmon, skin-side down, and cook, covered, for 10-12 minutes, or until the fish flakes easily. Use a spatula to loosen the fish from its skin, which will stick to the pan.

8) Divide the vegetables among 4 plates, top with salmon and serve immediately.

Serves 4

Phase	Meal	V	C	H	Wheat free	Dairy free
2	Fat			✓	✓	✓

Chicken Curry Salad

This is a cold dish that you just have to try. It is rich and creamy and never fails to disappear at any buffet or summer meal. It is a serious fat dish, so don't be tempted to serve it with bread or rice. There are a couple of tablespoons of mango chutney, but this gives just a tiny bit of carb and the taste 'value added' is more than worth it.

Ingredients:

For the substance:	For the dressing:
500g cooked chicken, diced (strip meat off a roast chicken or cook some chicken breasts)	6 tablespoons sugar-free mayonnaise (bought, or use the recipe in this book)
1 green pepper, deseeded & chopped	100ml double cream, (lightly whipped)
1 red pepper, deseeded & chopped	1-2 tablespoons curry powder or paste (mild or hot – as you like it) dissolved in the juice of the other ½ of the lemon
2 celery sticks, chopped	
Juice of ½ lemon	
A pinch of cayenne pepper	1-2 tablespoons mango chutney, sugar-free (optional, if you can't find a sugar-free version)
Salt & ground black pepper	
	1 onion, finely chopped

Method:

1) Put everything in the first column together in a bowl and mix well.

2) Put everything in the second column together and mix well.

3) Pour the sauce (the second column) over the meat and salads (the first column) and mix in really well.

4) Serve on a bed of crispy lettuce and garnish with fresh parsley.

TIP 1 – Use spring onions instead of mango chutney and this can be suitable for Candida sufferers.

Serves 4

Phase	Meal	V	C	H	Wheat free	Dairy free
2	Fat		Can be	✓	✓	

Chicken Caesar Salad

This is a Harcombe friendly version of the classic dish. An Italian born Mexican, Caesar Cardini, is credited with the invention of this recipe. The story goes that unusually high demand at the restaurant on Independence Day, 1924, led to stocks running out and this was created from what was left. Apparently the original recipe did *not* feature anchovies or Worcester sauce (which can give anchovy flavour). So we'll stick to the original as far as possible, but we will have bacon croutons instead of bread.

Ingredients:

2 romaine lettuces	1-2 cloves garlic, finely chopped
Sea salt for cooking	
4 boneless chicken breasts	Juice of 1 lemon
	6 tablespoons olive oil
50g bacon pieces, diced	6 tablespoons Parmesan cheese, grated
1 egg, coddled (step 4)	
Pinch of sea salt	Freshly ground pepper

Method:

1) Separate the lettuce leaves and discard the outer leaves. Wash and thoroughly drain the leaves in a salad spinner, or pat them dry with kitchen paper. Put the leaves in a tub in the fridge to chill.

2) Sprinkle some sea salt on a griddle and dry fry the chicken for approximately 5 minutes each side, or until cooked. If you don't have a griddle, you can use a normal grill, but the griddle will give the authentic char grill markings.

3) At the same time, fry the bacon pieces in their own fat in a small frying pan. Set them aside.

4) Coddling the egg makes the yolk become slightly thicker and warm. You should keep eggs at room temperature but, if you don't, cover the egg with warm water so that it doesn't crack during the next stage. Place the egg in a mug and pour boiling water over it to completely cover it. Let it stand for exactly 1 minute. Then run cold water into the mug until the egg is cool enough to handle. Crack the egg into a bowl ready for the next step.

5) In a food processor, blend the coddled egg, a pinch of sea salt, garlic and lemon juice until the mixture is thick (approximately 1 minute).

6) Slowly add the olive oil, 1 tablespoon or 2 at a time, gently blending.

7) When the dressing is well mixed, add 2 tablespoons of the Parmesan cheese and some freshly ground black pepper and give the mixture a quick final blend.

8) Remove the lettuce leaves from the fridge. Tear the leaves into bite size pieces (don't chop or the edges will brown). Place the leaves in a large bowl and toss them in the dressing until fully coated.

9) Arrange the dressed leaves on 4 plates. Sprinkle a tablespoon of Parmesan over each plate. Place a char grilled chicken breast on each serving and sprinkle the bacon croutons on top.

TIP 1 – You can add a couple of anchovies and/or a couple of drops of Worcester sauce at step 5 if desired.

Serves 4

Phase	Meal	V	C	H	Wheat free	Dairy free
2	Fat		✓	✓	✓	

Moroccan Chicken

This is an amazing dish – the mixture of flavours really works. It is impressive enough to serve when entertaining, or it makes a quick meal if you fancy a special dinner one night. Yes, there is a bit of orange juice in this recipe, which is refined, and there is real orange to garnish but the relative quantities are so small that it won't make a difference. Hence this is still a fat meal – and a very healthy one at that.

Ingredients:

3 teaspoons olive oil	Salt & ground black pepper
4 chicken-breasts, boneless & cut into bite-sized chunks	250g rocket leaves
	100g fennel, thinly sliced
1 clove garlic, finely chopped	2 oranges, peeled, sectioned & sliced into chunks
1 teaspoon ground cumin	
6 tablespoons orange juice	4 green olives, pitted & thinly sliced
60ml balsamic vinegar	50g goats cheese, crumbled
2 tablespoons Dijon mustard	

Method:

1) Warm 2 teaspoons of oil in a large frying pan, over a medium-high heat.

2) Fry the chicken for 2 minutes.

3) Add the garlic and cumin and fry for 2 more minutes.

4) Reduce the heat to low. Stir in the orange juice, vinegar and mustard. Slowly stir in the final

teaspoon of oil to make a warm dressing. Add the salt and pepper to taste.

5) Divide the rocket leaves among 4 dinner plates. Sprinkle with fennel and oranges. Spoon the warm chicken mixture over the salad and top with olives and goats cheese.

TIP 1 – Leave out the cheese garnish to make this dairy-free.

TIP 2 – Squeeze your own oranges and keep the pulp and bits to make the juice as unrefined as possible and hence a good carbohydrate.

Serves 4

Phase	Meal	V	C	H	Wheat free	Dairy free
2	Fat			✓	✓	Can be

Hunter's Chicken

You may know this by the French name – "Chicken Chasseur". Chicken can be such a healthy food, if you buy quality meat from a reputable source. Animals need to have been freely grazing on grass in sunlight to provide humans with optimal nutrition.

We really hope that this recipe book will encourage you to eat real food and to stop eating low-fat/low-taste everything. You may have lived on grilled chicken in recent years – now is the time to enjoy succulent chicken, with all its natural juices, simply enhanced with staple vegetables and the aroma of bouquet garni.

Ingredients:

4 chicken pieces (legs or breasts – as desired)	100g mushrooms, sliced
1 tablespoon corn flour	120ml cider or dry white wine
Salt & ground black pepper	75g tomato purée
2 tablespoons olive oil	Bouquet garni sachet
2 onions, sliced	1 tablespoon parsley, chopped
2 carrots, peeled & sliced	

Method:

1) Preheat the oven to 350° F, 175° C, gas mark 4.

2) Season the corn flour with salt and pepper; use this to coat the chicken pieces.

3) Heat the oil in a large frying pan, add the chicken pieces and fry until browned. Put the chicken in a large oven-proof dish.

4) Stir-fry the vegetables (onions, carrots & mushrooms) until soft and then add these to the casserole dish too.

5) Add the cider/wine and tomato purée to the casserole dish and place the bouquet garni in the juices.

6) Cover and cook in for approximately 60-90 minutes, or until the chicken is tender.

7) Before serving, remove the bouquet garni sachet and sprinkle with chopped parsley.

TIP 1 – Most recipes for chicken advise removing the skin at some stage. We don't, as this is one of the tastiest and healthiest parts of the chicken.

Serves 4

Phase	Meal	V	C	H	Wheat free	Dairy free
2	Fat			✓	✓	✓

Coq au Vin

The classic Coq au Vin does not normally have brandy or cream, but this version makes for a really rich and creamy alternative. This dish is indulgent and rich in natural fats. Remember, any fats found in real food are good for us – it is just the manufactured (trans) fats that we need to avoid. This will be a real treat for your dinner party guests.

Ingredients:

75g butter	2 tablespoons mixed herbs
100g unsalted, non-smoked, bacon, chopped	Salt & ground black pepper
4-6 portions of chicken (legs, breasts or mixture, as you like)	240ml chicken stock
	240ml red wine
2 cloves garlic, crushed	60ml brandy (optional)
200g button mushrooms	120ml double cream (optional)
12 shallots (or small onions)	Fresh parsley

Method:

1) Preheat the oven to 350° F, 175° C, gas mark 4.

2) Melt the butter and fry the bacon in a large frying pan.

3) Add the chicken and cook until brown (5-10 minutes).

4) Add the garlic, mushrooms, shallots, mixed herbs and seasoning and fry them in the juices, taking care not to break up the chicken pieces.

5) Add the stock, red wine and brandy (optional) while the mixture is simmering.

6) Cook everything in a casserole dish in the oven for 60-90 minutes.

7) Add the cream to thicken just before serving (optional).

Serve with fresh parsley on top and with a selection of fresh vegetables for a pure fat meal.

TIP 1 – Do try to use shallots – the difference in taste between shallot and normal onions, especially with this quantity in the recipe, is quite significant.

Serves 4-6

Phase	Meal	V	C	H	Wheat free	Dairy free
2	Fat			✓	✓	

Mustard Roast Chicken

If anyone still worries about eating the fat and skin of animals – where many invaluable nutrients are found – this is the recipe to have you fighting over the skin. This is delicious cold, so you may like to add extra chicken portions for lunches during the week ahead.

Shop bought Dijon mustard need only have the following ingredients: water, mustard seeds, vinegar and salt. Some will also have citric acid, or an alternative preservative, and some will have white wine. These options are all fine – what you don't need is any variety with added sugar.

Ingredients:

| 1 free range chicken (and additional portions) | 1 onion, quartered |
| 4 cloves of garlic in their skin and chopped in half | Dijon mustard |

Method:

1) Preheat the oven to 350° F, 175° C, gas mark 4.

2) Stuff the chicken with the garlic cloves and the onion.

3) Place the chicken breast down in a roasting dish and cook in the oven for 15-20 minutes.

4) Remove the chicken from the oven. Turn it over so that the breast is up and then rub the mustard liberally over the skin before returning it to the oven.

5) Cook for a further 1 hour, or until the juices run clear from the chicken.

6) To serve, carve the chicken or serve it jointed as an alternative – 2 legs, 2 wings and 2 breasts.

Pour some of the juices from the roasting dish over the carved meat for added succulence.

7) Serve with a selection of fresh vegetables for a pure fat meal.

TIP 1 – We have not ticked the Candida box because of the vinegar in Dijon mustard but, unless you have severe Candida, you should be fine with this recipe.

Serves 4-6

Phase	Meal	V	C	H	Wheat free	Dairy free
2	Fat			✓	✓	✓

Chicken Cordon Bleu

The classic ingredients for chicken cordon bleu are chicken, ham or prosciutto and a rich cheese, like Gruyère. Traditionally, however, the whole thing is invariably coated in breadcrumbs, so we are doing a Harcombe friendly version here.

Ingredients:

2 courgettes, sliced	A handful of basil leaves
4 tomatoes, quartered	100g strong cheese – e.g. Gruyère, parmesan, grated
1 aubergine, diced	
4 tablespoons olive oil	8 slices prosciutto (air-dried ham)
4 boneless chicken breasts	
4 teaspoons pesto sauce	Salt & ground black pepper

Method:

1) Preheat the oven to 400° F, 200° C, gas mark 6.

2) Put the courgettes, tomatoes and aubergine in a roasting tray and spoon the olive oil over them.

3) Cut a pocket in each chicken breast and fill each one with a teaspoon of pesto, a few basil leaves and some of the grated cheese.

4) Wrap each chicken breast with 2 slices of prosciutto and then place them in the roasting tray on top of the vegetables and olive oil.

5) Add seasoning (a sprinkling of black pepper, if not the salt).

6) Roast for 35-40 minutes until the chicken juices run clear and the vegetables are soft to a fork touch.

7) Just before serving, add the remaining grated cheese for the last couple of minutes in the oven. This will give the golden glaze of the classic cordon bleu, but without the golden breadcrumbs.

TIP 1 – You should be able to get a pesto sauce with no sugar, flour or unnecessary ingredients. The base ingredients can include tomatoes, tomato purée, onions, olive oil, lemon juice, salt, parsley, basil, black pepper – any variations of these real ingredients are fine.

TIP 2 – If you can't find a pesto sauce with all natural ingredients, make our version in this book.

TIP 3 – The classic cordon bleu recipe would advise removing the chicken skin. We would always recommend keeping the skin on, as it's the tastiest bit.

Serves 4

Phase	Meal	V	C	H	Wheat free	Dairy free
2	Fat		✓	✓	✓	

Tarragon Cream Chicken

Tarragon is considered a perfect match for chicken and the tang of the lemon, with the richness of the crème fraîche, makes for four perfectly balanced ingredients. This is one of the simplest dinner party dishes to have in your repertoire.

Ingredients:

4 chicken breasts, diced	2 tablespoons fresh parsley, finely chopped
2 tablespoons butter	2 tablespoons Dijon mustard
400ml crème fraîche	Juice of ½ lemon
2 tablespoons fresh tarragon, finely chopped (or 2 teaspoons dried)	Salt & ground black pepper

Method:

1) Melt the butter in a frying pan and heat it until it starts to bubble. Add the chicken to the pan and fry until it is cooked through and starting to brown at the edges. Turn the heat down low.

2) Add the crème fraîche, herbs and mustard to the pan and stir well.

3) Heat to a simmer. Add the lemon juice and some seasoning.

4) Serve with fresh tarragon garnish.

Serves 4

Phase	Meal	V	C	H	Wheat free	Dairy free
2	Fat		✓	✓	✓	

Turkey Steaks with Ham Wrap

This is our only turkey recipe, but it's a good one. We should enjoy turkey more often – not just for Christmas and Thanksgiving. Turkey has a stronger flavour than chicken, so it works better with complementary strong flavours like ham.

Ingredients:

4 turkey breast steaks	4 slices Parma ham
Freshly ground black pepper	25g butter
Juice of ½ lemon	A dozen peppercorns, crushed
1 tablespoon fresh tarragon, chopped or 1 pinch dried tarragon	150ml single cream
	Tarragon sprigs to garnish (optional)

Method:

1) Season the turkey steaks with black pepper, lemon juice and tarragon.

2) Wrap each steak in a slice of Parma ham.

3) Heat the butter in a frying pan. Fry the steaks for 3-5 minutes on each side, or longer for thicker steaks (until they are just cooked through).

4) Add the crushed peppercorns and cream. Stir everything together until it is heated through. To make the sauce thicker, boil the mixture so that some water evaporates.

Serves 4

Phase	Meal	V	C	H	Wheat free	Dairy free
2	Fat		✓	✓	✓	

Roast Pork & Autumn Apple

This can be done at any time of year, but it is particularly tasty and healthy when the autumn apples fall and you can use them fresh from the ground. If you live in a city, do make every effort to find wild seasonal fruit somewhere near you. What could be better than free real food?

Ingredients:

Leg of pork or rolled shoulder of pork, with the skin on (allow at least 250g per person) 1 onion, quartered 4 cloves of garlic in their skin and chopped in half	1 large carrot & 1 large parsnip, cleaned with skin on, cut into chunks Sprigs of fresh thyme 2 or more large cooking apples (Bramleys are ideal), peeled & chopped into chunks

Method:

1) Preheat the oven to 300° F, 150° C, gas mark 2.

2) Line a roasting dish with tin foil and place the pork in the middle. Pack the prepared vegetables and thyme around the joint and tightly wrap the foil around the joint. Cover with an extra piece of foil if needed, to seal the joint.

3) Slow roast in the oven for 3-4 hours. You can leave it longer if you like, as the moisture will stay around the joint if you sealed it well.

4) Half an hour before you are ready to eat, drain the juice from the joint and return it to a hot oven (400° F, 200° C, gas mark 6) with the foil peeled back from the joint to expose and crisp the skin.

5) Place the chopped apple chunks in a saucepan with just enough water to cover the bottom of the pan

(the saucepan should be such that the apples are piled quite high rather than spread out). Steam the apples with the saucepan lid on, for about 10-15 minutes, stirring frequently, until the apples mix to a mushy consistency.

6) Serve with the autumn apple and a selection of fresh vegetables. Include the vegetables used in cooking the joint – these will be the tastiest ones.

TIP 1 – The secret to great crackling is step 4 of the recipe. Andy always manages to get our crackling 'teeth breakingly' good!

TIP 2 – Keep any leftover pork tightly wrapped in tin foil to retain the moisture.

TIP 3 – The apples strictly make this a slight "mixes" meal, but cooking apples are so sharp that a spoonful for garnish and taste will make little difference. If you are very carb sensitive, don't have the apple sauce and argue for extra crackling instead!

Serves 4-6

Phase	Meal	V	C	H	Wheat free	Dairy free
2	Fat		✓	✓	✓	✓

Cream & Mustard Pork

This is a really decadent fat dish – with pork, butter and cream. Saturated fat has, quite wrongly, been accused of many crimes – including being the cause of heart disease. Humans and our ancestors have been eating animals and their by-products for hundreds of thousands of years. The idea that these foods are responsible for a killer disease is absurd. Far more likely culprits are the sugar and refined carbohydrates that we have started consuming in unprecedented quantities in the past century or so.

Ingredients:

30g butter	240ml double cream
600g pork, diced	4 teaspoons Dijon mustard
225g button mushrooms	
8 tablespoons dry white wine	Salt & ground black pepper

Method:

1) Heat the butter gently in a large frying pan and add the pork and fry until it is brown (approximately 5 minutes).

2) Add the mushrooms and fry them until golden brown (push the pork pieces to the outer edge of the pan to let the mushrooms cook in the centre).

3) Add the white wine, cream and mustard. Bring to the boil stirring continuously. Reduce the heat and simmer for 2-3 minutes.

4) Season to taste and serve.

TIP 1 – The mushrooms make this unsuitable for Candida.

TIP 2 – Make sure that the mustard doesn't have any unnecessary added sugars or other ingredients.

Serves 4

Phase	Meal	V	C	H	Wheat free	Dairy free
2	Fat			✓	✓	

Pork & Apricot Salad

If you like the idea of pork and apple, this pork and apricot variation is something else. The creamy yoghurt, tangy mustard and well-chosen herbs, blend together in a quite unforgettable dish. The dried apricots are refined fruits and, therefore, they do add a bit of carbohydrate to a fat dish, but they are in such small quantities that you shouldn't worry. Each serving ends up with just a few grams of dried apricots and the taste and nutrients more than make this little 'cheat' worth while.

Ingredients:

½ lettuce, shredded	2 tablespoons olive oil
1 red pepper, deseeded & cut into strips	400g boneless pork, cut into strips
1 green pepper, cut into strips	Juice & zest of 1 lemon
150g Natural Live Yoghurt	50g dried apricots, chopped
1 clove garlic, finely chopped	2 teaspoons thyme
1 teaspoon Dijon mustard	2 teaspoons sage
Salt & ground black pepper	1 tablespoon pine nuts (optional)

Method:

1) Place the shredded lettuce into a large bowl. Add the red and green peppers and mix together.

2) Blend together the yoghurt, garlic and mustard with salt and pepper to taste.

3) Put the salad on 4 plates, or into 4 large bowls, and pour over equal quantities of the yoghurt dressing.

4) Heat the oil in a large frying pan. Add the pork, lemon zest and juice and fry for 5 minutes or until the pork is cooked.

5) Add the chopped apricots, thyme and sage and heat through.

6) Spoon the cooked pork over the salad. Sprinkle with pine nuts, if desired.

Serves 4

Phase	Meal	V	C	H	Wheat free	Dairy free
2	Fat		✓	✓	✓	

Duck in Plum Sauce

Duck is a much underused meat. It tends to be a dish ordered in restaurants and yet it is so easy to do at home. Duck has a stronger flavour than chicken, so it doesn't need to be overpowered with a strong sauce. The perfect accompaniment to duck is simple plum flavouring.

Like all grass grazed meat, duck is so healthy – it is quite a dense meat, with a relatively low water content (approximately 50%, whereas pork is nearer 75%). The remaining 50% is 39% fat and 11% protein. As with virtually all meat on the planet, the majority of the fat is unsaturated – not that unsaturated is better or worse than saturated. We share this just to undermine the notion that meat is predominantly saturated fat.

Ingredients:

4 duck quarters, breasts or legs, as you prefer, with the skin on 1 red onion, finely chopped	500g ripe plums, stoned and cut in quarters

Method:

1) Preheat the oven to the lowest setting, ready to keep the duck just warm.

2) Prick the duck skin and then fry the duck pieces skin side down for approximately 10 minutes and then turn the pieces over to do the other side. The duck skin will release fat quite quickly and you will be cooking the duck in its own juices.

3) Transfer the duck to an oven-proof dish and keep it warm in the oven.

4) Add the chopped onion to the frying pan and lightly fry in the duck juices for 5 minutes.

5) Add the plums and cook for a further 5 minutes, stirring occasionally.

6) Return the duck to the pan and cook for a further 5-10 minutes, depending on how pink you like your duck.

7) Serve with simple vegetables, like cauliflower and broccoli, to avoid competing flavours.

TIP 1 – To avoid mixing, serve most, if not all, of the plums to any non Harcombe dieters at the meal. The plums will have done their job flavouring your duck and making the juice rich and dark.

Serves 4

Phase	Meal	V	C	H	Wheat free	Dairy free
2	Fat		✓	✓	✓	✓

Beef & Pepper Casserole

Red meat has taken a battering in recent years, as people have shunned it in an obsession with 'low-fat everything'. Did you know that the main fat in beef is monounsaturated fat? This is the main fat in olive oil, which we are told to eat more of. We have been fed too much nonsense about fat and this book is here to celebrate real food. Nature is not going to deliver food in a form that is bad for us. That's the job of food manufacturers.

Ingredients:

1 tablespoon corn flour	1 beef stock cube
Salt & ground black pepper	500ml water
	60ml red wine
600g stewing beef, diced	1 red pepper, deseeded & diced
2 tablespoons oil	
2 onions, sliced	1 green pepper, deseeded & diced
1 clove garlic, crushed	
2 carrots, peeled & chopped	50g button mushrooms
	Black olives (optional)

Method:

1) Preheat the oven to 350° F, 175° C, gas mark 4.

2) Mix the corn flour, salt and pepper in a mixing bowl.

3) Toss the diced beef in the dry mixture to coat it.

4) Heat the oil in a large frying pan, and cook the meat, onions and garlic until the onions are soft and the meat lightly browned.

5) Transfer to a large oven-proof dish (ideally a casserole dish).

6) Put the carrots, remaining seasoned corn flour and crumbled stock cube into the pan and add the water and the wine.

7) Stir and bring to the boil and then pour over the meat in the oven dish.

8) Cover and cook for 90 minutes.

9) Add the peppers and mushrooms and continue cooking for 30 minutes.

10) Garnish with black olives before serving, if desired.

TIP 1 – Leave out the mushrooms for this to be suitable for Candida.

Serves 4

Phase	Meal	V	C	H	Wheat free	Dairy free
2	Fat		Can be	✓	✓	✓

Boeuf Bourguignon

This is a really simple version of the French classic. This dish can be done as a 'cooking in a hurry meal' if you have a slow-cooker. You can put the slow-cooker on the lowest setting before work and return home to a rich aroma and delicious casserole.

Ingredients:

1 tablespoon olive oil	1 carrot, peeled & sliced
1kg braising steak, diced	350ml red wine
100g bacon, diced	1 tablespoon tomato purée
150g button mushrooms	
2 cloves garlic, crushed	Salt & ground black pepper
8 shallots (or small onions)	Bouquet garni sachet
	1 tablespoon corn flour

Method:

The simplest option is to gently brown the steak, shallots and bacon in the oil and then to put all the ingredients in a slow-cooker on high for 3-4 hours or on low for the day. The casserole option is as follows:

1) Preheat the oven to 350° F, 175° C, gas mark 4.

2) Heat the oil in a large frying pan.

3) Brown the steak in the hot oil and then add the bacon and mushrooms and cook for a further 1-2 minutes.

4) Add the garlic and shallots and stir-fry until soft.

5) Put all the other ingredients, except the corn flour, in an oven-proof casserole dish (i.e. the carrot, red wine, tomato purée, salt & pepper, bouquet garni).

6) Cook in the oven for 60-90 minutes.

7) Just before serving remove the bouquet garni sachet (like a teabag) and add the corn flour to the juices to thicken them.

Serve with a selection of fresh vegetables (steamed cauliflower, green beans and broccoli accompany this dish particularly well).

Serves 4

Phase	Meal	V	C	H	Wheat free	Dairy free
2	Fat			✓	✓	✓

Chilli Con Carne

Adults can have chilli con carne in Phase 2, but the hardest thing about this dish will be getting used to having meat chilli without rice. When you are close to your ideal weight, or in Phase 3, you can have meat chilli with brown rice as you are then mixing good fats and good carbs. When you are trying to lose weight, however, you should get used to having a bowl of meat chilli with a rocket, or similar dark leaf, salad. Children can lap this up at any time – with whole wheat pasta, whole wheat spaghetti, brown rice, baked potatoes or any unrefined carbs.

Ingredients:

2 tablespoons olive oil	50g mushrooms, chopped
400g minced beef	400g tin kidney beans, drained & rinsed
1 red onion, finely chopped	
1 onion, finely chopped	400g tin chopped tomatoes
2 cloves garlic, crushed	75g tomato purée
3 carrots, peeled & chopped	2 teaspoons mixed herbs
	2 teaspoons chilli powder
1 red & 1 green pepper, deseeded & finely chopped	250ml beef or vegetable stock

Method:

1) Brown the mince in a large frying pan, over a moderate heat.

2) Add the onions and garlic and cook until soft.

3) Add the chopped carrots, peppers, mushrooms and cook for approximately 3-4 minutes.

4) Add the beans, tomatoes, tomato purée, herbs, chilli powder and stock.

5) Continue to simmer until the carrots are tender, which will be approximately 20-25 minutes.

TIP 1 – Add a teaspoon each of ground cumin and coriander and a pinch of ground cinnamon, for a really authentic chilli taste. Garnish with a small bunch of fresh coriander, finely chopped.

TIP 2 – Substitute peppers for the mushrooms, or just leave out the mushrooms, for this dish to be suitable for Candida.

Serves 4

Phase	Meal	V	C	H	Wheat free	Dairy free
2	Fat		Can be	✓	✓	✓

Veal Escallops in a Creamy Mushroom Sauce

Please only buy veal from the butcher and ensure that it has been reared to welfare standards endorsed by compassion in world farming. Pork chops will work just as well with this wonderfully rich recipe.

Ingredients:

2 tablespoons butter	300ml dry white wine
1 tablespoon ground nut oil	200ml double cream
4 veal escallops (200g each approximately)	Salt & ground black pepper
175g mushrooms, sliced	Fresh parsley, chopped for garnish (optional)
1 tablespoon Calvados (apple brandy) (optional)	

Method:

1) Heat the butter and oil in a large frying pan, on a moderately high heat. Add the escallops (you may need to do 2 at a time) and fry them on both sides until the meat is cooked as you like it. Set the meat to one side, on a plate, keeping it warm.

2) Fry the mushrooms in the pan, stirring occasionally, for 4-5 minutes. Transfer the mushrooms to the veal plate to keep them warm.

3) Add the Calvados and wine to the pan. Bring to the boil and then simmer for 4-5 minutes.

4) Add the cream to the pan and simmer for a further 4-5 minutes.

5) Return the veal and mushrooms to the pan and cook them until hot. Season the dish.

6) Serve with a parsley sprinkling on top. This would go really well with simple French vegetables like green beans or even exotic salsify.

TIP 1 – As a frying guide, veal escallops that are approximately 1cm thick will need 2-3 minutes frying each side. Cook for slightly longer if the meat is thicker. The overriding principle is how you like your meat, however.

TIP 2 – Don't worry about using alcohol for cooking in Phase 2 – the French rarely make a main meal without using some alcohol and the French person who eats French food is rarely overweight. The alcohol burns off and the flavour is the thing that is left.

Serves 4

Phase	Meal	V	C	H	Wheat free	Dairy free
2	Fat			✓	✓	

Steak au Poivre (Phase 2 version)

This Phase 2 variation produces an even tastier version of this classic dish, but without taking much more time.

Ingredients:

4 steaks (fillet, sirloin, entrecote – whatever you can buy)	25g butter
1-2 tablespoons black peppercorns, crushed	2 tablespoons brandy, warmed
1 tablespoon olive oil	250ml single cream
	Salt & ground black pepper

Method:

1) Press the crushed peppercorns into both sides of the steaks.

2) Heat the oil and butter together in a frying pan and fry the steaks quickly (on a high heat) for approximately 2 minutes on each side.

3) Lower the heat and cook for a further 3-7 minutes on each side (as you like your steak done).

4) Transfer the steaks to a serving dish and keep hot.

5) Add the brandy and cream to the pan. Season and simmer for 2 minutes, stirring constantly.

6) Pour over the steaks and serve with your choice of vegetables. Green beans, courgettes, fried onions and mushrooms go really well with this dish.

Serves 4

Phase	Meal	V	C	H	Wheat free	Dairy free
2	Fat		✓	✓	✓	

Andy's Cheese Burgers

We have a Phase 1 burger recipe (meatballs), a Phase 2/easily adaptable to Phase 1 burger recipe (Lird's) and two Phase 2 burger recipes – Andy's and Mat's.

Ingredients:

500g fresh minced beef	2 teaspoons hot horseradish sauce (with no added sugar)
1 onion, very finely chopped	
1 clove garlic, crushed	Freshly ground pepper
100g cheddar or similar hard cheese, grated	

Method:

1) Preheat the oven to 400° F, 200° C, gas mark 6 (there are other cooking options below).

2) Place all the prepared ingredients in a mixing bowl and mix thoroughly with your hands.

3) Take a handful of the mixture and form a small but tight ball with your hands. Place the meat ball on a baking tray and lightly pat down to make a burger shape. Repeat until all the mixture is used up.

4) Bake in the oven for approximately 15-30 minutes. Alternatively, you can fry the burgers in a frying pan with some olive oil. Or, you can char grill them on a very hot griddle for 2-3 minutes on each side. Or, weather permitting, you can barbecue them.

Makes 4-6 burgers, depending on their size.

Phase	Meal	V	C	H	Wheat free	Dairy free
2	Fat		✓	✓	✓	

Mat Burgers

This is our spiciest burger recipe, thanks to Mat. You can replace the Tabasco with even hotter sauces – there are whole web sites dedicated to such things. Worcester sauce tends to include vinegar, anchovies, onions, garlic, spices and sugar. A tiny amount of sugar in a tiny amount of sauce will be fine for Phase 2.

Ingredients:

500g fresh minced beef	1 teaspoon Dijon mustard
1 onion, very finely chopped	5 drops of "ludicrously hot Tabasco sauce"
1 teaspoon lemon juice	2 shakes of Worcester sauce (leave out if your Candida is severe)
1 tablespoon crushed garlic, minced with 1 teaspoon salt	Freshly ground pepper

Method:

1) Ideally barbecue these but, if the weather is bad, preheat the oven to 400° F, 200° C, gas mark 6.

2) Place all the prepared ingredients in a mixing bowl and mix thoroughly with your hands.

3) Take a handful of the mixture and form a small but tight ball with your hands. Place the meat ball on a baking tray and lightly pat down to make a burger shape. Repeat until all the mixture is used up.

4) Bake in the oven for approximately 15-30 minutes.

Makes 4-6 burgers, depending on their size.

Phase	Meal	V	C	H	Wheat free	Dairy free
2	Fat		(✓)	✓	✓	✓

PHASE 2 – SIDE DISHES & SAUCES

Orange Mash

If you're missing potatoes, this could be your saving dish. This can go with either fat or carb meals, but it is safer with carb meals, as the veg are high carb ones.

Ingredients:

100g carrots, peeled & sliced	100g butternut squash, peeled, deseeded & diced
100g swede, peeled & diced	1 tablespoon crème fraîche
1 spring onion, chopped	Salt & ground black pepper

Method:

1) Boil the vegetables in a saucepan of water until they are very soft.

2) Drain the vegetables and mash them with a potato masher in the saucepan, adding the crème fraîche as you would butter.

3) Season to taste and serve quickly, as the crème fraîche will cool the mash.

TIP 1 – You can make more of a purée by blending the vegetables with the crème fraîche instead of mashing them.

TIP 2 – Cook the vegetables in vegetable stock, rather than water, for added flavour.

Serves 4

Phase	Meal	V	C	H	Wheat free	Dairy free
2	Either	✓	✓	(✓)	✓	

Bulghar Wheat Salad

Bulghar wheat makes a great base for a salad. It has a high carbohydrate content (76%), so it can be a useful dish for fitness enthusiasts. It is quite useful for B vitamins and very good, for a non-animal food, for minerals, providing iron, magnesium, phosphorous, copper and especially manganese in good quantities. It is an ideal grain for those suffering from pure wheat intolerance, so it is an excellent all-rounder.

Ingredients:

225g bulghar wheat, (dry weight)	8 tablespoons olive oil
100g fresh tomatoes, finely chopped	2 tablespoons lemon juice, ideally fresh
100g cucumber, finely chopped	2 tablespoons fresh basil, finely chopped
1 onion, finely chopped	Salt & ground black pepper
1 spring onion, finely chopped (optional)	

Method:

1) Just cover the bulghar wheat with boiling water and leave it to soak for 30 minutes.

2) Drain well and squeeze out the excess water.

3) Add in the finely chopped tomatoes, cucumber and onions.

4) Mix the olive oil, lemon juice, basil and seasoning in a small bowl.

5) Add this mixture to the bulghar wheat and stir well.

TIP 1 – We put brackets around the 'wheat-free' tick below because bulghar wheat is strictly in the wheat family. However, as with couscous, many people find that they can tolerate bulghar on occasions whereas they can't cope with pure wheat.

TIP 2 – This can be a really useful dish to take to work in a tub for lunch. Add more chopped salad vegetables to make the serving more substantial.

TIP 3 – This also works really well with couscous or quinoa, for grain alternatives.

Serves 4

Phase	Meal	V	C	H	Wheat free	Dairy free
2	Carb	✓	✓	✓	(✓)	✓

Mayonnaise

This version is so easy to make and it is delicious. You need never buy mayonnaise from a shop again.

Ingredients:

1 egg – very fresh, yolk only	2 teaspoons cider or wine vinegar
½ teaspoon salt	300ml olive or sunflower oil
½ teaspoon Dijon mustard	Freshly ground black pepper

Method:

1) With a blender:

- Separate the egg yolk and put this in a blender; add the salt, mustard and vinegar and blend for approximately 10 seconds.

- Slowly add the oil and continue to blend (feed the oil through the lid ideally, or keep turning the blender off to add more oil).

- As the oil is added, the mayonnaise will thicken.

- Season with black pepper.

2) Without a blender:

- Separate the egg yolk and beat it thoroughly with a whisk in a small bowl.

- Add the salt, mustard and vinegar and continue to beat well.

- Slowly add the oil, continuing to beat, until the mayonnaise thickens.

- Season with black pepper.

This makes approximately 300ml of dressing.

Mustard Salad Dressing

This is a great variation of the basic Mayonnaise recipe. As you can see, it takes two of the ingredients and increases their quantities – the vinegar is doubled and the mustard increases more than ten-fold. This makes for a really rich and tangy dressing.

Ingredients:

1 egg – very fresh, yolk only	4 teaspoons cider or wine vinegar
½ teaspoon salt	300ml olive or sunflower oil
2 tablespoons Dijon mustard	Freshly ground black pepper

Method:

1) Follow the method for mayonnaise.

- Separate the egg yolk and put this in a blender; add the salt, mustard and vinegar and blend for approximately 10 seconds.

- Slowly add the oil and continue to blend (feed the oil through the lid ideally, or keep turning the blender off to add more oil).

- As the oil is added, the mayonnaise will thicken.

- Season with black pepper.

This makes approximately 300ml of dressing.

The Mayonnaise and mustard salad dressing have the following properties:

Phase	Meal	V	C	H	Wheat free	Dairy free
2	Either	✓		✓	✓	✓

French Vinaigrette Dressing

Andy's years in France helped him perfect the true French Vinaigrette. As with all French cooking, the secret is in simple, high quality, ingredients. Maille is a good brand of Dijon mustard and the olive oil should be extra virgin. The French go for 3-4 parts oil to vinegar; they don't use balsamic, as it's too sweet and they save the black pepper for sprinkling over the salad leaves.

Ingredients:

¼ teaspoon sea salt	1 teaspoon Dijon mustard
2 tablespoon sherry or red wine vinegar	6-8 tablespoons olive oil
1 shallot, finely chopped	

Method:

1) Mix the salt, vinegar and shallot in a small bowl and leave to stand for at least 10 minutes.

2) Mix in the mustard and then 6 tablespoons of olive oil. Stir well, then taste. If too sharp, add the remaining olive oil and more salt, if necessary. You can add more mustard – as you like it.

3) Toss the salad leaves in the dressing and serve.

TIP 1 – This version of vinaigrette is best used immediately. If you want to make some dressing to keep in the fridge, the shallots don't keep well so you can either add them at the time of serving (which loses the opportunity of marinating them) or you can choose a shallot-free option from our vinaigrette recipe variations.

Variations of Vinaigrette Salad Dressing

Keep to the French ratio of 3 measures of oil to 1 of vinegar/lemon and make sure that you mix everything thoroughly. Try the following variations:

1) Olive oil and balsamic vinegar for a sweeter, non-French, version;

2) Olive oil and cider vinegar (will give a slightly different taste with cider vinegar being apple based and wine vinegar being grape based);

3) Olive oil and lemon, or lime, juice (great for fish dishes);

4) Olive oil and fruit vinegar (e.g. raspberry).

TIP 1 – Add finely chopped garlic and leave to marinate for a few hours for added taste and anti-Candida properties.

TIP 2 – Add freshly chopped herbs, such as chives, basil, or oregano to give tasty variations.

The French Vinaigrette and its variations all have the following properties:

Phase	Meal	V	C	H	Wheat free	Dairy free
2	Either	✓		✓	✓	✓

Oil Free Dressing

This is for those of you who take a while to get used to not worrying about calories. A number of people do struggle with oily dressings and real food in the early stages. Hopefully you will keep repeating to yourself that it is the body's handling of carbohydrates that makes you fat and not fat itself.

In the meantime, here is an oil free dressing. For those of you who have an interest in calories, this provides approximately 10 calories per tablespoon. This dressing does have its other uses, as it is great for bean salad recipes. Beans are naturally high in carbohydrate, so oil free dressings can be quite useful.

Ingredients:

4 tablespoons concentrated apple juice	1 shallot, coarsely cut
5 tablespoons apple cider vinegar	1 teaspoon dry tarragon
2 tablespoons water	6-8 sprigs of fresh parsley or 1 teaspoon dry parsley
2 teaspoons mustard (sugar-free)	Salt & ground black pepper

Method:

1)   Put everything in a blender and whisk it together.

TIP 1 – Use lemon juice instead of apple cider vinegar to make this suitable for Candida.

Phase	Meal	V	C	H	Wheat free	Dairy free
2	Either	✓	Can be	✓	✓	✓

Pesto Sauce

In case you can't find a simple pesto sauce in the supermarket, here is a quick one that you can make.

Ingredients:

100g sun-dried tomatoes	2 tablespoons balsamic vinegar (optional)
2 tablespoons chopped fresh basil	2 tablespoons red wine (optional)
2 tablespoons chopped fresh parsley	6 tablespoons olive oil
½ red onion, chopped	50g Parmesan cheese, grated
4 cloves garlic, chopped	Salt & ground black pepper
25g pine nuts (optional)	
1 tablespoon tomato purée	

Method:

1) Blend the tomatoes, basil, parsley, onion, garlic and pine nuts until very fine.

2) Add the tomato purée, vinegar and red wine and blend thoroughly.

3) Stir in the olive oil and Parmesan cheese and season to taste.

TIP 1 – leave out the vinegar and wine if Candida is a problem for you.

Phase	Meal	V	C	H	Wheat free	Dairy free
2	Either	✓	Can be	✓	✓	

Madeira Sauce

This is a really adaptable sauce, which can be suitable for vegetarians or carnivores. Carnivores can use this with diced pork or chicken as a casserole, or as a pour on sauce over pork chops or chicken breasts. Vegetarians can make the sauce using vegetable stock and make a chunky quorn casserole.

Ingredients:

2 tablespoons olive oil	1 bay leaf
1 onion, finely chopped	1 sprig of fresh thyme
1 carrot, finely chopped	125ml Madeira
1 stick of celery, finely chopped	1 tablespoon tomato purée
1 clove garlic, crushed	500ml stock
25g mushrooms, finely chopped	

Method:

1) Heat the oil in a small saucepan and stir-fry all the vegetables, along with the bay leaf and thyme, until the vegetables begin to brown.

2) Add the Madeira and gently simmer to reduce the liquid by two thirds, which removes nearly all the alcohol but leaves the flavour.

3) Add the tomato purée and the stock; reduce the heat and simmer until the volume reduces to approximately half of what it was.

4) Sieve everything to leave a smooth sauce (you may as well dispose of the vegetables and herbs as you have taken the goodness from them already).

TIP 1 – Leave out the mushrooms, or use peppers instead, for this to be suitable for Candida.

Serves 4

Phase	Meal	V	C	H	Wheat free	Dairy free
2	Either	Can be	Can be	✓	✓	✓

(Cauliflower) Cheese Sauce

This sauce can be used to make either cauliflower cheese, or cheesy leeks, or any other cheese and vegetable dish. The recipe below uses cauliflower, but pour the sauce over any vegetable you fancy. This also goes surprisingly well with white fish, if you fancy a non-vegetarian meal.

Ingredients:

1 cauliflower, quartered, or 4 leeks, sliced or 4 white fish steaks	1 egg, whisked
240ml milk	100g Cheddar cheese, grated

Method:

1) Preheat the oven to 350° F, 175° C, gas mark 4.

2) For cauliflower cheese, or cheesy leeks, part cook the vegetables by lightly boiling or steaming them. Then place them in an oven-proof dish. For a white fish dish, brush the bottom of the oven-proof dish with butter and then place the fish steaks on top.

3) In a saucepan, bring the milk to the boil then turn off the heat. Allow the milk to cool for 2 minutes then mix in the whisked egg.

4) Add the grated cheese and stir continuously until the cheese has melted and you have a thick sauce.

5) Pour over the cauliflower, leeks or fish, sprinkle with a little grated cheese and place in the oven. Cook for 20-30 minutes. Serve hot.

TIP 1 – Serve the sauce with asparagus for a great fat starter.

TIP 2 – Sprinkle some fresh parsley, on top of the dish, just before serving, for a splash of colour and added taste.

TIP 3 – This also works really well with broccoli, instead of, or as well as, cauliflower.

Serves 4

Phase	Meal	V	C	H	Wheat free	Dairy free
2	Fat	Can be	✓	✓	✓	

Cheese Makers' Salad

Shallots are much milder and sweeter than onions, so you sadly can't substitute onions in any dish that specifies shallots. Banana shallots are a longer bulb version of normal shallots; but you can use normal shallots if you can't get the banana ones.

Ingredients:

2 banana shallots, finely sliced	1 iceberg lettuce, shredded or torn
2 tablespoons red wine vinegar	50-100ml single cream
	Sea salt

Method:

1) Place the finely sliced shallots in the bottom of a salad bowl. Add the vinegar and set the bowl aside, at room temperature, for at least an hour stirring the shallots occasionally.

2) Add the lettuce to the salad bowl. Pour the single cream over the salad leaves. Add sea salt to taste and mix the salad, ensuring that the softened shallots are dispersed throughout the salad.

3) Serve immediately as a rich accompaniment to any simple meat or fish.

TIP 1 – Substitute lemon juice for vinegar and this can be suitable for Candida.

Serves 4

Phase	Meal	V	C	H	Wheat free	Dairy free
2	Fat	✓	Can be	✓	✓	

PHASE 2 – SOUPS, STARTERS & LITE BITES

Oyster Mushrooms

This simple starter can be served hot or cold, so it makes a great dinner party dish if you want to save time for other things. Because there are so many mushrooms, treat this as a carb dish and therefore use low-fat crème fraîche to keep the fats away.

Ingredients:

1 tablespoon of olive oil	100ml low-fat crème fraîche
1 onion, chopped	A pinch of ground nutmeg
500g of wild oyster mushrooms, sliced & stems cut off	Salt & ground black pepper
½ teaspoon dried sage	

Method:

1) Place the oil in a large frying pan, over a high heat.

2) Add the onion, mushrooms and sage and fry until soft.

3) Turn off the heat and stir in the crème fraîche, nutmeg and seasoning.

4) Serve on a bed of rocket, spinach or other strong salad leaves.

TIP 1 – Boil the mushroom stems with a chopped shallot, in a little water, for a quick mushroom stock.

Serves 4

Phase	Meal	V	C	H	Wheat free	Dairy free
2	Carb	✓		✓	✓	

Hummus

Hummus is the Arabic word for "chickpea" and it is quite a historic food. It is referred to, as far back as 400BC, in the writings of Plato and Socrates and was a staple food in Europe by the Roman times. It took until 1910 to reach the US – brought in by European migrants and then it took another 70 years before it became a staple item in supermarkets. With this recipe, you will never have to shop for it again.

Chickpeas are carbs, but Hummus is often made in a base of (olive) oil, so it also has a measurable fat content. In 100g of Hummus there are 20g of carbohydrate and 9g of fat. Think of Hummus as a carb meal, therefore, but don't have 'lashings' of it with lots of brown bread, for example, or the fat content will start to add up. A good carb meal would be a wholemeal pita bread stuffed with grated carrot, salad leaves, pepper slices and Hummus.

Ingredients:

225g tin chickpeas, drained	3 tablespoons of olive oil
2 cloves garlic, crushed	Salt & ground black pepper
Juice of 1 lemon	Parsley to garnish
2 tablespoons Natural Live Yoghurt (low-fat – you need to avoid full fat yoghurt as this is a carb dish)	

Method:

1) Put the chickpeas, garlic, lemon juice, yoghurt and oil in a blender and blitz until smooth (will only take a few seconds).

2) Season to taste.

3) Garnish with parsley.

TIP 1 – To make the dish more authentic, add 1 tablespoon of tahini paste (sesame seed paste).

Serves 4

Phase	Meal	V	C	H	Wheat free	Dairy free
2	Carb	✓	✓	✓	✓	

Pear & Butternut Squash Soup

We would like to thank Val Smith for this recipe. Pear and ginger are wonderful enough together. When you add the sweetness and texture of butternut squash and the sharpness and creaminess of the Natural Live Yoghurt, the mix of flavours and textures is special.

Ingredients:

2 tablespoons olive oil (for cooking)	2 pears, peeled, cored & diced
500g butternut squash, peeled, deseeded & diced	500ml stock
1 onion, finely chopped	125ml Natural Live Yoghurt
3 cloves garlic, finely chopped	Freshly ground black pepper
25g fresh ginger, finely chopped	Small bunch chives (optional)

Method:

1) Preheat the oven to 350° F, 175° C, gas mark 4.

2) Brush a roasting tin with some olive oil. Roast the butternut squash pieces until soft to a fork touch. Remove them from the oven; allow them to cool slightly and then purée the squash in a blender.

3) Heat 1-2 tablespoons of olive oil in a large pan with a lid. Gently fry the onion, garlic and ginger for approximately 10-15 minutes (don't brown).

4) Add the diced pears and stir them in.

5) Add the stock and cover and cook for 20 minutes.

6) Add the puréed squash and NLY.

7) Add black pepper to taste.

8) Garnish with chives (optional).

TIP 1 – Make this a Phase 3 dinner party dish using cream instead of NLY.

TIP 2 – Use low fat NLY to keep this a pure carb meal.

Serves 4

Phase	Meal	V	C	H	Wheat free	Dairy free
2	Carb	✓	✓	✓	✓	

Falafel

This is the staple dish in Israel. While our children lunch on burgers and chips, Israeli children eat spicy chickpeas – guess which children get the healthier dish? This is a wonderful carb meal for adults and children.

Ingredients:

400g tin chickpeas, drained	For the Harissa sauce (this is quite spicy and definitely optional):
1 onion, finely chopped	200g red chillies, deseeded & chopped
50g parsley, chopped	6 cloves garlic, crushed
3 cloves garlic, crushed	1 teaspoon caraway seeds
1 tablespoon of the juice from the tin of chickpeas	1 teaspoon salt
½ teaspoon baking powder	1 teaspoon ground black pepper
1 teaspoon coriander	1 teaspoon cumin
1 teaspoon cumin	1 teaspoon coriander
Salt & ground black pepper	Olive oil
Whole wheat flour (or rice flour) for coating & olive oil for cooking	

Method:

1) For the falafel:

- Put everything in the first column (down to, and including, the salt & pepper) in a blender and blend until smooth.

- Place in a bowl in the fridge and leave for 20-30 minutes, until firm.

- Shape into approximately 12 balls, dust lightly with flour and fry in hot oil until browned and crisp.

2) For the Harissa:

- Put everything in the second column, except the olive oil, in a blender and blend until smooth.

- Store in a small jar, with some olive oil poured on top just covering the surface, to keep it fresh. Keep in the fridge until ready to use.

Serve stuffed into wholemeal pita breads, sliced open at the top. Add in shavings of lettuce and cucumber slices for extra crunch.

TIP 1 – Use rice flour to be suitable for Candida.

Makes 12 balls

Phase	Meal	V	C	H	Wheat free	Dairy free
2	Carb	✓	Can be	✓	Can be	✓

Sandwiches

The sandwich is the staple of the UK and US lunchbox, but it isn't in Europe. Our European friends favour cheeses, cold meats, salads and so on, if indeed they ever do make lunch boxes. Most European children have proper lunches either at school or back at home (which is why schools finish at about 1pm, or allow substantial time off at lunch time). If you are making sandwiches for yourself, or your children, here are some healthy tips:

The first thing you need is healthy bread so there are two options below:

1) Shop around and find a good source for a sugar-free 100% whole wheat loaf. A local organic supplier may be a good bet, health food shops are also worth a try and there may be the odd loaf in a supermarket (often the organic loaves), which have no sugar and very few ingredients overall.

2) The second option is to make your own, so here is a great base recipe to get you started. This base recipe is also perfect for serving with our carb soups – you don't have to make sandwiches.

Ingredients:

½ teaspoon salt	2 tablespoons warm water (tap water, warm to the touch)
350g whole wheat plain flour	
25g sunflower seeds	240ml of skimmed milk, lukewarm
1 packet of active dry yeast (7g net weight)	1 tablespoon olive oil

Method:

If you have a bread maker put in all the ingredients above and then set the loaf to be ready as desired.

If you don't have a bread maker then:

1) Preheat the oven to 400° F, 200° C, gas mark 6.

2) Mix the salt, flour and sunflower seeds in a bowl.

3) Run a small bowl under the hot tap to warm it up. Mix the yeast, the warm water and 2 tablespoons of the warm milk in this bowl. Cover with a tea towel and leave in a warm place for approximately 10-15 minutes.

4) Pour the yeasty liquid into the flour; add the olive oil and the rest of the warm milk and mix together thoroughly.

5) Put into a well greased bread tin and leave again in a warm place, covered with a tea towel, for 20-30 minutes.

6) Bake in the oven for approximately 30-40 minutes.

Here are some useful variations to this base recipe:

- For Candida sufferers use 2 level tablespoons of baking powder instead of the yeast, or use self raising flour. You will also need to use rice flour or buckwheat flour instead of whole wheat flour.

- For those with wheat intolerance, use rice flour or buckwheat flour instead of whole wheat flour (don't be fooled by the name – buckwheat flour is not from the wheat family as we know it).

- For a bit of spice, add up to a level teaspoon of nutmeg and/or cinnamon to the dry ingredients.

- For people with milk intolerance try real (unpasteurised) milk, or even just water.

For some perfect 'carb' sandwiches try the following fillings with your healthy bread:

- Marmite (only if you love it of course). (This is packed with B vitamins so we hope you do like it);

- Slices of tomato, cucumber and lettuce (no butter);

- Grated carrots and a few crushed peanuts (this is a delicious and moist sandwich filling);

- Low-fat cream cheese with, or without, cucumber or other salad garnish;

- Low-fat cottage cheese and chives or parsley;

- Low-fat cream cheese with a sprinkling of pine nuts and alfalfa;

- Hummus (try our recipe in this book);

- Fruit compote instead of jam (try our recipe).

Please note that none of the sandwiches above should have butter, as they are carb meals. You should never consume margarine or spreads, because they have been unnaturally solidified by food manufacturers.

For healthy fillings for Phase 3, where carbs and fats can be mixed, try the following:

- Sugar-free ploughman's – mature cheddar, iceberg lettuce, and use spring onions or pickled onions instead of the sweet pickle;

- Sugar-free peanut butter;

- Cold beef slices and horseradish sauce (make sure the sauce is sugar-free – most horseradish is). Or have beef with Dijon mustard;

- Ham and tomato, or ham and cheese, or just ham;

- Curried chicken (mix a tiny bit of curry powder with some thick yoghurt and use the yoghurt as a spread to 'butter' the bread. Then add the chicken slices);

- Home-made egg mayonnaise – mix a hard-boiled egg up with our mayonnaise recipe.

If you are caught out and about and have little alternative but to grab a sandwich for lunch, here are some tips:

- Try to buy from a sandwich 'deli', rather than from a shop, so that you can select the ingredients that go into the sandwich. In a deli you can ask for their brownest bread, with no spread and a salad filling.

- If you buy a pre-packed sandwich, go for the fewest ingredients listed overall (some have more than 50) and the 'most granary-like' bread that you can find.

- Because bread is a carb, try to limit the fat that you have with it. Go for the plain tuna, chicken, egg options with salad, not mayonnaise fillings.

We have seen people, especially at the height of Atkins, eating sandwiches at lunchtime but throwing away the bread. This is not as daft as it sounds. It is wasteful, but bread is generally better off in the dustbin than in your tummy. If you are caught out and a petrol/gas station sandwich is all that you can find, then a large baguette, with the bread thrown on the grass for the birds, can be quite a 'win win'. Many baguettes have very generous toppings of ham and cheese or mozzarella and tomato and you can use the bread as a 'plate' and eat the 'fat ingredients' on top.

Some people who have sandwiches during lunch meetings at work have been seen taking the filling out of the sandwiches – meat and cheese slices especially. Again – given the nutritional content of many processed breads, there are worse things that you could do.

Phase	Meal	V	C	H	Wheat free	Dairy free
2	Carb	Can be	Can be	✓	Can be	Can be

Roasted Vegetables with Pine Nuts & Parmesan

This is a really simple and colourful dish that is especially nice in the winter when the vegetables are in season. There are a few nuts and a bit of cheese in this recipe, but not enough to make any difference to your weight loss and they really add to the flavour.

Ingredients:

2 tablespoons olive oil	1 red pepper, deseeded & diced
2 onions, quartered	200g mixed salad leaves
1 clove garlic, crushed	Parmesan cheese, grated
1kg of mixed vegetables, peeled & diced (use butternut squash, aubergines & courgettes etc)	A sprinkling of pine nuts
	Balsamic vinegar

Method:

1) Preheat the oven to 400° F, 200° C, gas mark 6.

2) In a large frying pan, heat the oil and gently fry the onions and garlic for 2 minutes; then add all the other vegetables and stir-fry for a further 2 minutes.

3) Put the vegetables in a large oven-proof dish and roast in the oven for 30 minutes, stirring half way through.

4) To serve, place a small amount of mixed green lettuce in an open, pasta type bowl and spoon on the roasted vegetables. Sprinkle with the grated Parmesan cheese and pine nuts and place under a very hot grill for 2 minutes just to melt the cheese. Dribble a small amount of balsamic vinegar around the edge of the bowl and serve immediately.

TIP 1 – Go for the lower glycaemic index vegetables, like courgettes, rather than butternut squash, if you are very carbohydrate sensitive.

TIP 2 – Leave out the vinegar to be suitable for Candida.

Serves 4

Phase	Meal	V	C	H	Wheat free	Dairy free
2	Either	✓	Can be	✓	✓	Can be

Carrot & Coriander Soup

This classic soup is quick and easy to make and is absolutely delicious. It can be served as a meal on its own, or as a starter when entertaining. This is unusual in that the cream makes it a 'fat' vegetarian soup, whereas most vegetarian soups are carb meals. Hence no chunks of wholemeal bread with this soup, but it would be a perfect soup to mix with the 4 cheese salad in the winter.

Ingredients:

25g of butter	1 litre vegetable stock
1 onion, finely chopped	A handful of fresh coriander, chopped
1 clove garlic, crushed	150ml single cream
500g carrots, ¾ thinly sliced & ¼ grated	

Method:

1) Melt the butter in a large pan, over a low heat.

2) Fry the onion and garlic until soft.

3) Add the sliced carrots and give the mix a good stir.

4) Add the vegetable stock and bring to the boil.

5) Reduce the heat and simmer gently for approximately 30 minutes, or until the carrots are cooked.

6) Turn off the heat and allow the mixture to cool for 10 minutes.

7) Use a hand held blender to blend the mixture until smooth.

8) Stir in the grated carrots and coriander and then the cream.

9) Serve with a sprinkle of chopped coriander.

TIP 1 – This soup can be cooked in advance and re-heated as required. Don't keep it for too long though, as the cream goes off.

TIP 2 – If you can't get fresh coriander, add a teaspoon of crushed coriander seeds to the garlic and onions at step 2. If you really like the taste of coriander, you can add ½ teaspoon of crushed coriander seeds at step 2 in addition to the fresh coriander.

Serves 4-6

Phase	Meal	V	C	H	Wheat free	Dairy free
2	Fat	✓	✓	✓	✓	

Mediterranean Medley

This is a fabulous fat starter. This mixes all the special tastes of Italy and Greece in one dish. It looks really colourful and healthy and it tastes delicious. Top quality balsamic vinegar can be bought in any supermarkets – it costs more than the regular balsamic, but it is really thick and syrupy and makes all the difference to the dressing.

Ingredients:

Small packet of rocket leaves or lambs lettuce	For the Dressing:
4 'beef' tomatoes, thinly sliced	2 tablespoons top quality balsamic vinegar
8 sun dried tomatoes in oil, finely sliced	4 tablespoons, extra virgin olive oil
16 cherry tomatoes, halved	2 tablespoons oil from the bottle of sun dried tomatoes
100-200g feta cheese, crumbled	Salt & ground black pepper
16 pitted black olives, halved	
Fresh basil leaves, torn	
A few pine nuts (optional)	

Method:

1) Make the dressing in a small bowl by mixing the ingredients together.

2) Divide the leaves into 4 and place on 4 small serving plates.

3) Cover the leaves with the thinly sliced beef tomatoes.

4) Arrange 2 sun dried tomatoes and 4 cherry tomatoes on each plate.

5) Sprinkle the feta evenly across all 4 plates.

6) Arrange 4 olives, halved, on each plate.

7) Sprinkle on the torn basil leaves and a few pine nuts.

8) Drizzle the dressing on each plate and serve immediately.

Serves 4

Phase	Meal	V	C	H	Wheat free	Dairy free
2	Fat	✓		✓	✓	

Feta & Aubergine Salad

This makes a great starter or light snack for four, or a main meal for two. Feta and aubergine are two Mediterranean classics and they go together so well.

Ingredients:

2 aubergines	Freshly ground black pepper
4 tablespoons olive oil	
200g Greek Feta cheese, crumbled	Mixed salad leaves – enough for 4 salad bowls
Small bunch fresh coriander, chopped	

Method:

1) Preheat the oven to 400° F, 200° C, gas mark 6.

2) Slice the aubergines lengthways and drizzle half the olive oil over the flesh of the aubergines. Cook them in the oven for 20 minutes.

3) Carefully scoop out the flesh from the aubergines and mix it in a bowl with the crumbled feta, coriander and pepper. Spoon the mixture back into the aubergine skins. Return the loaded skins to the oven for a further 5 minutes.

4) Arrange the mixed salad leaves in a shallow bowl and drizzle with olive oil. Remove the aubergines from the oven and place one half in each salad bowl.

Serves 4

Phase	Meal	V	C	H	Wheat free	Dairy free
2	Fat	✓	✓	✓	✓	✓

Rocket, Pine Nut & Parmesan Salad

This is such a simple starter to make and it tastes delicious. The pine nuts add a lovely texture and flavour and the whole combination just makes you want to have more.

Ingredients:

2 tablespoons pine nuts	Balsamic vinegar
300g rocket salad	50g Parmesan cheese - shavings
2 tablespoons olive oil	

Method:

1) Heat a frying pan and toss in the pine nuts. Stir frequently and cook until they are a light brown all over. (They cook in their own natural oil).

2) Pile up the rocket salad on 4 plates and drizzle with olive oil. Add a few drops of balsamic vinegar around the edge of each plate.

3) Divide the pine nuts into 4 and sprinkle them over the rocket salad. Then add the parmesan shavings to each plate.

4) Serve immediately.

TIP 1 – Go for the richest balsamic you can find and afford. The more syrupy, the better for this dish.

TIP 2 – Don't worry about the balsamic for Candida – you only need a few drops for decoration and taste.

Serves 4

Phase	Meal	V	C	H	Wheat free	Dairy free
2	Fat	✓	(✓)	✓	✓	

Marinated Salmon & Avocado Salad

This is such an easy starter. It is ideal as you can make it late afternoon and then leave it in the fridge so that you can get on with the other courses. It also stays happily in the fridge so, if you have guests who arrive at flexible times, it won't ruin the dish. The smoked salmon and vinegar make this dish unsuitable for people with Candida.

Ingredients:

	Marinade:
½ avocado	
100g smoked salmon	1 tablespoon white vinegar
1 onion, sliced	
125g cherry tomatoes, halved	1 tablespoon lemon juice
	3 teaspoons olive oil
4 lettuce leaves (use romaine or the equivalent rocket leaves also works well)	1 clove garlic, crushed
	2 teaspoons drained capers, chopped
	2 teaspoons fresh parsley, chopped
	¼ teaspoon dry mustard

Method:

1) Peel and chop the avocado and cut the smoked salmon into strips.

2) Gently mix the avocado, salmon, onion and tomatoes in a bowl.

3) To make the marinade, combine all the ingredients in a screw top jar and shake well.

4) Add the marinade to the salmon mixture.

5) Arrange the mixture on the salad leaves and serve, or alternatively put the mixture in fridge for an hour to let the flavours come out.

TIP 1 – Avocados do contain good measures of both fat and carbohydrate, but the amount of avocado in each serving is too small to make a difference.

Serves 4

Phase	Meal	V	C	H	Wheat free	Dairy free
2	Fat			✓	✓	✓

Creamy & Spicy Prawns

This is a seriously rich starter, which you may like to follow with a simple roast meat main course to impress you guests with your range of culinary skills.

Ingredients:

1 tablespoon olive oil	1 teaspoon hot paprika, (optional)
3 rashers of bacon, cut into thin strips	500g shelled prawns
1 onion, finely chopped	300ml double cream
2 cloves garlic, finely chopped	Salt & ground black pepper
25g butter	50g strong cheddar cheese, grated
50g mushrooms, thinly sliced	

Method:

1) Preheat the oven to 350° F, 175° C, gas mark 4.

2) In a small frying pan, heat the oil and gently fry the bacon until cooked. Remove from the frying pan.

3) Fry the onion and garlic in the bacon fat, adding the butter until soft, but not coloured. Add the mushrooms and fry them with the garlic and onion. Add the paprika at this stage, if desired, and cook for a further minute.

4) When the mushrooms are cooked, remove the mixture from the heat. Stir in the uncooked prawns and the cooked bacon and mix everything together.

5) Divide the mixture between 4 oven-proof ramekins.

6) Pour the double cream over the mixture in each ramekin until everything is covered in cream.

7) Season and cook in the oven for 25 minutes.

8) Add the grated cheese to the top of each dish and place under a hot grill until browned.

TIP 1 – This can be served on a bed of salad as a main meal.

TIP 2 – Leave out the mushrooms for this to be suitable for Candida.

Serves 4

Phase	Meal	V	C	H	Wheat free	Dairy free
2	Fat		Can be	✓	✓	

French Onion Soup

This is a Harcombe friendly version of the French classic soup – you won't even miss the bread.

Ingredients:

50g butter	1 litre beef stock, ideally fresh using our beef stock recipe
1kg onions, thinly sliced	
2 garlic cloves, crushed	Salt & ground black pepper
2 tablespoons thyme, ideally fresh, but dried is fine	150g Gruyère, grated
3 tablespoons dry sherry	

Method:

1) Heat the butter in a large pan and gently cook the onions, garlic and thyme for approximately 20 minutes, until the onions are soft but not browned.

2) Increase the heat slightly and cook for 15 minutes, until the onions become caramelised, stirring occasionally to prevent sticking.

3) Reduce the heat. Add the sherry and simmer for 2-3 minutes. Add the stock and bring to the boil. Add the seasoning and then simmer for 10 minutes.

4) Serve into oven-proof soup bowls. Top each serving with a share of the grated cheese. Place under a grill and 'toast' until the cheese melts and browns.

Serves 4

Phase	Meal	V	C	H	Wheat free	Dairy free
2	Fat		✓	✓	✓	

Chicken Liver Paté

Liver is the most nutritious food on the planet, but it's not to everyone's taste. This is where liver paté can help. Those who don't like the taste of liver may well be able to enjoy a paté instead and, thereby, get the benefit of all the nutrients in this super food.

Ingredients:

100g butter	50ml brandy
1 onion, finely chopped	50ml double cream
1 clove garlic, crushed	Freshly ground black pepper
450g chicken livers, chopped	

Method:

1) Melt the butter in a frying pan and lightly fry the onion and garlic until transparent. Add the chicken livers and cook for a further 4-5 minutes until they are nicely browned.

2) Add the brandy to the pan and lightly simmer for 2-3 minutes. Allow to cool for 3-4 minutes.

3) Transfer the mixture from the pan to a blender. Add the double cream and ground pepper. Blend to a smooth mixture.

4) Transfer the blended mix to a number of small ramekins, or a small dish, and chill in the fridge for at least an hour before serving.

Serves 4

Phase	Meal	V	C	H	Wheat free	Dairy free
2	Fat		✓	✓	✓	

Devilled Kidneys

Meat is the most nutritious food group available to humans and offal – organ meat – is the most nutritious meat. Hence the liver, kidneys and heart of animals, which have been naturally reared, grazing on grass in sunlight, are the absolute top of the list of the healthiest things that we can consume.

Liver beats kidneys for most nutrients, but both are excellent sources of vitamin A, the B vitamins and the important minerals iron and zinc. The one nutrient that kidneys beat liver for is vitamin B12. This is the key nutrient that can only be found in animal foods (vegetarians can get it from eggs). Deficiency symptoms include signs of anaemia as the red blood cell production is impaired. B12 is also needed for nerve health and deficiency can lead to confusion, depression, forgetfulness and poor concentration.

Ingredients:

1 teaspoon cayenne pepper	30g butter
1 teaspoon mustard powder	50ml chicken stock
Freshly ground black pepper	Dash of Worcestershire sauce
6 lamb's kidneys	2 tablespoons double cream

Method:

1) Mix the cayenne pepper and mustard powder in a bowl and season with the black pepper.

2) Remove the membrane from the kidneys, slice them in half lengthwise and then roll them in the spice mixture.

3) Melt the butter in a frying pan. When it just starts to brown add the kidneys and quickly fry them for 2-3 minutes on both sides, until they are nicely browned.

4) Add the chicken stock and Worcestershire sauce and boil until the stock volume is reduced by half.

5) Turn off the heat to the frying pan and allow everything to cool for a minute. Then stir in the double cream and mix thoroughly so that you have a smooth, light brown coloured sauce.

6) Transfer to a warm dish and serve immediately.

Serves 2

Phase	Meal	V	C	H	Wheat free	Dairy free
2	Fat		✓	✓	✓	

PHASE 2 – DESSERTS & CAKES

People following The Harcombe Diet get used to some fundamental principles and these just become second nature: eating only real food is the main one; not mixing is another; managing the three conditions is critical and not snacking makes such a difference.

Another practice that the most successful Harcombe followers are adopting is that each of the three main meals a day only needs to be one course. The concept of starters, main courses and desserts is best kept for special occasions. Every day meals should feature a substantial serving of meat, fish, eggs, dairy and vegetables/salads and there should *not* be a regular need for more than one course.

People often have a main 'main meal' each day (usually dinner in the evening) and you may like dessert with this meal. If you continue to lose well in Phase 2 having berries with cream or yoghurt, or a cheese platter, after a fat meal, then carry on. For many people, the carb content of dairy is proving too high to be able to eat cream and cheese so freely.

So, take care with desserts in Phase 2 and you may find them best kept for special occasions. The dessert recipes in this section are certainly ideal for special occasions.

The final tip is that many people are doing well in Phase 2 having a square or two of at least 85% cocoa content dark chocolate at the end of one main meal – often lunch, due to the reasonable caffeine content. So long as you carry on losing well and stay craving free – do what works for you. A bit of dark chocolate, with a decaffeinated cappuccino, could round off a meal beautifully for you.

Raspberry Dip with Berries

Berries are the one fruit that you can have with fat desserts as they are so low in carbohydrate. Try to get a selection of berries in season – raspberries, strawberries and blackberries, even blueberries if you can get hold of them. If you are entertaining in the winter, you can always buy frozen berries and defrost them.

Ingredients:

Approximately 200g of berries	2 tablespoons kirsch (optional)
250ml double cream	More berries to use as 'dips'
250ml Natural Live Yoghurt	

Method:

1) Put the berries, cream, yoghurt and kirsch in a blender and blend until creamy and smooth.

2) If you have a 'Lazy Susan' dish this looks great with the creamy mixture in the middle and then different berries in the trays on the outside.

3) If you don't have a 'Lazy Susan', you can put a small bowl in the middle of a platter and then surround it by berries. Provide cocktail sticks, or dessert forks, so that people can stab the berries and dip them in the cream.

Serves 4

Phase	Meal	V	C	H	Wheat free	Dairy free
2	Fat	✓	✓	✓	✓	

Berry Pudding

This is as close to a Phase 2 pudding as something so delicious can be. Not for every day, but a real treat when berries are in season and a stunning dinner party dessert when served individually in ramekins.

Ingredients:

400g of frozen mixed berries (or fresh if preferred)	250ml double cream
	75g fresh raspberries
2-4 tablespoons raspberry liqueur, or similar fruit flavoured liqueur	75g fresh blueberries
	50g dark chocolate, ideally 85% cocoa content, grated

Method:

1) Defrost the berries in a blender, to retain the liquid. When defrosted, liquidise them. Add raspberry liqueur to taste.

2) Whip the cream until it stands in peaks.

3) Divide the fresh raspberries and blueberries into ramekins. Pour the liquidised berry & liqueur mixture over the berries until they are covered.

4) Spoon the cream over the berry mixture and smooth it to the top of the ramekin. Grate chocolate on top and decorate with berries if required.

5) Chill for an hour before serving.

Serves 4

Phase	Meal	V	C	H	Wheat free	Dairy free
2/3	Fat	✓	✓	✓	✓	

Berry Pudding (by the book)

This is the Phase 2 version of the Berry Pudding recipe. Still not to have with every fat meal in Phase 2, sadly. Dairy products, like yoghurt, milk or cream, have approximately a 5% carbohydrate content, so this will start to add up if you have too much too often.

Ingredients:

400g of frozen mixed berries (or fresh if preferred) 75g fresh raspberries 75g fresh blueberries	500ml Greek yoghurt (must be a naturally thick variety, not runny) 100% cocoa powder

Method:

1) Defrost the berries in a blender, to retain the liquid. When defrosted, liquidise them.

2) Divide the fresh raspberries and blueberries into ramekins. Pour the liquidised berry mixture over the berries until they are covered.

3) Spoon the thick yogurt over the berry mixture and smooth it to the top of the ramekin. Sprinkle cocoa powder on top.

4) This one can, and should, be eaten immediately.

TIP 1 – You can use frozen berries for the whole dish. Freeze berries in season and then separate some whole berries to line the ramekins and liquidise the rest.

Serves 4

Phase	Meal	V	C	H	Wheat free	Dairy free
2	Fat	✓	✓	✓	✓	

Chocolate Orange Strawberries with Ginger Cream

We would like to thank Melissa Barton for the next two recipes. Many of you continue to lose weight well while including some 85% dark chocolate in Phase 2. This is a delicious 'close to Phase 2' dessert, but don't have such treats daily or you will likely slow weight loss.

Ingredients:

500g strawberries, hulled & quartered	100g bar of 85% dark chocolate
250ml double cream	Orange essence (no added sugar)
Ground ginger	

Method:

1) Place the prepared strawberries in a small dish.

2) Whip the double cream until stiff and add a pinch of ground ginger.

3) Break most of the bar of 85% dark chocolate into small pieces. Place the chocolate pieces in a bowl and add a few drops of orange essence. Melt in the microwave, removing to stir occasionally, until all the lumps have gone and the mixture is smooth.

4) Spoon the whipped cream over the strawberries and pour on the melted orange chocolate.

5) Grate the remainder of the dark chocolate for sprinkles on top.

Serves 4

Phase	Meal	V	C	H	Wheat free	Dairy free
2	Fat	✓	✓	✓	✓	

Melissa's Taste of Paradise

This is Melissa's version of Bounty Bars. We think coconut and chocolate taste even better in their natural state, and with berries and cream, than they do processed and with sugar and emulsifiers. Melissa dedicates this recipe to Zoë for naming it!

Ingredients:

500g mixed berries 300ml double cream 2 tablespoons coconut cream	50g 90% cocoa dark chocolate, grated 10g flaked almonds

Method:

1) Divide the berries into 4 small dishes.

2) Pour the cream and coconut cream into a bowl with the grated chocolate and whisk until thick.

3) Spoon the creamy chocolatey mixture over the berries and sprinkle with the flaked almonds.

TIP 1 – If you are able to get hold of a whole real coconut, you could use the milk from it instead of the coconut cream. If you can crack the coconut in two, you can serve the mixture in a 'coconut' bowl for a special occasion, leaving the coconut 'meat' in the shell to be spooned out, as part of the dessert.

Serves 4

Phase	Meal	V	C	H	Wheat free	Dairy free
2	Fat	✓	✓	✓	✓	

Sugar-free Orange Sorbet

The Harcombe Diet does not encourage artificial sweeteners (as they have no nutritional benefit and do little to get rid of a sweet tooth). However, dinner parties are times to 'cheat' and this sorbet will amaze your guests, as they won't believe it is sugar-free.

Ingredients:

4 tablespoons lemon juice	300ml unsweetened concentrated orange juice
2 teaspoons liquid sweetener	2 egg whites
240ml water	Orange slices (use the rest of the oranges from which the zest was taken)
The zest of 2 oranges	

Method:

1) Mix the lemon juice and sweetener with 240ml of water.

2) Add the orange zest and orange juice and pour into an ice cube tray.

3) Freeze until just firm. Turn into a mixing bowl and mash with a fork until the crystals are broken down.

4) Whisk the egg whites until stiff and fold them into the frozen mixture.

5) Put the mixture in a plastic container and return it to the freezer, freezing until firm.

6) Remove the mixture from the freezer 10-15 minutes before serving to give the sorbet time to soften.

7) Garnish with orange slices.

TIP 1 – Squeeze your own oranges and keep the pulp and bits to make the juice as unrefined as possible and hence a good carbohydrate.

TIP 2 – We have ticked 2/3 in the table below, largely because of the sweetener, but this is just about as close to the Phase 2 rules as a dessert can be.

TIP 3 – (H) is in brackets in case you are very carbohydrate sensitive and then the orange juice in this recipe may be too much for Hypoglycaemia sufferers.

Serves 4

Phase	Meal	V	C	H	Wheat free	Dairy free
2/3	Carb	✓	✓	(✓)	✓	✓

Sugar-free Ice cream

It never ceases to amaze us, and anyone who tastes this, that this recipe is sugar-free. It just shows that nature provides all the sugar we need in fruit. As with our smoothie recipes, keep peeled and chopped fruit in tubs in the freezer at all times.

Ingredients:

Approximately 200g of frozen berries – strawberries, raspberries – whatever you fancy	250ml double cream 250ml Natural Live Yoghurt An ice cream machine

Method:

1) Put the frozen berries into a blender with enough cream and yoghurt to cover them and start blending them. Once the frozen fruit is broken down, keep adding the rest of the yoghurt and cream until they are all blended in.

2) Put the mixture in an ice cream machine (follow the machine instructions) and then put it in the freezer once done.

You can make lots of variations to this recipe:

- Add more berries for a more fruity flavour;

- Add more yoghurt and less cream for a more tangy flavour;

- You can substitute fresh unsweetened orange juice for the yoghurt to make the recipe sweeter and more like a sorbet (Phase 3 only);

- You can add chopped frozen bananas to the recipe to make the consistency thicker (Phase 3 only, as this would mix carbs and fats too much).

Serves 4

Phase	Meal	V	C	H	Wheat free	Dairy free
2	Fat	✓	✓	✓	✓	

Here are two alternative carb recipes:

Banana & Mango Ice cream

Ingredients:

3 bananas, peeled, sliced & frozen in advance 1 large mango (or 2 peaches), peeled, diced & frozen in advance	150ml low fat milk or Natural Live Yoghurt An ice cream machine

Method: as with the main sugar-free ice cream recipe.

Strawberry & Peach Sorbet

Ingredients:

200g frozen strawberries 2 peaches, peeled, diced & frozen in advance	100ml freshly squeezed unsweetened orange juice An ice cream machine

Method: as with the main sugar-free ice cream recipe.

Serves 4

Phase	Meal	V	C	H	Wheat free	Dairy free
2/3	Carb	✓	✓	(✓)	✓	Can be

Tropical Fruit Fool

This works with any soft tropical fruit – mango or papaya would be perfect. Peaches or nectarines would also work well.

Ingredients:

400g mango or papaya (or a mixture), peeled & diced Zest & juice of 1 lime 150ml crème fraîche	100ml Greek Natural Live Yoghurt Fresh fruit slices to decorate (optional)

Method:

1) Put the mango/papaya and the zest and lime juice in a blender and blend until smooth.

2) Put the crème fraîche and yoghurt in a bowl and whisk until thick.

3) As soon the crème fraîche and yoghurt thickens, add the mango purée and whisk them briefly together (or fold the mango into the cream).

4) Spoon the tropical mix into 4 small glasses and chill for 1-2 hours before serving.

5) Decorate with slices of fresh mango or papaya or banana slices or sprigs of fresh mint.

TIP 1 – We didn't tick the 'H' box as tropical fruit is high in carbohydrate. Unless you are highly carb sensitive, this small amount should be fine.

Serves 4

Phase	Meal	V	C	H	Wheat free	Dairy free
2	Fat	✓	✓		✓	

Phase 3

(P342) Main Meals

(P356) Healthy cheats

PHASE 3 – MAIN MEALS

Tangy Apple Nut Roast

This is the Christmas dinner of the vegetarian world. It can be served when entertaining, or baked at the weekend to eat for main meals during the week. Remember that nuts are one of the rare foods that have fat and carb in reasonable quantities, so this is a Phase 3 dish.

Ingredients:

175g brown rice (dry weight)	175g mixed nuts, chopped (hazelnuts, cashews, almonds & brazils work really well)
600ml of vegetable stock	
2 smalls onions, finely chopped	1 sprig fresh rosemary
1 clove garlic, finely chopped	1 sprig fresh thyme
4 mushrooms, finely chopped	(or ½ teaspoon of each herb dried if you can't get fresh)
1 stick celery, finely chopped	Salt & ground black pepper
2 tablespoons olive oil	1 egg (optional)
	1 apple, (cooking or eating)

Method:

1) Preheat the oven to 400° F, 200° C, gas mark 6.

2) Part cook the brown rice in the vegetable stock (cook for half the recommended time).

3) Drain the rice through a sieve and put it in a mixing bowl and leave it to one side.

4) Stir-fry the vegetables in the olive oil. Then add them to the rice.

5) Add the chopped nuts to the mixing bowl with the rice & vegetables.

6) Add in the rosemary, thyme, salt & pepper.

7) Crack the egg into a small bowl and beat with a fork until mixed in.

8) Add the egg to everything else (without the egg the mixture doesn't bind and will be crumbly but this doesn't affect the taste).

9) Put half the mixture into a loaf (glass) oven dish and press it down well into the dish.

10) Core & slice the apple on top of the mixture until it makes an apple layer. Put the rest of the mixture on top (pressing it down well again) so that you have made an apple sandwich.

11) Cover the loaf dish with tin foil.

12) Bake for 30-45 minutes, or until the top of the roast is golden.

TIP 1 – Substitute peppers for the mushrooms, or just leave out the mushrooms, for this dish to be suitable for Candida.

Serves 4-6

Phase	Meal	V	C	H	Wheat free	Dairy free
3	Mixes	✓	Can be	✓	✓	✓

Spicy Lentils

This could also be called curried lentils and it is delicious with minted cucumber yoghurt. This mixes fats (butter and coconut milk) and carbs (lentils), in fairly even proportions, so it should only be eaten for special occasions in Phase 2, or whenever you like in Phase 3.

Ingredients:

2 onions, finely chopped	275ml water
75g butter	400g unsweetened coconut milk
6 cloves garlic, crushed	4 thick slices fresh ginger
1 carrot, peeled & grated	400g tin chopped tomatoes
2 level teaspoons cumin seeds	Salt & ground black pepper
2 level teaspoons mustard seeds	Juice of 1 lime
3 level teaspoons ground turmeric	15g of fresh coriander
250g split red lentils	

Method:

1)   Fry the onions in the butter until soft.

2)   Add the garlic, the grated carrot, the cumin and mustard seeds and cook gently for approximately 5 minutes.

3)   Stir the turmeric in and cook for another couple of minutes.

4)   Add the lentils, the water, coconut milk, ginger, tomatoes, salt & pepper, lime and coriander.

5) Simmer, uncovered, stirring occasionally, for 30-40 minutes, until the lentils are soft.

6) Remove the slices of ginger before serving if you can find them. Warn your guests if not!

Serve with brown rice as an Indian dish or eat this as a lentil dish on its own or serve it as a side dish with lamb.

Serves 4

Phase	Meal	V	C	H	Wheat free	Dairy free
3	Mixes	✓	✓	✓	✓	

Brazil Nut Bake

This is a delicious nut roast bake. The tangy nut roast recipe uses brown rice as the staple instead of breadcrumbs. This recipe uses the traditional bread crumbs and, therefore, is not good for those with wheat intolerance. Make sure you bake your own bread for the breadcrumbs, or find sugar-free bread from a health food shop or supermarket.

Ingredients:

200g Brazil nuts, shelled	1 red pepper, deseeded & finely chopped
200g wholemeal breadcrumbs	1 teaspoon marjoram
200g carrot, grated	Salt & ground black pepper
150g onions, finely chopped	3 eggs
3 celery sticks, finely chopped	3 tablespoons tomato purée

Method:

1) Preheat the oven to 400° F, 200° C, gas mark 6.

2) Break the Brazil nuts into small pieces and put them in a medium mixing bowl (crush them finely if you like a smooth roast and leave them a bit chunky if you like it crunchy).

3) Add the breadcrumbs, carrot, onions, celery, pepper, marjoram and seasoning.

4) Beat the eggs in a small bowl.

5) Add the tomato purée to the eggs and mix well.

6) Pour the eggs and tomato purée into the dry ingredients and mix well.

7) Put the mixture in an oven-proof loaf dish, ideally a glass dish so that you can see when the roast is cooked.

8) Bake for 30-45 minutes. The dish is ready when the top of the roast is golden.

TIP 1 – This is strictly a Phase 3 recipe, as the nut quantities are quite significant and nuts are natural mixtures of fat and carbohydrate. However, as an occasional treat, this won't hurt in Phase 2.

Serves 4

Phase	Meal	V	C	H	Wheat free	Dairy free
3	Mixes	✓		✓		✓

Whole Wheat Pancakes with Spinach & Walnuts

This is a wonderful vegetarian dish, which can be presented to look as good as it tastes. It does mix good fats (cheese, butter) with good carbs (wholemeal flour) but it really is worth it. You can use the pancake base recipe to make healthy stand-alone pancakes at any time.

Ingredients:

For the pancakes:	For the filling:
100g wholemeal plain flour, sifted	50g butter
2 eggs	200g spinach, (pre-cooked weight)
240ml milk	100g Emmental cheese, grated
	50g walnuts, roughly chopped

Method:

1) To make the pancakes:

   - Sift the flour into a bowl, make a well in the middle and crack the eggs into it.

   - Whisk the eggs into the flour, collecting as much of the flour as possible.

   - Then, pour in the milk, a little at a time, while continuing to whisk. Continue to whisk until the mixture is smooth, with no lumps.

   - Put aside until ready to use.

2) For the filling:

   - Melt the butter in a saucepan and then add the spinach. Reduce the heat and 'sweat' the spinach for approximately 5 minutes, stirring occasionally.

- Add the Emmental and walnuts and stir into the spinach. Put the lid on the pan and simmer over a very low heat, for 5 minutes, stirring occasionally.

3) To cook the pancakes:

- In a frying pan, melt 25g of butter and, when hot, add one quarter of the pancake mix, making sure that the base of the pan is completely covered.

- Cook over a moderate heat for 2-3 minutes until the mixture becomes firm, then, flip over the pancake with a plastic spatula (or toss it if confident) and cook the other side for another 2-3 minutes.

- When cooked, transfer to a warmed plate and keep warm. Repeat for the remaining mixture until you have 4 large pancakes.

4) To serve:

- Place each pancake on a plate and divide the filling between the 4 plates. Then, roll the pancakes into a sausage shape and serve immediately.

Serves 4

Phase	Meal	V	C	H	Wheat free	Dairy free
3	Mixes	✓		✓		

Wholemeal Pizza

This is the healthiest way to do pizza for children and this is also one of the tastiest treats you can allow yourself. It is a perfect Phase 3 dish, as it mixes good carbs and good fats. It is also great, when friends come round, to have a pizza in the freezer ready to feed and impress.

Ingredients:

1 portion of the sugar-free wholemeal bread recipe (see our recipe under sandwiches) Tomato purée or paste 200g mozzarella 100g cheddar, grated 150g mushrooms, sliced	1 red pepper, deseeded & sliced 1 teaspoon dried basil, or fresh leaves 1 teaspoon dried oregano, or fresh leaves Salt & ground black pepper

Method:

1) Preheat the oven to 425° F, 220° C, gas mark 7 and grease some pizza trays.

2) Make the bread dough as per our sugar-free bread recipe, under "Sandwiches".

3) Roll out the dough and shape into rounds to fit the pizza trays. You can buy flat pizza trays for 'thin & crispy' pizzas or deep trays for 'deep pan' pizzas. The choice is yours, or make one of each.

4) Smear tomato purée, or paste, all over the pizza bases.

5) Slice the mozzarella and arrange on top of the tomato base.

6) Grate the cheddar on top of everything.

7) Slice the mushrooms and peppers and arrange on top of the cheese.

8) Sprinkle on the basil, oregano and seasoning.

9) Bake in the oven for 15-25 minutes, depending on the size of the pizza trays used.

TIP 1 – Use low-fat cheddar and mozzarella to reduce the amount of fat that is being mixed with carbs.

TIP 2 – Try different toppings e.g. sweet corn and pineapple chunks, pepperami and olives – whatever you can invent.

TIP 3 – The bread base makes this unsuitable for people suffering from Candida.

Serves 4

Phase	Meal	V	C	H	Wheat free	Dairy free
3	Mixes	Can be		✓		

Mushroom Burgers

This is a not good for people with Candida or wheat intolerance, as it contains wheat and yeast. It also mixes carbs and fats (breadcrumbs and eggs) but eggs are not as high in fat as, say, butter so the mixing could be worse. This is a great dish for children or for adults in Phase 3.

Ingredients:

4 tablespoons olive oil	75g of wholemeal bread crumbs (or 3 slices of wholemeal bread crumbled up by hand)
1 onion, finely chopped	
225g mushrooms, chopped	
50g wholemeal flour	1 egg, beaten
150ml water	Salt & ground black pepper
1 teaspoon yeast extract	
1 teaspoon lemon juice	For the coating – 100g wholemeal breadcrumbs & 2 beaten eggs
½ teaspoon rosemary	
½ teaspoon thyme	

Method:

1) In a large frying pan, heat 2 tablespoons of olive oil and gently fry the onion & mushrooms until soft.

2) Add the flour, water, yeast extract, lemon juice, rosemary and thyme and cook gently for a further 5 minutes.

3) Off the heat, stir in the breadcrumbs and the beaten egg.

4) Season to taste.

5) Leave until cold.

6) With floured hands, to stop sticking, shape the mixture into 8 burger shapes.

7) Brush with the beaten egg and then coat with the breadcrumbs.

8) Bring 2 tablespoons of olive oil to sizzling point in a frying pan and then cook the burgers for 5 minutes until each side is golden brown.

Serve with parsnip chips or ratatouille.

Serves 4 (Makes 8 burgers)

Phase	Meal	V	C	H	Wheat free	Dairy free
3	Mixes	✓		✓		✓

Caribbean Chicken

This dish does mix good fats (chicken & olive oil) with good carbs (apricots, pineapple & kidney beans) but, for dinner parties, this is the best 'rule' to drop for one evening. It still means you and your guests are eating only healthy and delicious ingredients but, let's face it, you're going to cheat a bit with wine anyway!

Ingredients:

1 tablespoon olive oil	100g tin red kidney beans, drained & rinsed
4 chicken breasts, sliced	½ teaspoon honey
2 tablespoons mild curry powder	½ teaspoon mixed spice
1 tablespoon corn flour	½ yellow pepper, deseeded & chopped
100g pineapple chunks in sugar-free juice (you will need the juice)	½ red pepper, deseeded & chopped
100g dried apricots, chopped	Salt & ground black pepper
300ml boiling water	
2 teaspoons tomato purée	

Method:

1) Heat the oil in a large frying pan, and fry the chicken until golden brown on both sides.

2) Add the 2 tablespoons of mild curry powder and mix thoroughly. Fry for a further 2-3 minutes.

3) Blend the corn flour with the pineapple juice and add to the pan with the pineapple chunks, dried apricots, water, tomato purée, kidney beans,

honey and mixed spice. Cover the pan and simmer gently for 20-25 minutes.

4) Add the red and yellow peppers; salt and pepper to taste and simmer for a further 5-10 minutes.

Serve with a green or mixed salad to be really healthy, or with brown rice and peas to be really 'Caribbean'.

Serves 4

Phase	Meal	V	C	H	Wheat free	Dairy free
3	Mixes		✓	✓	✓	✓

PHASE 3 – HEALTHY CHEATS

Chocolate Balls

This is one of Zoë's favourite desserts – anything with chocolate in gets her vote. This one is seriously special too as it doesn't have any added sugar. There is some sugar in the dark chocolate but this recipe keeps the sugar intake to a minimum.

Ingredients:

225g dark chocolate with at least 70% cocoa content (85% is even better)	20g butter, softened
	Cocoa powder or additional dark chocolate, grated (optional)
100ml double cream	
1 vanilla pod, split lengthways	

Method:

1) Break the chocolate into pieces and put them into a heat-proof bowl and place this bowl in a saucepan with a bit of boiling water in it. Make sure that the water is just deep enough to melt the chocolate but not too deep to splash into the chocolate.

2) Put the cream in another saucepan, add the vanilla pod and heat it up to just below boiling point. Take it off the heat just before it boils.

3) Let it cool and then remove the vanilla pod.

4) Beat the butter until very soft. Mix it into the chocolate.

5) Add in the vanilla cream mixture and put the mixture in the fridge until it goes firm.

6) Shape into small balls (like hand made chocolates) and roll in sieved cocoa powder, or chocolate shavings – as desired.

TIP 1 – Use a teaspoon of vanilla extract if you can't be bothered with the vanilla pod.

TIP 2 – Use dark chocolate bars with orange or mint flavouring if you can find them. Or add a tablespoon of rum or whisky to the mixture – all for added flavour.

TIP 3 – We have put '2/3' under Phase below. This is not strictly a Phase 2 recipe but it is quite a healthy 'cheat'.

Serves 4

Phase	Meal	V	C	H	Wheat free	Dairy free
2/3	Fat	✓	✓	✓	✓	

Cappuccino & Chocolate Mousse

This is a fabulous 'close-to-sugar-free' dessert – there is just a bit of sugar in the chocolate.

The carbohydrate content of chocolate is very interesting: a 100g bar of milk chocolate has over 50g of carbohydrate; a 100g bar of 70% cocoa chocolate has 33g of carbohydrate and a 100g bar of 85% cocoa chocolate has just 19g of carbohydrate (about the same as one apple). So, we list this dish as one that mixes, but go for the darkest chocolate you can to make this more of a fat meal, than a carb meal. Dark chocolate is also rich in iron, magnesium and anti-oxidants, so it is firmly on the 'good for you' list.

Ingredients:

175ml milk	2 eggs
2 tablespoons coffee granules (decaff advised)	1 tablespoon dark rum
	¼ teaspoon cinnamon
175g dark chocolate with at 70% cocoa content and ideally 85%	Whipped fresh cream and chocolate coffee beans to decorate

Method:

1) In a small saucepan, heat the milk and the coffee granules until simmering.

2) Pour this into a blender, add the dark chocolate, broken into small pieces, and blend for approximately 30 seconds.

3) Add the eggs, rum and cinnamon and blend again until smooth and well combined.

4) Pour the mixture into 4 individual serving dishes and leave to set in the fridge for at least a couple of hours.

5) Just before serving, cover each dish with whipped cream and a couple of coffee beans for decoration.

TIP 1 – The dishes can be left overnight if desired.

TIP 2 – Ideally use decaffeinated coffee to help your guests sleep if you are serving this late at night and to avoid the blood sugar stimulus that caffeine gives. There will be enough caffeine in the dark chocolate to keep them awake long enough to get home!

Serves 4

Phase	Meal	V	C	H	Wheat free	Dairy free
3	Mixes	✓	✓	✓	✓	

Classic French Chocolate Mousse

If you love chocolate this recipe is to die for. You can stand a spoon up in it and it will give you a chocolate high like you can't imagine. It is also as close to the rules of this book as chocolate can get as it is a fat meal in essence. Eat it at the end of a 'fat' dinner party and enjoy.

Ingredients:

225g chocolate with at least 70% cocoa content (85% cocoa content makes the dessert even richer)	3 tablespoons sugar 1 teaspoon vanilla extract 2 tablespoons of dark rum
60ml of a cup of black coffee (decaffeinated ideally) 2 eggs – very fresh	240ml double cream (suitable for whipping)

Method:

1) Separate the egg yolks and whites. Put the yolks in one mixing bowl and the whites in another.

2) Using an electric whisk beat the egg yolks until they are mixed. Gradually add in 1 tablespoon of sugar, while whisking all the time. Continue whisking for approximately 5 minutes, or until the yolks turn pale yellow.

3) Whisk in the rum and vanilla. Leave to one side for a moment.

4) Break the chocolate into squares and put it into a saucepan with the liquid coffee. (Literally make a cup of coffee and measure out 60ml of it). Stir together, over a low heat, until all the chocolate is melted.

5) Add the melted chocolate and coffee to the egg yolks, rum and vanilla mixture. Leave to one side.

6) Clean the whisk beaters thoroughly and then start to whisk the egg whites. Gradually add in the remaining 2 tablespoons of sugar to the egg whites and whisk the whole lot until stiff peaks form.

7) Fold the egg white mixture gently into the mixture of egg yolk, rum, vanilla, chocolate and coffee.

8) Using the empty egg white mixing bowl, whip the cream until just stiff and then add this to the other ingredients. Fold everything in together to mix it thoroughly and then pour and spoon the whole lot into a nice bowl ready for a dinner party.

9) Place in the fridge and leave for at least 2 hours (it can be made the night before and left for 24 hours).

TIP 1 – This is best served at room temperature, so get the mousse out in good time before dessert.

Serves 4-8

Phase	Meal	V	C	H	Wheat free	Dairy free
3	Fat	✓	✓	✓	✓	

The Speedy Alternative!

This is for when you want a chocolate dessert but you don't have the time to do the full French Chocolate Mousse extravaganza. This one is also for the end of a fat dinner party.

Ingredients:

225g chocolate with at least 70% cocoa content (85% cocoa content makes the dessert even richer)	300ml double cream 1 tablespoon of dark rum 1 teaspoon vanilla extract

Method:

1) Break the chocolate into small pieces.

2) Gently heat the cream in a small saucepan over a low heat. Don't let it boil.

3) When it begins to simmer, remove from the heat and add the chocolate pieces stirring well until they are all dissolved.

4) Stir in the rum and extract of vanilla.

5) Pour the mixture into small serving pots (espresso cups will be perfect).

6) Allow to cool and then put in the fridge for at least an hour, or even overnight.

Serves 4-8

Phase	Meal	V	C	H	Wheat free	Dairy free
3	Fat	✓	✓	✓	✓	

Healthy Muffins

Children love muffins and these home-made versions have no additives, as little sugar as we can get away with and whole wheat carbohydrates. They also take little more than 20 minutes to make and children can join in with the cooking. This is the kind of snack that you can prepare for unexpected guests in the time it takes for them to meet the cat and for you to make a cup of coffee (in that order of course).

Ingredients:

400g wholemeal plain flour	20g butter
2 teaspoons baking powder	240ml milk
50g brown sugar	2 tablespoons golden syrup
1 egg beaten	1 teaspoon bicarb of soda

This is the basic recipe. You then need to pick one of the following variations to make the relevant muffin:

Carrot Muffins:

2 carrots, grated (any size carrots you like – use bigger carrots for more 'carroty' muffins).

Carrot & Coconut Muffins:

2 carrots, grated;

50g desiccated coconut.

Banana Muffins:

4 mashed bananas (make them as 'bananary' as you like).

Banana & Nut Muffins:

2-3 mashed bananas;

50g nuts, chopped.

Ginger & Date Muffins:

2 teaspoons ground ginger;

100g dates, chopped.

Bran & Raisin Muffins:

Substitute 50g of flour with 50g of bran;

50g raisins.

Method:

1) Preheat the oven to 400° F, 200° C, gas mark 6 and grease a muffin tray, which can hold 12 muffins, or place paper cases in the tray holes.

2) Put the flour, baking powder, brown sugar and egg in a mixing bowl.

3) Add the flavouring that you have chosen into this bowl.

4) Put the butter and milk in a saucepan and stir until the butter is melted and the milk is on the verge of boiling.

5) Add in the golden syrup and stir in well.

6) The 'finale' is when you sprinkle in the bicarb of soda and the mixture rises up the pan as if it is going to spill over (children love this bit).

7) Before it spills over, pour it on top of the dry ingredients in the mixing bowl and stir it in thoroughly.

8) Spoon the mixture into the muffin holes evenly.

9) Bake in the oven for approximately 10-15 minutes (until golden).

TIP 1 – Use rice flour, or buckwheat, flour to make it wheat-free.

Serves 4 hungry children (makes approximately 12 small to average muffins)

Phase	Meal	V	C	H	Wheat free	Dairy free
3	Mixes	✓		✓		

Cheese Scones

This recipe mixes fats and carbs, so adults watch out. For children, however, mixing good carbs and fats is fine. If children have a weight problem just keeping them off refined carbs will help enormously. If you can give overweight children either fat meals or carb meals, without them complaining, this will really help too. What we must never do with children is to cut back their calorie intake while they are still growing. It is *what* they eat, rather than *how much* that is so important.

Ingredients:

450g wholemeal plain flour	300g hard cheese, grated (cheddar is ideal)
2 tablespoons baking powder	300ml milk
A good pinch of salt & the same of pepper	A scone shape cutter (fun shapes for children are best – we have Homer Simpson)
50g butter	

Method:

1) Preheat the oven to 400° F, 200° C, gas mark 6.

2) Put the flour, baking powder, salt & pepper in a mixing bowl.

3) Rub in the butter.

4) Stir in almost all the cheese and milk (leaving just a little of each to one side) and knead into a manageable dough.

5) Roll out to approximately 2cm thickness, cut into shapes and place on a lightly greased baking tray.

6) Brush the tops and sides with a dash of the remaining milk and sprinkle a bit of the remaining grated cheese on top of each scone.

7) Cook in the oven for approximately 20 minutes (until golden).

TIP 1 – Use rice, or buckwheat, flour to make the recipe wheat-free.

Serves 4 (makes approximately 8-12 scones, depending on the scone cutter).

Phase	Meal	V	C	H	Wheat free	Dairy free
3	Mixes	✓		✓		

Chestnut Carob Mousse

You can buy carob from any health food shop and sometimes in the gluten free section in good supermarkets. It is a great alternative to chocolate and has the advantage of generally being sugar-free. Take care to select a sugar-free version, just in case there are some sugared bars around.

This dessert does mix fats and carbs – the cream is obviously a fat but the carob and chestnuts are, interestingly, carbs. Carob has 13 times the amount of carbohydrate to fat in its content and chestnuts have 48 times the carb to fat content. Chestnuts are often called 'un-nuts' as they are so unlike the other foods with 'nut' in the name.

Ingredients:

225g carob 1 egg 250g tin unsweetened chestnut purée	300ml double cream (suitable for whipping)

Method:

1) Break the carob into chunks and melt them in a bowl placed within a saucepan of boiling water (keep the water shallow enough not to spill into the bowl but deep enough to melt the carob). When melted, remove from the heat.

2) Separate the egg yolk and white and add the yolk to the melted carob, stirring gently but continuously so that you don't end up with chocolate scrambled egg!

3) Add in the chestnut purée, stirring all the time.

4) Whip the egg white and cream in a separate bowl, until they form peaks. Fold it into the carob mixture.

5) Pour into 4-8 small serving bowls and leave them in the fridge so that the dessert sets.

6) Serve with a swirl of whipped cream on top if desired and/or carob drops (if you can find these).

Serves 4-8

Phase	Meal	V	C	H	Wheat free	Dairy free
3	Mixes	✓	✓	✓	✓	

Chestnut Soufflé

This is another fabulous dessert with chestnuts in it. It is another one that mixes fats and carbs sadly (hence dinner parties only, or Phase 2 as you are getting close to your natural weight). Try it first without any sugar or sweetener and then, at least, you will only be having good fats and carbs. Chestnuts are a treasure of the 'un-nut' world as they are so low in fat and calories compared to other 'nuts'. They have substantial quantities of vitamin C, surprisingly, and are generally very nutritious.

Ingredients:

4 eggs, separated	3 tablespoons milk
240ml unsweetened chestnut purée	1 tablespoon brandy
1 tablespoon liquid sweetener or 3 tablespoons sugar (optional) or no sweetener at all	240ml cream (suitable for whipping)

Method:

1) Preheat the oven to 350° F, 175° C, gas mark 4.

2) With an electric mixer, beat the eggs yolks in one mixing bowl for a couple of minutes until creamy and pale yellow.

3) In another bowl whisk the chestnut purée, sweetener/sugar (optional), milk and brandy until well combined.

4) Add the egg yolks to the chestnut mixture and blend everything together well.

5) Wash the beaters thoroughly and then whisk the egg whites until stiff peaks form.

6) Fold the eggs whites into the rest of the mixture.

7) Turn into an ungreased soufflé dish.

8) Bake in the oven for 35-40 minutes.

9) Serve with the whipped cream.

Serves 4

Phase	Meal	V	C	H	Wheat free	Dairy free
3	Mixes	✓	✓	✓	✓	

Tropical Ice Cake

This can be made a week ahead and kept in the freezer if desired. It does have honey, which is strictly refined, but the quantities are too small to make any difference. The orange juice is also 'refined' but squeeze your own and keep the pulp and bits to make the juice as unrefined as possible.

Ingredients:

For the coconut cream:	For the mango bit:
400ml unsweetened coconut milk	2 eggs, separated
300ml Natural Live Yoghurt	2 mangoes, peeled & diced
2 tablespoons honey	2 teaspoons orange zest
1 tin with a push up bottom (approximately 20cm diameter)	300ml freshly squeezed orange juice
	2 tablespoons honey

Method:

1) Line just the bottom 'disc' of the push-up-bottom tin, with cling film.

2) For the coconut cream:

- Whisk together the coconut milk, yoghurt & honey in a bowl.

- Pour this into the tin, cover with tin foil and freeze until partly frozen.

3) For the mango bit:

- Put the egg yolks, mangoes, orange zest, orange juice and honey in a blender and blitz until smooth.

- Whisk the eggs whites until stiff and then fold these into the rest of the mango mixture.

4) Pour the mango mixture evenly on top of the frozen coconut mixture and put the whole lot back in the freezer with tin foil on top again.

5) Remove from the freezer 15-30 minutes before serving, remove from the tin and place slices of mangoes on top for decoration.

TIP 1 – The dish can also be done with fresh or unsweetened tinned pineapple instead of mangoes for when mangos are out of season.

Serves 4

Phase	Meal	V	C	H	Wheat free	Dairy free
3	Mixes	✓	✓		✓	

Fig Rolls

Supermarket fig rolls are a children's favourite – here is the home-made healthy alternative. This can also be made with dates instead of figs, or with a mixture of the two. This recipe has a bit of sugar, but the dried fruit and apple juice provide the natural sweetness. Sadly this is not for adults trying to lose weight.

Ingredients:

350g dried figs, chopped	175g wholemeal plain flour
250ml unsweetened apple juice	75g porridge oats (jumbo oats make the bars chunkier)
150g butter	
2 tablespoons brown sugar	2 tablespoons nuts, chopped

Method:

1) Preheat the oven to 350° F, 175° C, gas mark 4 and grease a baking tin thoroughly (the tin should be approximately 20-30cm in size and at least 4cm deep).

2) Put the figs and apple juice in a saucepan; bring them to the boil, simmer for approximately 5 minutes with a lid on. Leave to cool.

3) Whisk the butter and sugar in a medium bowl.

4) Stir in the cooled fig mixture.

5) Add the flour, oats and nuts; mix well.

6) Spread the mixture evenly across the greased tray.

7) Cook in the oven for approximately 40 minutes, or until golden brown.

TIP 1 – Use rice, or buckwheat, flour to make this wheat-free.

Can be cut into approximately 12 slim bars, or cut as you like them.

Phase	Meal	V	C	H	Wheat free	Dairy free
3	Mixes	✓			Can be	

Sugar-free Carrot Cake

This is the traditional carrot cake classic, varied to be sugar-free by using dried fruit instead of sugar. This recipe is a healthy cake option for children, or for adults in Phase 3. If you are asked to make a cake for a school or charity event, taking a sugar-free offering, with wholemeal flour, might make people think about the amount of white flour and sugar that we consume daily.

Ingredients:

175g wholemeal plain flour	75g raisins, or sultanas
2 teaspoons baking powder	100g butter
A pinch of salt	Zest of half an orange
1 teaspoon cinnamon (optional)	2 eggs
125g carrots, grated	A few tablespoons of milk (to adjust the consistency)
50g walnuts, chopped	

Method:

1) Preheat the oven to 325° F, 165° C, gas mark 3 and grease a 20cm diameter cake tin.

2) Put the flour, baking powder, salt and cinnamon in a bowl and mix well.

3) Add in the grated carrot, chopped walnuts and raisins or sultanas and mix well again.

4) Cream the butter until very soft and then add the orange zest.

5) Beat the eggs well (ideally with an electric whisk) and then add these to the butter gradually. To prevent curdling, add a little of the flour mixture.

6) When both eggs are beaten in, add the egg and butter mixture to the dry ingredients and mix thoroughly.

7) Add some milk to give the mixture a soft, but not runny, consistency.

8) Put the mixture into the greased cake tin and bake for 45-60 minutes.

TIP 1 – Use rice, or buckwheat, flour to make this wheat-free.

TIP 2 – If you want some icing on top, mix 100g icing sugar with the zest of half an orange and 4 teaspoons of orange juice and spread this over the cake – this is obviously not sugar-free but it looks and tastes great.

Makes 1 cake

Phase	Meal	V	C	H	Wheat free	Dairy free
3	Mixes	✓			Can be	

Banana Whips

This mixes fats and carbs but it still only has good fats and good carbs and the 'not mixing' rule is the easiest one to drop for dinner parties. It makes a great dessert for children as well.

Ingredients:

3 bananas	150ml double cream
1 ripe avocado	Slices of kiwi fruit, strawberries & mint sprigs to decorate if serving at a dinner party
2 tablespoons lemon juice	

Method:

1) Slice the bananas into a blender. Scoop out the flesh from the avocado, add this to the blender and blend it all until smooth.

2) Mix in the lemon juice until combined.

3) Whip the cream with an electric whisk until it forms soft peaks and then fold this into the banana mixture.

4) Chill in the fridge for at least an hour.

5) Serve in nice bowls or glasses and decorate with the kiwi slices, a strawberry and mint sprigs (as desired) before serving. As an alternative you could decorate with slices of banana and shavings of 70+% cocoa chocolate – literally grate the chocolate over the servings.

Serves 4

Phase	Meal	V	C	H	Wheat free	Dairy free
3	Mixes	✓	✓		✓	

USEFUL TABLES

MEASURES & CONVERSIONS

We don't use 'cups' at all in this recipe book, as we can never work out what they are. Australian cups are also different to American cups, so it all seems a bit tricky to us. All of our recipes are in metric measurements.

Hopefully your scales will measure both metric and imperial but if you like to always work in one version, and convert from the other, here are the definitive tables for you to use. We have used American cup measures here, just in case you always wondered how to convert other recipes you may have into 'normal' measures. The first table is for volume/liquids and the second and third tables are for weight.

Conversion table for volume & liquids:

USA	Universal	Imperial	Imperial	Metric	Other
Cups	Tablespoons	Fluid oz	Pints	ml	
1/16	1			15	= 3 teasp
1/8	2	1		30	
¼	4	2	1/8	60	
½	8	4	¼	120	
¾	12	6	1/6	180	
1	16	8	½	240	
2	32	16	1	480	
4.2	68	34	2.1	1000	= 1 litre

Conversion table for weight (Imperial to Metric):

Imperial	Imperial	Metric	Metric
oz	lbs	g	kg
1	1/16	28	0.028
4	¼	113	0.113
8	½	227	0.227
16	1	454	0.454

Conversion table for weight (Metric to Imperial):

Metric	Metric	Imperial	Imperial
g	kg	oz	lbs
100	0.1	3.5	0.22
250	0.25	8.75	0.55
500	0.5	17.5	1.1
1000	1	35	2.2

Please note that:

1 teaspoon is approximately 5g of dry weight;
1 dessert spoon is approximately 10g of dry weight; &
1 tablespoon is approximately 15g of dry weight.

Please note that:

1 teaspoon is approximately 5ml of liquid;
1 dessert spoon is approximately 10ml of liquid; &
1 tablespoon is approximately 15ml of liquid.

Oven Temperature Conversions:

This table is the definitive oven conversion table. All of our recipes list Fahrenheit, centigrade and gas marks to cater for all kitchens. However, this may help you with other recipe books that you may have.

FAHRENHEIT	CENTIGRADE	GAS MARK	DESCRIPTION
225 – 275 f	110 – 135 c	0 – 1	Very Cool
300 – 325 f	150 – 165 c	2 – 3	Cool
350 – 375 f	175 – 190 c	4 – 5	Moderate
400 – 425 f	200 – 220 c	6 – 7	Hot
450 – 475 f	230 – 245 c	8 – 9	Very Hot

US/UK Food conversions:

This final table is for the different names of foods in the US and UK. We use the UK names in our recipes:

UK	US	UK	US
Aubergine	Eggplant	Mince	Ground meat
Biscuit	Cookie	Muesli	Granola
Chips	Fries	Porridge	Oatmeal
Coriander (herb)	Cilantro	Prawn	Shrimp
Courgette	Zucchini	Rocket (salad)	Arugula
Crisps	Chips	Sweets	Candy

THE INDEX

The contents page at the front of the book will be the best starting point if you are looking for a Phase 1 breakfast, a Phase 2 fat meal or a healthy cheat. This index has every recipe listed in alphabetical order, along with all egg/fish/meat recipes listed together and soups/salads grouped together. Chicken Curry Salad, for example, appears in alphabetical order under C *and* under "Curries" *and* under "Salads".

A

Aioli – Garlic Mayonnaise (1 & 2. Either) P157
Aioli (Herb) (1 & 2. Either) P158
Andy's Cheese Burgers (2. Fat) P287
Asparagus & Basil Pasta (2. Carb) P206
Aubergine Bake (2. Fat) P224
Aubergine Boats (2. Fat) P226
Aubergine Pasta (2. Carb) P218

B

Bacon & Eggs (Simple) (1 & 2. Fat) P26
Baked Potatoes (2. Carb) P210
Banana & Mango Ice cream (2. Fat) P338
Banana Whips (3. Mixes) P378
Basque Pork Stew ((1 &) 2. Fat) P112
Bean & Tomato Chilli (2. Carb) P220
Bean Paella ((1 &) 2. Carb) P40
Beef & Pepper Casserole (2. Fat) P278
Beef à la Grecque ((1 &) 2. Fat) P114
Beef Stock (1 & 2. Either) P150
Berry Pudding (2/3. Fat) P332
Berry Pudding (by the book) (2. Fat) P333
Berry/Fruit Compote (2. Carb) P195
Bhuna Masala Curry ((1 &) 2. Either) P129
Boeuf Bourguignon (2. Fat) P280
Bolognaise (Spaghetti) ((1 &) 2. Fat) P118
Brazil Nut Bake (3. Mixes) P346
Brown Rice Risotto Base ((1 &) 2. Carb) P46

Bubble & Squeak (1 & 2. Either) P138
Bulghar Wheat Salad (2. Carb) P290
Burmese Curry (1 & 2. Fat) P50
Butternut Squash Curry (1 & 2. Either) P36

Beef & Steak

Beef & Pepper Casserole (2. Fat) P278
Beef à la Grecque ((1 &) 2. Fat) P114
Boeuf Bourguignon (2. Fat) P280
Carpaccio of Beef (1 & 2. Fat) P180
Moroccan Beef ((1 &) 2. Fat) P116
Roast Rib of Beef (1 & 2. Fat) P93
Steak au Poivre (Phase 1 version) (1 & 2. Fat) P92
Steak au Poivre (Phase 2 version) (2. Fat) P286

Burgers

Andy's Cheese Burgers (2. Fat) P287
Chickpea Burgers with Chive Relish (2. Carb) P208
Lird Burgers ((1 &) 2. Fat) P121
Mat Burgers (2. Fat) P288
Meatballs (1 & 2. Fat) P74
Mushroom Burgers (3. Mixes) P352

C

Cajun Seasoning (1 & 2. Either) P144
Cappuccino & Chocolate Mousse (3. Fat) P358
Caribbean Chicken (3. Mixes) P354
Carpaccio of Beef (1 & 2. Fat) P180
Carrot & Coriander Soup (2. Fat) P316
Cauliflower & Courgette Bake (2. Fat) P231
Cauliflower Vichyssoise with Chive Cream ((1 &) 2. Fat) P182
Celeriac Chips (1 & 2. Either) P141
Char grilled Vegetables ((1 &) 2. Either) P164
Cheese Makers' Salads (2. Fat) P302
Cheese on Cod (2. Fat) P239
Cheese Sauce (Cauliflower) (2. Fat) P300
Cheese Scones (3. Mixes) P366
Chef's salad ((1 &) 2. Fat) P94

Chestnut Carob Mousse (3. Mixes) P368
Chestnut Soufflé (3. Mixes) P370
Chicken Cacciatore ((1 &) 2. Fat) P108
Chicken Caesar Salad (2. Fat) P256
Chicken Cordon Bleu (2. Fat) P266
Chicken Curry Salad (2. Fat) P254
Chicken Liver Paté (2. Fat) P327
Chicken Livers with Marsala & Sage (1 & 2. Fat) P56
Chicken Stock (1 & 2. Either) P149
Chickpea Burgers with Chive Relish (2. Carb) P208
Chilli Con Carne (2. Fat) P282
Chocolate Balls (2/3. Fat) P356
Chocolate Mousse – Speedy Alternative (3. Fat) P362
Chocolate Mousse (Classic French) (3. Fat) P360
Chocolate Orange Strawberries with Ginger Cream (2. Fat) P334
Coconut Curry Chicken (1 & 2. Fat) P62
Cod with Lemon & Coriander Relish ((1 &) 2. Fat) P98
Cod with White Wine Sauce (2. Fat) P236
Coq au Vin (2. Fat) P262
Coriander Marinated Salmon & Lime (1 & 2. Fat) P177
Cream & Mustard Pork (2. Fat) P272
Creamy & Spicy Prawns (2. Fat) P324
Creamy Fish in Sherry Sauce (2. Fat) P232
Creole Fish Casserole (2. Fat) P240
Crunchy Coleslaw ((1 &) 2. Either) P162
Crustless Quiche (2. Fat) P201
Cumin & Coriander Lamb (1 & 2. Fat) P91

Cheese

Andy's Cheese Burgers (2. Fat) P287
Aubergine Bake (2. Fat) P224
Aubergine Boats (2. Fat) P226
Cheese on Cod (2. Fat) P239
Cheese Sauce (Cauliflower) (2. Fat) P300
Cheese Scones (3. Mixes) P366
Chef's salad ((1 &) 2. Fat) P94
Chicken Caesar Salad (2. Fat) P256
Chicken Cordon Bleu (2. Fat) P266

Creamy & Spicy Prawns (2. Fat) P324
Crustless Quiche (2. Fat) P201
Egg & Asparagus Bake (2. Fat) P230
Feta & Aubergine Salad (2. Fat) P320
Four Cheese Salad (2. Fat) P222
French Onion Soup (2. Fat) P326
Halibut in Cheese Sauce (2. Fat) P234
Lentil Moussaka (2. Carb) P212
Mediterranean Medley (2. Fat) P318
Parmesan & Garlic Fish Fillets (2. Fat) P246
Pesto Sauce (2. Either) P297
Red Pepper Chicken ((1 &) 2. Fat) P105
Roasted Vegetables with Pine Nuts & Parmesan (2. Either) P314
Rocket, Pine Nut & Parmesan Salad (2. Fat) P321
Whole Wheat Pancakes with Spinach & Walnuts (3. Mixes) P348
Wholemeal Pizza (3. Mixes) P350

Chicken

Caribbean Chicken (3. Mixes) P354
Chicken Cacciatore ((1 &) 2. Fat) P108
Chicken Caesar Salad (2. Fat) P256
Chicken Cordon Bleu (2. Fat) P266
Chicken Curry Salad (2. Fat) P254
Coconut Curry Chicken (1 & 2. Fat) P62
Coq au Vin (2. Fat) P262
Garden Chicken Supreme (1 & 2. Fat) P64
Hungarian Chicken (1 & 2. Fat) P60
Hunter's Chicken (2. Fat) P260
Merguez Spiced Chicken (1 & 2. Fat) P66
Mexican Chicken ((1 &) 2. Fat) P106
Moroccan Chicken (2. Fat) P258
Mustard Roast Chicken (2. Fat) P264
Red Pepper Chicken ((1 &) 2. Fat) P105
Roast Chicken with Garlic & Lemon (1 & 2. Fat) P71
Spicy Moroccan Roast Chicken (1 & 2. Fat) P70
Tandoori Chicken (1 & 2. Fat) P68
Tarragon Cream Chicken (2. Fat) P268

Thai Coconut Chicken Salad (1 & 2. Fat) P72
Warm Chicken Salad ((1 &) 2. Fat) P123

Chilli

Bean & Tomato Chilli (2. Carb) P220
Chilli Con Carne (2. Fat) P282
Quinoa Chilli with Walnuts & Beans (2. Carb) P221
Vegetable & Pulse Chilli (2. Carb) P204
Vegetarian Chilli (2. Carb) P216

Chips

Celeriac Chips (1 & 2. Either) P141
Harcombe Friendly Chips (2. Carb) P211
Parsnip Chips (1 & 2. Either) P79

Chocolate

Cappuccino & Chocolate Mousse (3. Fat) P358
Chocolate Balls (2/3. Fat) P356
Chocolate Mousse – Speedy Alternative (3. Fat) P362
Chocolate Mousse (Classic French) (3. Fat) P360
Chocolate Orange Strawberries with Ginger Cream (2. Fat) P334
Melissa's Taste of Paradise (2. Fat) P335

Curries & Indian Dishes

Bhuna Masala Curry ((1 &) 2. Either) P129
Burmese Curry (1 & 2. Fat) P50
Butternut Squash Curry (1 & 2. Either) P36
Chicken Curry Salad (2. Fat) P254
Dhansak Curry (1 & 2. Either) P131
Indian Curry (1 & 2. Either) P128
Indian Curry Sauce Base Recipe (1 & 2. Either) P127
Korma Curry (2. Fat) P130
Lamb Rogan Josh (1 & 2. Fat) P86
Mild Korma Curry (1 & 2. Either) P38
Seafood Curry ((1 &) 2. Fat) P102
Southern Indian Vegetable Curry (1 & 2. Carb) P34
Tandoori Chicken (1 & 2. Fat) P68

D

Devilled Kidneys (2. Fat) P328
Dhansak Curry (1 & 2. Either) P131
Duck in Plum Sauce (2. Fat) P276

Dips

Lird's Cacık (1 & 2. Either) P142
Tapenade (1 & 2. Fat) P156
Tomato Salsa ((1 &) 2. Either) P159
Tzatziki – Greek Dip ((1 &) 2. Fat) P181

Dressings

Aioli – Garlic Mayonnaise (1 & 2. Either) P157
French Vinaigrette Dressing (2. Either) P294
Herb Aioli (1 & 2. Either) P158
Mayonnaise (2. Either) P292
Mustard Salad Dressing (2. Either) P293
Oil Free Dressing (2. Either) P296
Vinaigrette Salad Dressing (Variations) (2. Either) P295

E

Egg & Asparagus Bake (2. Fat) P230
Egg & Bacon Salad (1 & 2. Fat) P179

Eggs

Bacon & Eggs (Simple) (1 & 2. Fat) P26
Cauliflower & Courgette Bake (2. Fat) P231
Crustless Quiche (2. Fat) P201
Egg & Asparagus Bake (2. Fat) P230
Egg & Bacon Salad (1 & 2. Fat) P179
Harcombe Protein Shake (1 & 2. Fat) P24
Omelette (Phase 1) (1 & 2. Fat) P28
Poached Egg Salad (1 & 2. Fat) P21
Salmon & Chive Omelette (2. Fat) P199
Scrambled Eggs (Phase 1) (1 & 2. Fat) P29
Spanish (Squash) Omelette (1 & 2. Fat) P22
Tuna & Broccoli Frittata (2. Fat) P200

F

Falafel (2. Carb) P308
Farmhouse Hot Pot (1 & 2. Fat) P84
Feta & Aubergine Salad (2. Fat) P320
Fig Rolls (3. Mixes) P374
Four Cheese Salad (2. Fat) P222
French Green Beans (1 & 2. Either) P140
French Onion Soup (2. Fat) P326
French Vinaigrette Dressing (2. Either) P294
Fruit Platters (2. Carb) P190

Fish

Cheese on Cod (2. Fat) P239
Cod with Lemon & Coriander Relish ((1 &) 2. Fat) P98
Cod with White Wine Sauce (2. Fat) P236
Coriander Marinated Salmon & Lime (1 & 2. Fat) P177
Creamy & Spicy Prawns (2. Fat) P324
Creamy Fish in Sherry Sauce. (2. Fat) P232
Creole Fish Casserole (2. Fat) P240
Haddock with Fennel (1 & 2. Fat) P25
Halibut in Cheese Sauce (2. Fat) P234
Honey Scallop & Chilli Stir-fry ((1 &) 2. Fat) P104
Hot Sizzling Prawns (1 & 2. Fat) P178
Mackerel with Basil (2. Fat) P242
Marinated & Grilled Mackerel (2. Fat) P244
Marinated Salmon & Avocado Salad (2. Fat) P322
Monkfish with Hoisin Sauce (1 & 2. Fat) P54
Mussels in Cider (2. Fat) P248
Parmesan & Garlic Fish Fillets (2. Fat) P246
Prawn & Cucumber Soup ((1 &) 2. Fat) P188
Roasted Fish with Dill & Spinach ((1 &) 2) P100
Salade Niçoise/Salmon Niçoise (1 & 2. Fat) P52
Salmon & Chive Omelette (2. Fat) P199
Salmon Mousse (Lemon & Chives) ((1 &) 2. Fat) P186
Salmon with Mediterranean Vegetables (2. Fat) P252
Seafood Chowder (2. Fat) P250
Seafood Curry ((1 &) 2. Fat) P102
Thai Tuna Salad ((1 &) 2. Fat) P96

Tuna & Broccoli Frittata (2. Fat) P200
Tuna with Crème Fraîche & Asparagus (2. Fat) P238

Fruit

Banana & Mango Ice cream (2. Fat) P338
Banana Whips (3. Mixes) P378
Berry Pudding (2/3. Fat) P332
Berry Pudding (by the book) (2. Fat) P333
Berry/Fruit Compote (2. Carb) P195
Fruit Platters (2. Carb) P190
Raspberry Dip with Berries (2. Fat) P331
Smoothies (2/3. Carb) P196
Strawberry & Peach Sorbet (2/3. Carb) P339
Tropical Fruit Fool (2. Fat) P340

G

Garden Chicken Supreme (1 & 2. Fat) P64
Gazpacho Soup (1 & 2. Either) P166
Ginger Spiced Pork ((1 &) 2. Fat) P110
Ginger Tofu & Okra ((1 &) 2. Carb) P48
Gravy (1 & 2. Either) P146
Grilled Tomato Soup (1 & 2. Either) P168

H

Haddock with Fennel (1 & 2. Fat) P25
Halibut in Cheese Sauce (2. Fat) P234
Harcombe Friendly Chips (2. Carb) P211
Harcombe Protein Shake (1 & 2. Fat) P24
Healthy Muffins (3. Mixes) P363
Herb & Peppercorn Sauce (1 & 2. Either) P143
Herb Aioli (1 & 2. Either) P158
Honey Scallop & Chilli Stir-fry ((1 &) 2. Fat) P104
Hot Sizzling Prawns (1 & 2. Fat) P178
Hummus (2. Carb) P304
Hungarian Chicken (1 & 2. Fat) P60
Hunter's Chicken (2. Fat) P260

I

Indian Curry (1 & 2. Either) P128

Indian Curry Sauce Base Recipe (1 & 2. Either) P127

K

Korma Curry (2. Fat) P130

L

Lamb Casserole (1 & 2. Fat) P76
Lamb Kebabs (1 & 2. Fat) P80
Lamb Rogan Josh (1 & 2. Fat) P86
Lamb with Oregano & Basil (1 & 2. Fat) P75
Lentil Moussaka (2. Carb) P212
Lird Burgers ((1 &) 2. Fat) P121
Lird's Cacık (1 & 2. Either) P142
Liver with Bacon & Onion (1 & 2. Fat) P58

Lamb

Cumin & Coriander Lamb (1 & 2. Fat) P91
Lamb Casserole (1 & 2. Fat) P76
Lamb Kebabs (1 & 2. Fat) P80
Lamb Rogan Josh (1 & 2. Fat) P86
Lamb with Oregano & Basil (1 & 2. Fat) P75
Roast Leg of Lamb with Rosemary (1 & 2. Fat) P90
Spiced Roast Lamb ((1 &) 2. Fat) P120
Sunday Roast Lamb (1 & 2. Fat) P78

M

Mackerel with Basil (2. Fat) P242
Madeira Sauce (2. Either) P298
Marinated & Grilled Mackerel (2. Fat) P244
Marinated Beef, Lamb or Pork (1 & 2. Fat) P82
Marinated Olives (1 & 2. Either) P139
Marinated Salmon & Avocado Salad (2. Fat) P322
Mat Burgers (2. Fat) P288
Mayonnaise (2. Either) P292
Meat Ball Kebabs ((1 &) 2. Fat) P122
Meatballs (1 & 2. Fat) P74
Mediterranean Medley (2. Fat) P318
Mediterranean Quinoa (1 & 2. Carb) P32
Melissa's Taste of Paradise (2. Fat) P335

Merguez Spiced Chicken (1 & 2. Fat) P66
Mexican Chicken ((1 &) 2. Fat) P106
Mild Korma Curry (1 & 2. Either) P38
Minced Meat Stuffed Peppers (1 & 2. Fat) P73
Monkfish with Hoisin Sauce (1 & 2. Fat) P54
Moroccan Beef ((1 &) 2. Fat) P116
Moroccan Chicken (2. Fat) P258
Mushroom Burgers (3. Mixes) P352
Mushroom Stroganoff (2. Fat) P228
Mussels in Cider (2. Fat) P248
Mustard Roast Chicken (2. Fat) P264
Mustard Salad Dressing (2. Either) P293

Meat Other & Multiple Options

Andy's Cheese Burgers (2. Fat) P287
Bolognaise (Spaghetti) ((1 &) 2. Fat) P118
Duck in Plum Sauce (2. Fat) P276
Farmhouse Hot Pot (1 & 2. Fat) P84
Lird Burgers ((1 &) 2. Fat) P121
Marinated Beef, Lamb or Pork (1 & 2. Fat) P82
Mat Burgers (2. Fat) P288
Meat Ball Kebabs ((1 &) 2. Fat) P122
Meatballs (1 & 2. Fat) P74
Minced Meat Stuffed Peppers (1 & 2. Fat) P73
Pork, Chicken or Beef Kebabs (1 & 2. Fat) P88
Turkey Steaks with Ham Wrap (2. Fat) P269
Veal Escallops in a Creamy Mushroom Sauce (2. Fat) P284

Nuts

Brazil Nut Bake (3. Mixes) P346
Roasted Vegetables with Pine Nuts & Parmesan (2. Either) P314
Tangy Apple Nut Roast (3. Mixes) P342
Whole Wheat Pancakes with Spinach & Walnuts (3. Mixes) P348

O

Oil Free Dressing (2. Either) P296

Omelette (Phase 1) (1 & 2. Fat) P28
Orange Mash (2. Either) P289
Oyster Mushrooms (2. Carb) P303

Offal

Chicken Liver Paté (2. Fat) P327
Chicken Livers with Marsala & Sage (1 & 2. Fat) P56
Devilled Kidneys (2. Fat) P328
Liver with Bacon & Onion (1 & 2. Fat) P58

P

Parmesan & Garlic Fish Fillets (2. Fat) P246
Parsnip Chips (1 & 2. Either) P79
Pea Soup (1 & 2. Either) P167
Pear & Butternut Squash Soup (2. Carb) P306
Perfect 'Carb' Breakfast (2. Carb) P192
Perfectly Cooked Vegetables (1 & 2. Either) P154
Pesto Sauce (2. Either) P297
Poached Egg Salad (1 & 2. Fat) P21
Pork & Apricot Salad (2. Fat) P274
Pork, Chicken or Beef Kebabs (1 & 2. Fat) P88
Prawn & Cucumber Soup ((1 &) 2. Fat) P188

Pasta

Asparagus & Basil Pasta (2. Carb) P206
Aubergine Pasta (2. Carb) P218
Spinach, Bean & Tarragon Pasta (2. Carb) P202

Pork

Basque Pork Stew ((1 &) 2. Fat) P112
Cream & Mustard Pork (2. Fat) P272
Ginger Spiced Pork ((1 &) 2. Fat) P110
Pork & Apricot Salad (2. Fat) P274
Roast Pork & Autumn Apple (2. Fat) P270

Pulses

Bean & Tomato Chilli (2. Carb) P220
Bean Paella ((1 &) 2. Carb) P40
Chickpea Burgers with Chive Relish (2. Carb) P208

Lentil Moussaka (2. Carb) P212
Quinoa Chilli with Walnuts & Beans (2. Carb) P221
Spicy Lentils (3. Mixes) P344
Spinach, Bean & Tarragon Pasta (2. Carb) P202
Vegetable & Pulse Chilli (2. Carb) P204
Whole Wheat Couscous & Chickpeas (2. Carb) P214

Q

Quinoa Chilli with Walnuts & Beans (2. Carb) P221

R

Raspberry Dip with Berries (2. Fat) P331
Ratatouille (1 & 2. Either) P136
Red Pepper & Tomato Soup (1 & 2. Either) P176
Red Pepper Chicken ((1 &) 2. Fat) P105
Roast Butternut Squash Soup (1 & 2. Either) P174
Roast Chicken with Garlic & Lemon (1 & 2. Fat) P71
Roast Leg of Lamb with Rosemary (1 & 2. Fat) P90
Roast Pork & Autumn Apple (2. Fat) P270
Roast Rib of Beef (1 & 2. Fat) P93
Roasted Fish with Dill & Spinach ((1 &) 2) P100
Roasted Peppers ((1 &) 2. Either) P160
Roasted Vegetables with Pine Nuts & Parmesan (2. Either) P314
Rocket, Pine Nut & Parmesan Salad (2. Fat) P321
Root Vegetable Soup (1 & 2. Carb) P172

Rice/Quinoa

Bean Paella ((1 &) 2. Carb) P40
Brown Rice Risotto Base ((1 &) 2. Carb) P46
Mediterranean Quinoa (1 & 2. Carb) P32
Quinoa Chilli with Walnuts & Beans (2. Carb) P221
Special Fried Rice (1 & 2. Mixes) P124
Spinach & Sun Dried Tomato Risotto (1 & 2. Carb) P30
Stuffed Peppers/Tomatoes ((1 &) 2. Carb) P44

S

Salade Niçoise/Salmon Niçoise (1 & 2. Fat) P52
Salmon & Chive Omelette (2. Fat) P199

Salmon Mousse (Lemon & Chives) ((1 &) 2. Fat) P186
Salmon with Mediterranean Vegetables (2. Fat) P252
Sam's Spicy Soup (1 & 2. Either) P170
Sandwiches (2. Carb) P310
Scrambled Eggs (Phase 1) (1 & 2. Fat) P29
Seafood Chowder (2. Fat) P250
Seafood Curry ((1 &) 2. Fat) P102
Smoothies (2/3. Carb) P196
Southern Indian Vegetable Curry (1 & 2. Carb) P34
Spanish (Squash) Omelette (1 & 2. Fat) P22
Special Fried Rice (1 & 2. Mixes) P124
Spiced Roast Lamb ((1 &) 2. Fat) P120
Spicy Lentils (3. Mixes) P344
Spicy Moroccan Roast Chicken (1 & 2. Fat) P70
Spinach & Sun Dried Tomato Risotto (1 & 2. Carb) P30
Spinach Paté ((1 &) 2. Fat) P184
Spinach, Bean & Tarragon Pasta (2. Carb) P202
Sprout Salad (1 & 2. Either) P134
Steak au Poivre (Phase 1 version) (1 & 2. Fat) P92
Steak au Poivre (Phase 2 version) (2. Fat) P286
Stir-fry Vegetables (1 & 2. Either) P132
Strawberry & Peach Sorbet (2/3. Carb) P339
Stuffed Peppers/Tomatoes ((1 &) 2. Carb) P44
Sugar-free Carrot Cake (3. Mixes) P376
Sugar-free Ice cream (2. Fat) P339
Sugar-free Orange Sorbet (2/3. Carb) P336
Sunday Roast Lamb (1 & 2. Fat) P78

Salads

Bulghar Wheat Salad (2. Carb) P290
Cheese Makers' Salad (2. Fat) P302
Chef's salad ((1 &) 2. Fat) P94
Chicken Caesar Salad (2. Fat) P256
Chicken Curry Salad (2. Fat) P254
Crunchy Coleslaw ((1 &) 2. Either) P162
Egg & Bacon Salad (1 & 2. Fat) P179
Feta & Aubergine Salad (2. Fat) P320
Four Cheese Salad (2. Fat) P222
Marinated Salmon & Avocado Salad (2. Fat) P322

Poached Egg Salad (1 & 2. Fat) P21
Pork & Apricot Salad (2. Fat) P274
Rocket, Pine Nut & Parmesan Salad (2. Fat) P321
Salade Niçoise/Salmon Niçoise (1 & 2. Fat) P52
Sprout Salad (1 & 2. Either) P134
Thai Coconut Chicken Salad (1 & 2. Fat) P72
Thai Tuna Salad ((1 &) 2. Fat) P96
Warm Chicken Salad ((1 &) 2. Fat) P123

Sauces

Cajun Seasoning (1 & 2. Either) P144
Cheese Sauce (Cauliflower) (2. Fat) P300
Gravy (1 & 2. Either) P146
Herb & Peppercorn Sauce (1 & 2. Either) P143
Madeira Sauce (2. Either) P298
Pesto Sauce (2. Either) P297
Thai Inspired Stir-Fry Sauce (1 & 2. Either) P151
Tomato Sauce (15 Minute) (1 & 2. Either) P152

Sorbets/Ice cream

Banana & Mango Ice cream (2. Fat) P338
Strawberry & Peach Sorbet (2/3. Carb) P339
Sugar-free Ice cream (2. Fat) P339
Sugar-free Orange Sorbet (2/3. Carb) P336
Tropical Ice Cake (3. Mixes) P372

Soups

Carrot & Coriander Soup (2. Fat) P316
Cauliflower Vichyssoise ((1 &) 2. Fat) P182
French Onion Soup (2. Fat) P326
Gazpacho Soup (1 & 2. Either) P166
Grilled Tomato Soup (1 & 2. Either) P168
Pea Soup (1 & 2. Either) P167
Pear & Butternut Squash Soup (2. Carb) P306
Prawn & Cucumber Soup ((1 &) 2. Fat) P188
Red Pepper & Tomato Soup (1 & 2. Either) P176
Roast Butternut Squash Soup (1 & 2. Either) P174
Root Vegetable Soup (1 & 2. Carb) P172
Sam's Spicy Soup (1 & 2. Either) P170

Stocks

Beef Stock (1 & 2. Either) P150
Chicken Stock (1 & 2. Either) P149
Vegetarian Stock (1 & 2. Either) P148

T

Tandoori Chicken (1 & 2. Fat) P68
Tangy Apple Nut Roast (3. Mixes) P342
Tapenade (1 & 2. Fat) P156
Tarragon Cream Chicken (2. Fat) P268
Thai Coconut Chicken Salad (1 & 2. Fat) P72
Thai Inspired Stir-Fry Sauce (1 & 2. Either) P151
Thai Tuna Salad ((1 &) 2. Fat) P96
Tomato Salsa ((1 &) 2. Either) P159
Tomato Sauce (15 Minute) (1 & 2. Either) P152
Tropical Fruit Fool (2. Fat) P340
Tropical Ice Cake (3. Mixes) P372
Tuna & Broccoli Frittata (2. Fat) P200
Tuna with Crème Fraîche & Asparagus (2. Fat) P238
Turkey Steaks with Ham Wrap (2. Fat) P269
Tzatziki – Greek Dip ((1 &) 2. Fat) P181

V

Veal Escallops in a Creamy Mushroom Sauce (2. Fat) P284
Vegetable & Pulse Chilli (2. Carb) P204
Vegetable Hot Pot ((1 &) 2. Carb) P42
Vegetarian Chilli (2. Carb) P216
Vegetarian Stock (1 & 2. Either) P148
Vinaigrette Salad Dressing (Variations) (2. Either) P295

W

Warm Chicken Salad ((1 &) 2. Fat) P123
Wholemeal Pizza (3. Mixes) P350
Whole Wheat Couscous & Chickpeas (2. Carb) P214
Whole Wheat Pancakes with Spinach & Walnuts (3. Mixes) P348